Rhetoric, Rememb₁

Routledge Studies in Rhetoric and Communication

Rhetoric, Remembrance, and Visual Form

Sighting Memory

Edited by Anne Teresa Demo and Bradford Vivian

Routledge
Taylor & Francis Group
NEW YORK   LONDON

First published 2012
by Routledge
711 Third Avenue, New York, NY 10017

Simultaneously published in the UK
by Routledge
2 Park Square, Milton Park, Abingdon, Oxon OX14 4RN

*Routledge is an imprint of the Taylor & Francis Group,
an informa business*

© 2012 Taylor & Francis

The right of Anne Teresa Demo and Bradford Vivian to be identified as
the authors of the editorial material, and of the authors for their individual
chapters, has been asserted in accordance with sections 77 and 78 of the
Copyright, Designs and Patents Act 1988.

Typeset in Sabon by IBT Global.

First issued in paperback in 2013

Library of Congress Cataloging-in-Publication Data
Rhetoric, remembrance, and visual form : sighting memory / edited by
    Anne Teresa Demo, Bradford Vivian.
        p. cm. — (Routledge studies in rhetoric and communication ; 5)
    Includes bibliographical references and index.
    1. Memory.   2. Visual perception.   3. Visual communication.
4. Memory (Philosophy)   5. Material culture.   6. Mass media.
I. Demo, Anne Teresa, 1968–   II. Vivian, Bradford.
    BF371.R437 2011
    153.1'2—dc22
    2011011782

ISBN13: 978-0-415-74416-4 (pbk)
ISBN13: 978-0-415-89553-8 (hbk)
ISBN13: 978-0-203-80340-0 (ebk)

for Noah—
the brightest and most memorable part of our lives

Contents

PART III
Media and Mediums

Figures

Acknowledgments

We thank our contributors for their excellent work, good cheer, and care with deadlines at every stage in the process of producing this book. We would also acknowledge the generous support of the Central New York Humanities Corridor (Visual Arts and Culture cluster), funded by the Andrew W. Mellon Foundation, for making possible the Visible Memories Conference, held in Syracuse, NY, in October of 2008, from which this volume emerged. Kendall Phillips, Joanna Spitzner, and Roger Hallas deserve special recognition for the vital roles they played in planning and executing that event. Our colleagues in the Department of Communication and Rhetorical Studies and the administration in the College of Visual and Performing Arts at Syracuse University also provided valuable assistance in organizing the conference and in supporting our research efforts since that time. We likewise thank the Syracuse University Humanities Center, particularly its director, Gregg Lambert, for contributing to the development of this work. This volume is an outgrowth of the Public Memory Project at Syracuse University (http://vpa.syr.edu/initiatives/public-memory-project), of which are grateful to be a part. Finally, we wish to thank Elizabeth Levine and Diana Castaldini for their diligent work and expert assistance throughout the review and production phases of this book.

An earlier version of Paul Duro's essay (Chapter 3) appeared as "The Return to the Origin: Heidegger's Journey to Greece," *Art Journal* 66 (2007): 88–101. Revised portions of Frances Guerin's essay, "Memory through the Perpetrator's Lens: Witnessing via Images Taken by *Wehrmacht* Soldiers and Officers on the Eastern Front" (Chapter 9), have been taken from her volume, *Through Amateur Eyes: Film and Photography in Nazi Germany* (Minneapolis: University of Minnesota Press, forthcoming 2011). A quotation in Emily Godbey's essay (Chapter 13) is taken from Laurie Windham McGill, comment on "Memory Book," The Sixth Floor Museum at Dealey Plaza, http://www.jfk.org/go/about/memory-book/, comment posted on October 19, 2006. We gratefully acknowledge permission to reprint these materials.

Introduction

Bradford Vivian and Anne Teresa Demo

Enter the word "memory" into any internet search engine. The majority of results will include information on purchasing memory cards, flash drives, random access memory upgrades, and all manner of hardware and software for personal computing. Memory is increasingly synonymous in popular usage with processes of information storage and retrieval through visually-based technologies. The profound influence of such media on basic definitions of memory is evident in the rapidly expanding list of English terms that associate the work of remembering with the workings of computer technology: *memory mapping, memory chip, memory cycle, memory cell, memory card, memory caching, memory disk, memory bank, memory store*, and others.[1] Already plentiful associations between memory and visual media will be even more axiomatic in the future. In January of 2010, the Apple corporation released its eagerly anticipated tablet computer, the "iPad," which technology analysts have described as a possible "fifth" or "final" screen, meaning that it would seamlessly integrate all previous media screens—film, television, personal computers, and portable communications devices—into one portal. To remember in late modernity is to store, send, or retrieve content through a digital constellation of increasingly integrated visual channels.

But the results of one's hypothetical internet search will also yield, interspersed among these predominant findings, a smaller number of old-fashioned resources: personal memory aids. One can easily access in cyberspace a variety of organizations boasting improved memory skills for a diversity of personal applications, from college students studying for exams to elderly people hoping to offset the cognitive effects of aging. Such resources of personal memory training represent contemporary self-help equivalents to the classical *ars memoriae*, the art of memory with which students in the Greco-Roman and later European traditions acquired copious knowledge of the arts, humanities, and sciences by acquiring habits of powerful mental recall. A simple internet search thus provides a suggestive juxtaposition between contemporary technologies of memory and the classical art of memory, between impersonal media of instant data retrieval and the personal discipline of rigorously honing one's capacities for memorization and cognitive agility over the course of a lifetime.

Associations between memory and visual phenomena supply the common denominator between these apparently antithetical paradigms of memory (the one impersonal and technological, the other personal and artistic). Memory is fundamentally visual in either case. The panoply of available memory hardware and software fuels the omnipresent visual environments of late modernity. Memory in computational or digital form is noteworthy not only for its technological aspects but because the reorganization of space and time it engenders has accordingly transformed the content and appearance of cultural memory writ large. The mediated sum of popular culture forms is now preserved indefinitely, on any number of viewable databases, and the historical artifacts that populate museums or other archives are increasingly accessible in virtual as well as physical space.

Individual proficiency in the classical art of memory depended on a host of visual exercises, and contemporary techniques of memory improvement continue to rely on visually-based learning. The *ars memoriae* required orators to conjure elaborate mental images of roomy palaces or public spaces in order to memorize lengthy and complex discourses. "The classical sources" of this art, Frances Yates remarks, "seem to be describing inner techniques which depend on visual impressions of almost incredible intensity." Hence, she surmises, "the ancient memories were trained by an art which reflected the art and architecture of the ancient world, which could depend on faculties of intense visual memorization"—on capacities for "*seeing* the places, *seeing* the images stored on the places" of what one wished to remember.[2] Present-day programs of personal memory enhancement embrace psychological models of sensory input that prioritize visual memorization and recall (as in the examples of flash cards or object-recognition memory quizzes). Both personal and computational, or artistic and digital, memories find their *raison d'être* in the visual media upon which they rely. To remember, then as now, is to see.

A variety of historical roots nourish modern metaphorical affinities between images and memory. Plato's likening of the memory in our souls to a wax tablet upon which experiences or sensations leave impressions of varying endurance remains one of the most canonical representations of memory as visual media.[3] Traditional associations between memory and images have acquired renewed importance in contemporary society, at a time when visually-based technologies are routinely employed in both grand and modest efforts to preserve the past amid rapid social change. Numerous studies of visual culture explore the artistic, social, and political significance of myriad visual artifacts; numerous studies of public memory analyze diverse ways in which communities fashion, preserve, and transform representations (or images) of their shared past. *Rhetoric, Remembrance, and Visual Form* investigates myriad intersections among visual and memorial forms in modern art, politics, and society. The subtitle of this volume—*Sighting Memory*—is a trope meant to express its basic theme: the following chapters generate valuable insights concerning not only how memories may be seen (or sighted) in visual form but also how visual forms constitute noteworthy material sites of memory.

The case studies that comprise this book expand our understanding of intersections among visual and memorial forms by scrutinizing the simultaneous preservation and loss of memory that can occur through visual means—or, by the same token, the simultaneous permanence and transience of images that assist personal and collective recollection alike. The operating principles of both the classical *ars memoriae* and contemporary technologies of memory suggest that visual media can efficiently and reliably hypostasize the putative contents of memory. Whether in digital storage or in one's well-kept mental storehouse, we presume an ability to mechanistically retrieve either part or all of our memories through some form of sight (be it externally or internally directed). Our volume is motivated not by the goal of simply identifying metaphorical associations between visual and memorial forms; we propose, more substantively, that one may glean a host of insights into material intersections among visual culture and practices of memory by exploring in equal measure the potency and fallibility of images as mediums of the past or, conversely, by examining the simultaneously authentic yet manipulated qualities of memory as conjured through visual modes. This collection adds to existing scholarship on visual culture and collective memory an enhanced awareness of the profoundly significant paradoxes of presence and absence, of preservation and dissolution, inherent in efforts to remember through visual means or to render visible the contents of memory.

One of the most spectacular (in the full sense of that term) contemporary illustrations of these paradoxes concerns the digital alteration of photographs documenting the 2006 Israel-Lebanon conflict. Reuters news agency became embroiled in an international scandal when it was forced to admit that at least two images of the conflict it published were photographically manipulated before being widely distributed. The most widely reported incident concerned Adnan Hajj, a longtime Reuters photographer based in the Middle East, who altered one of his photographs of an Israeli air strike on Beirut by dramatically multiplying and enhancing the plumes of dark smoke rising from the city, thereby suggesting an even more destructive Israeli assault.[4] Hajj's photojournalistic doctoring was only one instance of a more general wave of photojournalistic manipulations featured in press coverage of the Israel-Lebanon conflict apparently intended to turn international opinion against Israel. Presumably raw and unmediated visual evidence of Israeli aggression, however, was extensively fabricated. The wildly reversible status of such images, which signified both objective truth and subjective fabrications of truth, indicates profound implications for popular memories of local, national, and international events. Hajj's dramatically embellished photographs were globally reproduced and disseminated via numerous media outlets, thus becoming immediately affixed in international memories of a historic and geopolitically significant military conflict.

Yet the memories in question changed dramatically when the visual sham was revealed. Hajj's photojournalistic manipulations—originally published as seemingly authentic documents of death and destruction—now document the very ease with which one may employ commonly available digital software in order to influence public perceptions of historical events. Image and memory, then, not only share the same material substance; we are increasingly habituated to experiencing that substance as a source of verisimilitude and chicanery at once.

Rhetoric, Remembrance, and Visual Form presents a detailed and thematically organized analysis of such complex material (and not merely metaphorical) intersections among memory and visual forms that will broaden our understanding of their mutual provenance. The volume builds upon and synthesizes a hitherto loosely related cluster of inquires into past and present associations between visual and memorial forms. Its primary contribution is to demonstrate more concretely the potentially indivisible union of seeing and remembering in modern art, society, and politics—to show how visual artifacts materially facilitate practices of remembrance and, conversely, how the work of memory consists in viewing the past from an artful or strategically selected vantage. Our contributors aptly address these thick imbrications among visual and memorial dynamics from international as well as interdisciplinary perspectives: the case studies to come feature a wide spectrum of not only disciplinary perspectives but also cultural experiences, encompassing Cuban, European, North American, and Pacific (in other words, global) practices of spectatorship and remembrance. Any narrowly defined disciplinary or cultural approach to the central theme of this volume, we contend, would fail to account sufficiently for the patently transnational and intercultural character of seeing as a mode or remembering, or of remembering as a mode of seeing, in modern public culture.

Modern scholars of memory frequently analyze the use of visual artifacts to commemorate the past, as in the cases of public monuments, memorials, architecture, cinema, or other visual media. The respective work of Andreas Huyssen, James Young, and Barbie Zelizer are especially prominent examples of such scholarship.[5] Each of these commanding figures in the field of memory studies investigates the form and function of collective memory through visual phenomena, ranging from urban environments, conceptual art, and monumental symbolism to photojournalism, documentary film, and popular culture artifacts.

The diverse interdisciplinary field of visual culture concomitantly demonstrates how visual artifacts gain their social, political, and moral significance by representing noteworthy historical events or by manipulating dynamics of time and space. Indeed, early commentaries on photography and cinema marveled at their ability to preserve the past in palpable authenticity. Preoccupations with these dimensions of photography suffuse classic volumes on the subject by Roland Barthes, Susan Sontag, and Alan Trachtenberg.[6] The notion that photography is inherently a medium of memory is palpable in Sontag's famous claim that "To collect photographs is to collect the world," that they "appropriate the thing photographed."[7] Contemporary studies of visual culture examine the dynamic ways that visual representations in general acquire historical or memorial meaning as a result of their cultural and technological circulation. The respective scholarly projects of W. J. T. Mitchell, James Elkins, and Robert Hariman and John Louis Lucaities emphasize the intrinsically malleable significance of images as such.[8]

Numerous contemporary visual artists and designers, finally, explore cultural preoccupations with memory characteristic of the present era. Artists of all stripes, ranging from Art Spiegelman's graphic novel *Maus* to Doris Salcedo's post-minimalist sculpture, exhibit delicate sensitivies to how one's chosen visual aesthetic either accommodates or forecloses specific kinds of recollection.[9] From photography and digital media to public art installations and conceptual performances, contemporary artists routinely demonstrate the power of visual forms to evoke compelling senses of memory while also dramatizing its personal, cultural, and technological variability.

These different realms of academic study and cultural activity, concerning either memory or visual form, draw from scattered sources and exemplars among their counterparts; yet they remain substantially separate domains of inquiry or endeavor. Some of the most authoritative anthologies on either subject include individual studies of images that involve themes of memory or individual studies of memory grounded in visual representations; in either case, however, one *topos* retains notable primacy over the other.[10] Artists whose work explores questions of memory and vision and scholars of visual culture or public memory, moreover, seldom appear in a common venue for the expressed purpose of concerted interdisciplinary exchange. *Rhetoric, Remembrance, and Visual Form* furnishes that venue.

Interspersing the work of visual artists and designers among more conventional academic scholarship is crucial to the aims of this volume. Artistic works reproduced and analyzed in chapters to come illustrate vividly the curious paradox that defines material intersections among visual cultures and cultures of remembrance in late modernity: the perception that visual representations of temporal events are both trustworthy and illusory, that the recollected past in visual artifacts can seem not only authentic but hyper-real; yet the past as such and the visual media through which we view it (or re-member it) are ephemeral and inherently polysemic cultural forms. Such is the state of both spectatorship and remembrance, or remembrance as spectatorship, in late modernity (as illustrated by the example of the Reuters agency's embarrassingly refutable visual evidence). The forms of visual media that we entrust to preserve memories of the past (photography, recorded testimonies, online archives, and more) function selectively, and are inherently susceptible to distortion, such that they deprive us of sight and memory precisely in appearing to furnish them. The academic and artistic works collected in this volume share an acute sensitivity to this interplay of presence and absence, of constant conjunction and disjunction among visual and memorial forms, which shapes not only aesthetic but also material intersections among memory and images in contemporary art, politics, and society. Memory in these cases is not merely a metaphor with which to describe bytes of data signified on digital screens; and the visual dimensions of such intersections are not simply metaphorical substitutes for cognitive mental operations, as in the classical *ars memoriae*. The notion that visual forms and forms of memory share the same ostensible substance is one of the most deeply engrained structures of feeling in late modernity.

The studies collected in this volume offer richly varied paths to a common end: the *rhetorical* form and function of the materiality that inheres between images and memory. We contend that images powerfully invoke memory, and that memory is profoundly informed by visual media, through rhetorical dynamics: visual and memorial forms coalesce according to the ways in which practices of interpretation, argumentation, or communication assign shared meaning to them. Maurice Halbwachs's premise that even individual memories depend upon "collective frameworks" of interpretation, such that "the past is not preserved but is reconstructed on the basis of the present,"[11] has become a basic assumption of modern memory studies. Hariman and Lucaities symmetrically observe that "picture viewing" is an interpretive activity; all those who view a single image may "*seem* to see the same thing, yet the full meaning of the image remains unarticulated."[12] But the interpretive, argumentative, or communicative content of images as well as memories is—like the interplay of presence and absence that suffuses their shared materiality—radically indeterminate. The studies in this volume address the rhetorical confluences of visual and memorial forms—their relations as orchestrated through patterns of interpretation, argument, or communication—by investigating how images may express seemingly permanent *and* transient impressions of the past, or the ways in which the past acquires the appearance of simultaneous objectivity *and* distortion through visual means. Memories may be sighted, and images may provide material sites of memory, for some viewers rather than others. The relevant rhetorical question is why material intersections among images and memory sometimes succeed and sometimes fail as persuasively wrought depictions—or sightings—of past and present reality.

The following essays are grouped according to their illustrations of provocative and enduring questions about sight and memory in modern art, politics, and society. We seek, in every case, to locate the dynamism intrinsic to overlapping practices of seeing and remembrance in ways commensurate with James Young's approach to memory, meaning, and monumental form. He proposes, in his oft-cited analysis of Holocaust monuments, not "to fix the monument's meaning in time, which would effectively embalm it," but to "reinvigorate this monument with the memory of its acquired past, to vivify memory of events."[13] Our contributors "vivify" the co-production of sight and memory, of memory and sight, in order to animate rather than "fix" the profound resonance of *place and space, monuments and memorials*, and *media and mediums* as dynamic sites of artistic, social, or political exchange in modern public culture.

The works in Part I, "Places and Spaces," explore how physical locations and environments constitute deeply evocative loci of memory. Visible remainders of the past comprise the material substrate of memory in such locales and environs: to view landscapes and cityscapes is to remember the past imprinted and continuously reprinted on their natural or physical contours. Our contributors reveal that substrate to be neither static nor neutral but vital and ever changing in its spatial shape and significance.

One can see regional history, for instance, in landscape surveys. Andrea Hammer draws upon recent scholarly work that treats landscape as a vast mnemonic device while examining remnants of Simeon DeWitt's original 1790 topographical survey of central New York State. She documents how newly emerging imperial power in the Finger Lakes Region of New York State was inscribed on the ground and in the mind, erasing a prior landscape of cultural myth and memory before being partially written over by newly emerging identities. Urban art installations, in addition to rural landscapes, may prompt viewers to perceive multi-layered historical significance in seemingly mundane metropolitan environs. Margaret Ewing examines the art of Christian Boltanski, Shimon Attie, and Gunter Demnig, maintaining that their works elicit viewers' personal awareness of history. The manner of viewing that artists invite at sites of traumatic history, she argues, allows visitors to apprehend the full complexity of German history and identity in the newly reunified state more deeply than through written texts or other forms of art.

One may travel far and wide to explore places and spaces as loci of memory. Romantic tours of Greco-Roman ruins inspired by European travel literature exemplify how habits of seeing, remembering, and travelling materially intersect. Paul Duro investigates travel literature that chronicles voyagers' impressions of classical places, monuments, and artworks. These texts, he maintains, demonstrate an "anticipatory memory" or "preemptive nostalgia" based not on previous experience but on perceptions, expectations, and desires gleaned through memoirs, travel guides, prints, photographs, and films prior to one's visit to the actual sites. Hence, Duro shows how visual memory can ironically precede corporeal experience. The liminal space of cemeteries, which embody both landscape features and ornate architectural design, can also constitute a defining site of collective memory. Malcolm Woollen studies the Woodland Cemetery in Stockholm, Sweden (built between 1915 and 1941), for this reason. He argues that the cemetery reveals a unique Swedish attitude towards death and an understated declaration of national values based not on state-sponsored narratives of tragedies or heroic victories but on everyday life. The cemetery illustrates how memory may visibly and materially express quotidian national identity without relying on monumental histories of military heroism or sacrifice.

Part II, "Monuments and Memorials," is comprised of scholarly and artistic work that considers how subjects which resist both visual representation and coherent communal recollection compel us to question the material form and rhetorical function of conventional monuments and memorials. Our contributors seek to unsettle, in this context, the visual as well as commemorative conservatism or didacticism that often suffuses the officially sanctioned significance of monuments and memorials. Their work shows how the material features of monuments and memorials may organize a vibrant nexus of innovative and potentially transformative artistic, social, and political practices.

Memories of the often appalling indirect consequences of modern warfare defy the generic conventions of typical monuments and memorials. Ekaterina Haskins explores the dynamic possibilities of ephemeral grassroots memorials by examining the *Eyes Wide Open* traveling exhibit dedicated to casualties on both sides of the Iraq War. She considers how its symbolism enables multiple audiences to assume an active role in the commemorative process. Her analysis demonstrates the challenges that advocates of memory may face in seeking to render visible the tragedies of war conventionally withheld from state commemoration. An investigation of how to interpret the meaning of horrific historical events in monumental or memorial form would be incomplete without reflecting on the artistic process involved in producing those forms. Kingsley Baird discusses the creative processes and memorial functions of *The Cloak of Peace* (2006), his commissioned stainless steel sculpture in the Nagasaki Peace Park. Baird uses the sculpture to highlight a particular challenge that confronts memory artists as well as the viewing public: how to reconcile the charged space between two primary "forms" of memory—the work's inhabitation of an amorphous public space and viewers' reinterpretation of its memorial symbolism—in order to bear witness to unresolved historical traumas.

The characteristically modern and late modern experience of accelerating historical or temporal mobility poses additional challenges for those who attempt to memorialize frequently unnoticed, anonymous tragedies. Robert Bednar investigates how mass transit can both cause and complicate the need for collective remembrance. He analyzes roadside shrines that attempt to memorialize the thousands of motorists killed annually in automobile accidents by unexpectedly reminding drivers and passengers of the dangers which attend automobile travel. Efforts to memorialize private, or publicly excluded, processes of grief in still other contexts can also teach us much about the limits of conventional memorial forms. Dee Britton examines numerous challenges to the designation of *Dark Elegy*, a sculptural installation designed to commemorate those killed in the bombing of Pan Am Flight 103, as a national memorial to victims of terrorism. The essay documents trenchant bureaucratic objections to the design, due to its vivid representation of human vulnerability, thereby illustrating incidents of contestation between instrumental and cultural representations of collective memory.

The contributions collected in Part III, "Media and Mediums," investigate critical relationships between unusual media or mediums of memory and the rhetorically malleable aura they lend to objects of memory. In every case, the material properties of a given medium facilitate corresponding practices of visual remembrance. Here, as in the preceding sections of the volume, our contributors delineate the inherently plastic matter of the media or mediums in question, demonstrating that they function not as neutral channels of representation but as essentially animate forms in the production of sight as memory, of memory as sight.

Discovering uncommon vantages on historical atrocities compels us to remember events anew through atypical visual media. Frances Guerin explores the possible appropriation of amateur photographs taken by German perpetrators as both agents of and witnesses to the barbarous events of the Holocaust and World War II. She considers how military atrocities may be seen and thus memorialized from radically uncommon perspectives—in this case, amateur photographs taken by Nazi soldiers of the very mass killings on the Eastern Front in which they participated. The mediums of household possessions and intimate embodied experience may shape patterns of remembrance in similarly terrifying episodes of forced migration and geopolitical exile. Ernesto Pujol addresses the formation of artistic memory, spinning an autobiography of remembrance in order to demonstrate the role of personal recollection, from childhood to adulthood, in spurring the creative process. He evocatively meditates in both words and images upon the multi-form ways that familial belongings and even our bodies can manifest coalesced patterns of remembrance and migration, as in the case of his family's experiences during and after the Cuban Revolution.

The constitutive media of popular culture fundamentally inform the character and significance of widely disseminated memories in addition to intimately held recollections. Ned O'Gorman and Kevin Hamilton examine how the rise of the U.S. as a nuclear power depended on the careful negotiation and manipulation of collective memory. They propose that the U.S. did so by shifting the visual emphasis of nuclear armament in public discourse from such fearsome icons as the mushroom cloud to a new icon: the nuclear console operator, who demonstrated control and rightful dominion over an otherwise fearsome technology. Traditional visual arts, in comparison, hold equally important clues to major transitions in the development of modern public remembrance. Johanna Ruohonen discusses memories of war as expressed in and evoked by Finnish public art, especially public painting. She focuses on the political functions of such seemingly non-political works and, in doing so, demonstrates the critical functions of apparently innocuous public art in generating collective memories of national history and reproducing storied ideals of present-day national identity. Ordinary persons, finally, help to fashion new mediums of memory not merely as conventional spectators but as active documentarians of historical events. Travelers and tourists collect visual mementos of both ordinary and extraordinary sights, thereby illustrating ingrained habits of remembering through visual tokens. Emily Godbey examines how Americans have understood disaster and tragedy as sites of consumption and leisure. She explores the production of postcards, souvenirs, portrait-making, and personal photography in relation to historical disasters. Godbey seeks to explain how and why Americans have commemorated scenes of tragedy with mementoes and pictures much as they have learned to document or preserve tokens of family vacations.

The aforementioned chapters combine to form a robustly interdisciplinary investigation rooted in regional, national, and international experiences. Their findings illuminate how memories may be seen (or sighted) in visual form and how visual forms constitute noteworthy sites of memory. The chapters boast a diversity of methods and disciplines from the arts, humanities, and social sciences; such diversity, however, coheres in the volume's consistent focus on rhetorical practices of communication, interpretation, or argumentation that motivate conjunctions of visual and memorial forms. Our contributors provide, despite differences in method, literature, subject matter, and nationality, an especially rich and thematically unified exploration of strategies according to which the production of visual artifacts and the work of remembrance materially intersect in ongoing processes of artistic, social, and political expression. The following studies consequently attend, with especial nuance and insight, to the complicated ways in which groups and individuals strive to make meaning from the simultaneously durable and ephemeral material of memory and images alike.

NOTES

1. *Oxford English Dictionary*, 3rd edition, s.v., "memory."
2. France A. Yates, *The Art of Memory*, reprint ed. (Chicago: University of Chicago Press, 2001), 4.
3. Plato, "Meno," in *The Collected Dialogues of Plato*, ed. Edith Hamilton and Huntington Cairns (Princeton: Princeton University Press, 1989), 353–84; and "Phaedo," in *Collected Dialogues*, 40–98. See also Douwie Draaisma, *Metaphors of Memory*, trans. Paul Vincent (Cambridge: Cambridge University Press, 2000), chapter 2; Sigmund Freud, "A Note upon the 'Mystic Writing-Pad,'" in *The Complete Psychological Works of Sigmund Freud*, vol. 19., trans. James Strachey (London: The Hogarth Press, 1961); and Yates, *Art of Memory*, chapter 2.
4. "Reuters Toughens Rules after Altered Photo Affair," Reuters January 18, 2007. Retrieved May 4, 2010 from http://www.reuters.com/article/latestCrisis/idUSL18678707.
5. Huyssen, Andreas, *Present Pasts: Urban Palimpsests and the Politics of Memory* (Stanford: Stanford University Press, 2003) and *Twilight Memories:*

Marking Time in a Culture of Amnesia (New York: Routledge, 1994); James E. Young, *At Memory's Edge: After-Images of the Holocaust in Contemporary Art and Architecture* (New Haven: Yale University Press, 2000) and *The Texture of Memory: Holocaust Memorials and Meaning* (New Haven: Yale University Press, 1993); Barbie Zelizer, *Remembering to Forget: Holocaust Memory Through the Camera's Eye* (Chicago: University of Chicago Press, 1998) and *Covering the Body: The Kennedy Assassination, the Media, and the Shaping of Collective Memory* (Chicago: University of Chicago Press, 1993). See also Kendall R. Phillips, ed., *Framing Public Memory* (Tuscaloosa, AL: University of Alabama Press, 2004); Greg Dickinson, Carole Blair, and Brian L. Ott, eds., *Places of Public Memory: The Rhetoric of Museums and Memorials* (Tuscaloosa, AL: University of Alabama Press, 2010); and Marita Sturken, *Tangled Memories: The Vietnam War, the AIDS Epidemic, and the Politics of Remembering* (Berkeley: University of California Press, 1997) and *Tourists of History: Memory, Kitsch, and Consumerism from Oklahoma City to Ground Zero* (Durham: Duke University Press, 2007).

6. Roland Barthes, *Camera Lucida: Reflections on Photography*, trans. Richard Howard (New York: Hill and Wang, 1994) and *Image-Music-Text*, trans. Stephen Heath (New York: Hill and Wang, 1978); Susan Sontag, *On Photography* (New York: Picador, 2001); Alan Trachtenberg, *Classic Essays on Photography* (Stony Creek, CT: Leete's Island Books, 1980).

7. Sontag, *Photography*, 3, 4.

8. W. J. T. Mitchell, *What do Pictures Want?: The Lives and Loves of Images* (Chicago: University of Chicago Press, 2006) and *Picture Theory: Essays on Verbal and Visual Representation* (Chicago: University of Chicago Press, 1995); James Elkins, *On Pictures and the Words That Fail Them* (Cambridge: Cambridge University Press, 1998), *The Domain of Images, On the Historical Study of Visual Artifacts* (Ithaca, NY: Cornell University Press, 1999), *Why are Our Pictures Puzzles? On the Modern Origins of Pictorial Complexity* (New York: Routledge, 1999), *Visual Studies: A Skeptical Introduction* (New York: Routledge, 2003); Robert Hariman and John Louis Lucaites, *No Caption Needed: Iconic Photographs, Public Culture, and Liberal Democracy* (Chicago: University of Chicago Press, 2007). See also Lester C. Olson, *Benjamin Franklin's Vision of America, 1754–1784: A Study in Rhetorical Iconology* (Columbia: University of South Carolina Press, April 2004) and Emblems of American Community in the Revolutionary Era: A Study in Rhetorical Iconology (Washington, D.C.: Smithsonian Institution Press, 1991); Cara A. Finnegan, *Picturing Poverty: Print Culture and FSA Photographs* (Washington, D.C.: Smithsonian, 2003).

9. See Art Spiegelman, *Maus I and II* (New York: Pantheon, 1991) and Huyssen, *Present Pasts*, chapter 7.

10. Some of the most widely cited anthologies in visual culture include Jessica Evans and Stuart Hall, eds., *Visual Culture: The Reader* (London: SAGE, 1999); Nicholas Mirzoeff, ed., *The Visual Culture Reader* (New York: Routledge, 2002); Lester C. Olson, Cara A. Finnegan, and Diane S. Hope, eds., *Visual Rhetoric: A Reader in Communication and American Culture* (London: SAGE, 2008); Lawrence J. Prelli, ed., *Rhetorics of Display* (Columbia: University of South Carolina Press, 2006). Especially notable collections of or commentaries on key works in modern memory studies includes Astrid Erll and Ansgar Nünning, eds., *Cultural Memory Studies: An International and Interdisciplinary Handbook* (Berlin: Walter de Gruyter, 2008); Michael Rossington and Anne Whitehead, eds., *Theories of Memory: A Reader* (Baltimore, MD: The Johns Hopkins University Press, 2007); and Jeffrey K. Olick, Vered Vinitzky-Seroussi, and Daniel Levy, eds., *The Collective Memory*

Reader (New York: Oxford University Press, 2011); Susanna Radstone and Bill Schwarz, eds., *Memory: Histories, Theories, Debates* (New York: Fordham University Press, 2010); and Anne Whitehead, *Memory* (New York: Routledge, 2009).

11. Maurice Hallbwachs, *On Collective Memory*, trans. Lewis A. Coser (Chicago: University of Chicago Press, 1992), 40.

12. Hariman and Lucaites, *No Caption Needed*, 43–44. Authoritative methodological works on the interpretation of images or visual phenomena include Charles A. Hill and Marguerite Helmers, *Reading Visual Rhetorics* (New York: Routledge, 2004); Gunther Kress and Theo van Leeuwen, *Reading Images: The Grammar of Visual Design* (New York: Routledge, 2006); Gillian Rose, *Visual Methodologies: An Introduction to the Interpretation of Visual Materials* (London: SAGE, 2006).

13. Young, *Texture*, 14.

Part I
Places and Spaces

1 Memory Lines
The Plotting of New York's New Military Tract

Andrea Hammer

Every story is a travel story—a spatial practice.[1]

—Michel de Certeau

Plot:
1. (a) A small piece of ground, generally used for a specific purpose. (b) A measured area of land; lot.
2. A ground plan, as for a building; chart; diagram
3. The series of events consisting of the outline of the action of a narrative or drama
4. A secret plan to accomplish a hostile or illegal purpose; scheme[2]

—Peter Brooks

You can see it best from the air: central New York's regular grid of plots and lines, the spatial medium of its roads, streets, cities, and towns that literally directs our movement through and placement within the landscape.

These are the remnants of New York State Surveyor General Simeon De Witt's original 1789 survey of central New York State's New Military Tract, some 2,625 square miles of bounty lands carved out of the Six Nations territory to remunerate New York's Revolutionary War soldiers for their service. De Witt subdivided the land into twenty-eight townships, each 60,000 acres and as square as possible, each further subdivided into 100 square lots of 600 acres, with six lots reserved to support schools and churches, larger claims, and compensate for lands under water.[3] Such boundaries make enduring marks on the landscape.

It's been well over 200 years since this spatial order was inscribed onto a complex of older, indigenous cultural landscapes. In that time the materials, even the uses, of these boundaries have changed while the lines themselves persisted. They've evolved into dirt, gravel, and paved roads; they've become foot paths transformed into fence lines; they've emerged as hedgerows, edge conditions, field discontinuities, crop boundaries,

Figure 1.1 East of Cayuga Lake. Photo courtesy of Alex MacLean, May 2007.

tree lines, and other phenomena. Even housing developments have been contorted to fit within the lines of old agricultural fields.[4] Despite over 200 years of accumulating marks and traces on the landscape, remnants of this system remain, in palimpsest fashion, like old writing bleeding through new.

Imagine this landscape—any landscape—as a continually unfolding story and vast mnemonic device, a living, shifting repository of marks, lines, and erasures that "speak" of past lives, past events, past cultural myths and meanings. To perceive the landscape, Donald Meinig writes, is to understand that life "must be lived amidst that which was made before," an accumulation which is always becoming something else. To perceive the landscape, Tim Ingold claims, is therefore "to carry out an act of remembrance," to engage "perceptually with an environment that is itself pregnant with the past."[5]

This essay attempts such an act of remembrance. It reconstructs the New Military Tract's original boundary lines and interprets these still visible artifacts as evidence of a particular kind of plotting inextricably bound up with other forms of plotting: illicit land schemes; military accounts as travel narratives; surveying, charting and mapping; and foundation narratives justifying dispossession and a new imperialistic social and economic order. These multiple meanings of plot, in other words, intersect in the landscape's material form, a spatial text deeply imbricated with other textual forms.

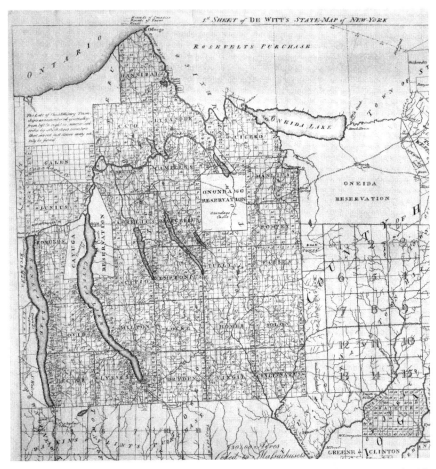

Figure 1.2   1ˢᵗ Sheet of Simeon De Witt's State Map of New York, 1792. Used with permission from New York State Library.

Plot refers variously to measured land as well as pieces of ground, to charts and diagrams as well as to secret schemes to accomplish hostile purposes, and, finally, to outlines or dramatic arcs of written and spoken narratives. To remember is to oscillate between these different forms of plotting in order to recuperate the "subterranean logic" that Peter Brooks suggests runs through plot's diverse semantic range. "Common to the original sense of the word is the idea of boundedness, demarcation, the drawing of lines to mark off and order,"[6] including the temporal orderings that create narrative and make stories. Just as boundaries function to found and articulate new spaces, so stories operate upon and across those spaces by launching interest in them, justifying them, delimiting who and who doesn't belong, and narrating, even adjudicating, what might be done within them.[7] Under the rubric of *plot,* then, things often kept apart come together: written military commands carried out by footsteps; military journals that narrate transgressive movement through space; survey notes, maps, and charts as transcriptions of journeys; progressive narratives of the meaning of the new republic and newly forming identities; and landscape as a text, readable against other sorts of texts.

Within a scant two decades following the Revolutionary War, newly emerging American imperial power became inscribed upon the ground and impressed in the mind, overlaying prior landscapes of indigenous cultural practice, myth, and memory, before being written over by newly emerging identities and possibilities, by new plots that contradict, challenge, elaborate, or tangle old plot lines, old story lines. From the emergence of the first maps that demarcated coveted Indian lands to that same ground reconfigured as a newly commodified and rationalized landscape, the plotting of upstate New York seems inseparable from a foundational violence at the heart of framing the new republic.

SIGHTING THE LINES

> [A]lthough the lines on the land have remained, their function has often changed, and in some places the continuity has been broken by landscape features imposed by subsequent generations; in other places, the landscape that reveals itself as an orderly geometry and purposeful pattern from the air becomes a jumble of abandoned field lines, rutted byways, and crossroads hamlets on the ground itself.[8]
>
> —William Wyckoff

As William Wyckoff noted in his work on western New York, "the landscape obscures as well as displays the intentions of past generations."[9] Recovering De Witt's 1789 boundaries—literally making them legible— has involved several phases. The first involved scanning individual De Witt township maps, georeferencing them to orthophotos, and displaying them as transparent layers over the infrared images. Findings echoed those of Wyckoff.[10] At a synoptic scale, fundamental and pervasive qualities of cardinality and rectilinearity are readily visible. A clear correspondence, if sometimes fragmented, exists between modern town line roads and original survey lines; in the townships of Ovid and Hector, for example, which lie between Seneca and Cayuga lakes, they conform quite precisely. Otherwise invisible modern civic (political) boundaries follow original survey lines. Substantially enlarging the superimposed images, moreover, shows how the integrity of individual lots falls apart most readily because of multiple subdivisions, woodland growth, farm and lot consolidation, and layers of new building. But even here remnants of old lot lines can be found, embedded within newer geometries.

Reading landscapes at the ground level, oddly enough, depends upon a constant movement back and forth between walking or driving the terrain in question and simultaneously orienting by virtue of aerial photographs, ideally a photographic series constructed over time. Following Lot 29 in old Ovid Township, No. 13, for instance, required taking bearings from a series of aerial photographs dating from 1938 and translating their abstract lines and squares into ground level phenomena: hedgerows of mature trees, ditches, windbreaks of small firs, chestnuts of 70 or 80 years' growth, a mature woodlot just off center. Its southern boundary, the gravel road called South Townline Road, borders a field of corn and, adjacent, a young woodland of undifferentiated, narrow saplings growing closely together. A raceway, circa 1960s, cut slightly into the woodland, is now a scrubby, un-mowed oval patch. Next to the woodland plot, a stand of walnuts and maples adjoins a thick field of fresh-cut wheat drying in windrows. This south side of Lot 29 gets the most sunlight and forms its densest edge. The eastern boundary has its own character: a paved road separated from the fields by a deep ditch alive with purple chicory, a tangle of wild grapevines, Queen Ann's lace, purple loose strife, yellow toadflax, clumps of thistle and milkweed, patches of cattails, and purple clover. Follow the northernmost boundary to the east and you'll see it disappear into a heavily wooded ravine before emerging on the other side as a discontinuity in an agricultural field. Without the abstract patterning from above, features on the ground appear clear in their immediate detail but an otherwise disorienting welter of phenomena.[11]

Yet simply bringing these lines into view is insufficient as a memorializing strategy. Invisible is the role that social conflict—arguably the key motivator of plots and plotting—plays in producing space, a role reconstructed here through historical documents and bent to the purpose of remembrance. Given the page limitations necessary for this volume, my examples are meant to be suggestive rather than exhaustive.

PLOTTING DISPOSSESSION: THE SULLIVAN-CLINTON CAMPAIGN AGAINST THE IROQUOIS

> The immediate objects are the total destruction and devastation of [British-allied and hostile Iroquois] settlements and the capture of as many prisoners of every age and sex as possible. It will be essential to ruin their crops now in the ground and prevent their planting more. . . . I would recommend, that some post in the center of the Indian Country, should be occupied with all expedition . . . whence parties should be detached to lay waste all the settlements round, with instructions to do it in the most effectual manner that the country may not be merely overrun, but destroyed.[12]
>
> —Gen. George Washington's orders to Gen. John Sullivan

[T]he Rebels . . . notwithstanding their fair Speeches, wish for nothing more, than to extirpate us from the Earth that they may possess our Lands.[13]

—Seneca Chief Sayengeraghta at Fort Niagara, 1779

Martin Bruckner makes a compelling case for why surveying in the early republic should command historical attention. Geographic literacy—manuals, maps, geometry—quite literally "enabled British Americans to . . . get their feet on the ground, granting them a sense of place and entitlement" and contributing to the rupture with their mother nation. But this same vehicle that "enabled a people to find and define themselves in a republican nation," he argues, itself led to a new imperial dynamic in the eastern states. Geographic literacy "was transformed into expressions of imperial self-identification and actions of territorial annexation."[14]

In 1779 Commander-in-Chief George Washington in effect ordered Generals John Sullivan and James Clinton, brother of New York's Governor George Clinton, to annex Iroquois lands. Washington ordered a campaign so destructive that it would push "the Indians to the greatest practicable distance from their own settlements and our frontiers" and make "the destruction of their settlements so final and complete as to put it out of their power to derive the smallest succor from them in case they should attempt to return this season."[15] By October, Sullivan had carried out Washington's orders, having burned to the ground approximately forty Indian towns, destroyed 160,000 bushels of corn, hundreds of acres of vegetables, peach, and apple orchards, including fifty- to seventy-year-old orchards at Kandaia along the eastern shore of Seneca Lake.

While the campaign initially escalated rather than halted Indian and British attacks on the frontier throughout 1778 and 1779, its immediate consequence was to open Indian lands to covetous eyes and future schemes. It opened to view, Barbara Graymont argues, "a hitherto uncharted country and revealed to the soldiers . . . a land of rich soil and luxuriant growth," a "state of civilization equal to, and often better than, that of the frontier whites."[16] Moreover, it enabled Surveyor General of the Continental Army, Robert Erskine, and his assistants Benjamin Lodge and Simeon De Witt literally to get their feet on the ground and produce some forty-four maps articulating the routes the army undertook that summer. De Witt, notably, would go on to succeed Erskine upon the latter's death in 1780 before taking up the new position of Surveyor General for New York State, a post he would hold for fifty years. In that position he would preside over the complete resurvey of the Six Nation's landscape as the New Military Tract and its transformation into a landscape of private property holders. Assisting him would be his cousin, Moses DeWitt, and Sullivan campaign soldiers Lieutenant John Hardenbergh and Hardenbergh's brother Abraham. All would invest heavily in the newly opened lands.

Historically, whoever held these lands wielded enormous geographic power. The heart of the Six Nations territory embraced a system of rivers and lakes that linked the east coast to western lands and the north to the south. Control of this network had been a source of Iroquois geographical power for generations, Daniel K. Richter notes, because it encompassed most of the major trade routes of the native Northeast, providing access both to European colonial markets and to peltries demanded by Euro-American traders.[17] While other reasons have been given for Washington's longest and most sustained scorched-earth campaign against the Iroquois—predominantly, the need to end Indian-Tory devastations on the frontier and to break Indian agriculture suspected of supplying British forces—"the American Revolution," concludes Max Mintz, "was not only a struggle for independence, but also for the lands of the Indians, and the jewel was the upstate New York domain of the Iroquois Six Nations."[18]

Besides its violence, the Sullivan campaign is noteworthy for the flood of narratives it produced through journals and diaries kept by the soldiers and officers, and for the abundance of drawings and maps made of this hitherto unknown (to whites) territory. "The river being forded," noted Reverend William Rogers in his journal while waiting for James Clinton's detachment to join Sullivan's,

> we entered upon what is properly called the Indian country, or that part of the wilderness claimed by the six nations. . . . The view of this was grand beyond description, as the ground for a great circuit was level and the grass was high and green. Drums were beating, fifes playing, colors flying. Getting to the mouth of the Tioga, we found it in width one hundred and forty-two yards, and the water much deeper than had been imagined. Verdant plains in our rear, the flowing Susquehanna on our right. Ourselves in the Tioga or Cayuga streem [sic], with a fine neck of land in our front and mountains surrounding the whole, afforded pleasant reflections though separated from friends and in an enemy's country." "Surely," Rogers mused, "a soil like this is worth contending for."[19]

At Newtown (now Elmira) Major John Burrowes judged the corn "superior to any I ever saw" and the land as "exceed[ing] any that I have ever seen." "Some corn stalks measured eighteen feet, and a cob one foot and a half long. Beans, cucumbers, watermelons, muskmelons, cimblens [sic] are in great plenty."[20] Thomas Grant, a member of the surveyor's party, kept up a running description of the country: "We came on the Head waters of the Sinica Creek which Emties itself into the River St Laurance 31/3 miles, entered a Great Swamp, The Timber chiefly white Pine and hemlock, which was 4 miles in Length; We then entred a fine Bottom. The Timber chiefly Sugar Tree & Walnut." Moving up the east side of Seneca Lake, Grant enthused about his march "this day 13 miles

Through a Contry which Exceeds any Land I ever saw, abonding with Locust, Walnut, hickry, and other Timber. The Good Land appears to be Extincive." Two days later: "The Good Land continues."[21] Major Jeremiah Fogg describes "the land between the Seneca and Cayuga lakes [as] good, level and well timbered; affording a sufficiency for twenty elegant townships, which in process of time will doubtless add to the importance of America." As for the Genesee flats, this "vast body of clear Intervale extending 12 or 14 miles up & down the river & several miles back from the river [is] cover'd with grass from 5 to 8 feet high & so thick that a man can git thro it but very slowly." Often the soldiers could see "nothing but the mens guns above the grass."[22] Chain-carrier Grant enthused: "these flats and the land Adjacent is allowed to exceed any thing in America."[23]

Such narratives comprise a tour—a narrative of movement *through* the country and accounts of what happened there and what might be done with it in the future—while extant maps transcribe that tour as flattened out and rationalized geographical plans. Upon accepting his appointment as geographer and surveyor to the Continental Army, Erskine wrote in 1777 to his fellow-surveyor George Washington "in order to shew what may really be accomplished by a Geographer, that more may not be expected than it is practicable to perform; and that an estimate may be made of the number of assistants required should the Map of any particular district be required in a given time." Erskine noted that "in planning a country a great part of the ground must be walked over, particularly the banks of Rivers and Roads; as much of which may be traced and laid down in three hours as could be walked over in one." *Planning* refers to making a plan of a piece of ground, to plotting. By laying out a ratio of three to one, Erskine estimates that it takes three times as long to measure the ground as it does to walk it. "Besides attending to the course and measuring the distance of the way he is traversing," Erskine notes, the surveyor "should at all convenient places where he can see around him, take observations and angles to Mountains, hills, steeples, houses and other objects which present themselves, in order to fix their site; to correct his work; and to facilitate its being connected with other Surveys." Such "information and computed distances" should yield "a tolerable idea of the Country."[24]

Staff officer Major Jeremiah Fogg observed that the Indians had taken every precaution "to prevent a survey of the country," wryly noting that "Maps of it hitherto taken seem rather to blind than enlighten a traveler," a tactic designed to keep "any civilized people [from getting] a foothold in their territories. . . ."[25] Washington's written orders (to poach from de Certeau), the subsequent march into foreign territory, the attendant narratives, the surveys made, and the maps produced are all interlocking narrative activities comprising this first phase of annexation: the opening up of new space and a founding theater for subsequent action.[26]

PLOTTING ENCLOSURE: SURVEYING THE NEW MILITARY TRACT

> Beginning at a beech tree standing on the West side of the Onon-
> daga River bearing S. 60 W. from the upper part of the Oswego
> Falls towards the east shore of the said River—this tree is marked
> on the west side—
>   N.E. corner
>   Township No. 1
>   Virtuous and Victorious Military
>   1789
> This tree likewise stands against a steep bank and around it the trees
> are all marked (that is, blazed) facing the corner and run from thence
> as the Needle now points Due West.[27]
>
> —Moses De Witt

The late historian J. B. Harley argues that "The surveyor . . . replicates
not just the 'environment' in some abstract sense but equally the territorial
imperatives of a particular political system."[28] Ten years after Sullivan's
army transformed a densely figured cultural landscape into a smoldering
ash heap, another army of surveyors—some veterans of that campaign—
returned to Indian country, this time to inscribe onto the landscape the
highly rationalized boundaries of the New Military Tract and, by implication, New York's newly consolidated power.

If maps can be tools in achieving spatial stability, as Denis Cosgrove
argues,[29] the new survey could be read as exemplum: the projection of an
authority that did not in fact exist, one among a series of competing schemes
as different modes of authority vied for the same prize. Similarly, Harley
has written persuasively of maps as "weapons of imperialism," charting
lands "claimed on paper before they were effectively occupied" and helping
to create myths "used to legitimate the reality of conquest and empire."[30]
Given, as Alan Taylor writes, that "the great vehicle for making property
and power in America [was] the control over the acquisition and disposition of Indian lands,"[31] the survey was a calculated, offensive strike in a
continuing battle for jurisdiction over Indian lands waged between New
York and its competitors: the substantially dispossessed and weakened Iroquois; Massachusetts; the Federal government; and a powerful group of
private speculators within New York State's legislative ranks led by Colonel
John Livingston.

New York's drive began almost immediately on the heels of Sullivan's
campaign in 1782, when the legislature expropriated nearly two million
acres of primarily Onondaga and Cayuga land as bounty payment for
New York soldiers, a promissory note to the victor. Their method was
based on the practices of the agrimensores, the Roman land surveyors
who marked, regulated, and distributed appropriated lands among the
veterans in its military colonies. They commenced, Taylor writes, without

benefit of treaty (Indian title would not be extinguished until 1788 and 1789) and in full defiance of federal authority as the sole arbitrator of Indian lands.[32] By 1789, the plan had undergone at least eight iterations. On February 28 the final draft was passed by the New York legislature, and De Witt was ordered to lay out the twenty-five townships (three were quickly added) and disperse the land by ballot.[33] Governor George Clinton wanted to settle Iroquoia as quickly as possible. Once again De Witt and his proxies would go over the ground he mapped under Sullivan and this time, remap it to function as a gridwork of exchangeable commodities within a free market system.

De Witt's approach was one of several experiments in the newly emerging practice of subdividing New World lands according to an abstract grid instead of the European practice of metes and bounds.[34] Under the latter system, surveyors had relied upon known topographic or geologic landmarks—a stone on the riverbank, an apple tree, a large stump— and a compass to perambulate a set of distances duly recorded in rods or poles. Subdividing lands according to a grid, however, substituted a formal mathematical elegance and rationalized solution to settlement for the vagrancies of topography and the transitory nature of landmarks. White expansion could press rapidly into Indian territory and (ideally, at least) with an orderly method for buying and selling lands. Transforming a densely forested land into a new republic of agricultural fields, villages, and towns might be accomplished more efficiently through a system of roads and transportation networks that quickly integrated settlers within a manufacturing and agricultural system and enfolded them within both national and world markets.[35] De Witt commissioned his young nephew, Moses, to oversee the survey, with John and Abraham Hardenbergh his assistants. Toward that end, Moses scrawled at the beginning of his 1789 journal an admonition to "Take time by the foretop," a figure of speech signifying the need for opportunistic haste.[36] Saturday, June 27, found De Witt in camp at Oswego Falls, "calculating & preparing for running Township No. 1" through well-timbered land that he judged would make "fine wheatland interspersed with beautiful upland." [37] Over the ensuing months and years as he and his men painstakingly surveyed the land, they kept a running inventory of the types of vegetation encountered, the quality of the soil and its fitness for agriculture:

> "Fabius . . . Lot 7: south bounds beginning at the southwest corner,
> thence east:
> 15 [chains]—entered a swamp timbered with tamarack and black
> alder;
> 35 [chains]—out of the swamp on beech and hemlock land.[38]

Such notations served not only as a way to calculate potential commodities (white pine for spars, boards, building timber and shingles; sugar trees for "the best fuel the forest yields"; hickory for farming utensils, etc.); they served as guides to soil type and quality. As Judge William Cooper noted in his earlier assessment of Otsego County:

> "Where the bass-wood, the butter-nut, the sugar-maple, white-ash, elm, and tall red-beech is the prevailing timber, you may be certain of a good soil both for grain and grass . . . The large topped, short mossy-beech denotes ungenerous land. The poplar in our climate promises good wheat . . . [S]uch tracts will be among the most valuable on account of the timber as I have before stated."[39]

By 1792, Richard Schein writes, "the woods of central New York . . . were filled with surveyors marks notched into trees at the corners of lots and townships . . . The result was a visible imprint of the survey, not unlike present day suburban subdivisions after the surveyors have set the stakes and flags in the ground but before the contractors have begun to work."[40] The completed surveys, Taylor notes, would allow the contested territory to be settled quickly.

By 1792, New York had inscribed a new spatial order on the ground and devised a balloting system for disbursing the parcels.[41] Such township names as Lysander, Cato, Brutus, Camillus, Cicero, Manlius, Aurelius, Romulus, Scipio, Fabius, and Ovid authorized a new meaning to the landscape, referencing ancient republican Roman and Greek foundational models rather than that of Great Britain. As for the Iroquois, Clinton quickly negotiated with sub-factions of the Cayuga and Onondaga to extinguish their claim to land in exchange for reservations of 100 square miles at the head of Cayuga Lake and the foot of Onondaga Lake. Head chiefs and power brokers, however, refused to recognize the Clinton treaties of 1788 and 1790, understanding that Clinton was set on flooding the territory with white settlers who would surround splintered Indian groups and seek to dislodge them altogether.

By 1794, the Cayuga reservation was divided again and, by 1799, it was eliminated altogether.[42] Concurrently, in 1795, developers including Moses De Witt petitioned the New York State Legislature to open up the Onondaga Reservation so that salt production from the Onondaga Lake could flow unimpeded.[43] Confident that reservation lands "would contribute to the increasing wealth, prosperity and importance of the State . . . (perhaps in preference to any other uncultivated part of the State)," De Witt promised a series of payments and guaranteed the settlement of some 200 farmers within ten years, or "one family to every 250 acres. . . ."[44] By 1822, what began as a tract of 100 square miles, or 64,000 acres, had been shaved to 7,300 acres, the reservation's current size.

The survey lines stand simultaneously as scheme and schemata for amassing power, wealth, and independence for some based on the systematic dispossession of others. They also enabled new settlers to locate themselves within a newly emerging social space and to carry out those labors that transform geometric space into lived landscapes.

PLOTTING A COMMODIFIED LANDSCAPE: ELKANAH WATSON'S TECHNOLOGICAL FOUNDATION NARRATIVE

> Our prospect [from Seneca Lake] extended south, over a bold sheet of water. The tops of the hills and trees were just tinged with the departing sun; the evening was serene; and my mind involuntarily expanded, in anticipating the period, when the borders of this lake will be stripped of nature's livery, and in its place will be rich enclosures, pleasant villas, numerous flocks, herds, etc. and it will be inhabited by a happy race of people, enjoying the rich fruits of their own labors, and the luxury of sweet liberty and independence, approaching to a millennial state.[45]
>
> —Elkanah Watson, *Memoirs*

David Nye has called attention to certain myths that framed American experience in the new republic. He calls these "America as Second Creation" stories, foundational myths recovered in diaries, letters, and journals that emphasize the self-conscious movement into a new space and its transformation into a prosperous, egalitarian society by new technologies—primarily surveying, mapping, and canal building. Projecting an endless supply of land and raw materials, the narratives describe a self-reliant individual who rises in the world by virtue of his personal powers and, through new technologies, completes the divine design latent within nature.[46]

If ever a man plotted his own life's story to conform to a progressive narrative of the developing New Military Tract—and by extension a triumphant new republic "approaching to a millennial state"—that man was Elkanah Watson, one of the tract's "unofficial proprietors."[47] Watson's handwritten journals, published memoirs, and numerous field books, maps, and surveys suggest a powerful convergence between the Second Creation plot and the active plotting of a commodified landscape. Watkins might easily serve as exemplum of Bruckner's description of the early American subject grounded in the performance of geographic literacy, a competence that allowed him to plot lands, transform them, and describe and define himself within what colonizers considered an inevitable, divinely sanctioned social and economic order.[48]

In September of 1791, during Moses De Witt's third summer of the survey, the Albany entrepreneur and speculator toured the region to assess its potential for an inland navigation system, a canal system to drive New York's development. Watson had been considering the scheme for years. Fellow travelers were Jeremiah Van Rensselaer, a former member of the U.S. Congress from New York and board member of the Bank of Albany;

Philip Van Cortlandt, a member of the New York State Senate; and Stephen Bayard. Both Cortlandt and Bayard had served in Sullivan's campaign, while Watson had been present during the contested 1788 treaty of Fort Stanwix, when Clinton extracted lands from the Onondaga. This group would form the Western Inland Lock Navigation Company, charged with opening water communication between the Hudson River and lakes Ontario and Seneca, a precursor to the Erie Canal completed in 1825.

It was during a visit to the country in 1788, Watson claims, while standing on the banks of the Mohawk River, that he first entertained the idea of "counteracting, at least by a fair competition" George Washington's plan to build a series of canals that would bring trade of the western regions to Alexandria. Returning three years later to implement his plan, Watson visited Whitesborough on the Mohawk's south side, where he noted "a promising new settlement . . . in the heart of a fine tract of land, and just dawning from a state of nature into civilization." Astonished at efforts made "to subdue the musky forest," he writes approvingly of log-houses "already thickly scattered in the midst of stumps, half burnt logs, girdled trees, and confusion" and observes with pleasure the well-filled log barns and, perhaps with even greater pleasure, that the price of the lands once purchased for a trifle had risen to three dollars an acre.[49]

Watson's hand-written journal account of his 1791 reconnaissance (later folded into the memoirs published by his son) is made with the selective eye of the engineer and the enthusiasm of the speculator. "What a glorious acquisition to agriculture and commerce," he writes, "do these fertile and extensive regions in the west present, in anticipation! And what a pity, since the partial hand of Nature has nearly completed the water communication from our utmost borders to the Atlantic ocean, that Art should not be made subservient to her and complete the great work!"[50] The language reflects the belief that the divine plan latent within the natural system of waterways, "nature's canals," simply awaited the completing hand of technology—and an appropriate visionary—to fulfill its inevitable destiny.

Along the way Watson had visions. Crossing Oneida Lake, he gazed "into futurity" and saw the newly opening territory "overspread with millions of freemen; blessed with various climates, enjoying every variety of soil, and commanding the boldest inland navigation on this globe; clouded with sails directing their course toward canals. . . ." Pausing to rest at Moses De Witt's Three River Point campsite, Watson predicted that "a large city will rise at this spot during the ensuing century. A canal communication from hence to Oswego harbor . . . is necessary to complete the great chain of water communication from Ontario to the Hudson. . . ."[51] On the eastern side of Seneca Lake, he pitched his tent at Appleton, formerly Kandaia, and wrote that the axe-marks of Sullivan's soldiers could "be seen in every direction," the few remaining apple trees girdled. He was "astonished" to find, in the place of the Senecas 150 people gathered at Appleton, "a prelude to the assembling of thousands, who are destined shortly to possess these fertile regions." This country between the lakes, he claimed "whenever it reaches a cultivated state, by the vigorous arm of freemen, it will become the paradise of America. . . ."[52]

Watson's belief that these lands, cultivated and linked by improved transportation networks, would usher in the millennial state was symptomatic of Enlightment belief in the grid (and its essential technologies) as a utopian gesture. Both David Nye and J. B. Jackson see New York's Military Tract townships as a conspicuous example of what would be repeated in the national grid, arguing that such an expression of space was symptomatic of profound cultural and environmental shifts in perception. In adopting the abstract grid over traditional practices of land division, colonists literally inscribed onto the land a set of new philosophical ideas: belief in free-market ideology, belief in natural abundance, belief in a Newtonian universe that was both rational and mathematical.[53] "Before the surveyor measured land according to a repeatable and verifiable system," Nye writes, "legal ownership was impossible. By dividing their land into units, Americans articulated an egalitarian sense of space that had no center and no past."[54]

Yet this "egalitarian sense of space" was egalitarian in concept only, certainly not in practice. Watson's narrative becomes more complex when read alongside his fieldbooks, letters, and surveys—documents outlining innumerable quarrels and insults as he fought with other speculators or laid claim to land already claimed by another, sometimes several others. What is clear is that the land so gridded and commodified promoted rampant speculation and outright fraud.[55]

Sometime shortly after the survey was completed in 1792, Watson opened a leather-bound journal and carefully ruled its pages into four narrow columns and one wide one. He labeled the narrow columns "good," "very good," "bad," and "very bad," reserving the wide section for "Remarks." On facing pages he drew in meticulous detail facsimiles of the township maps Moses De Witt and his surveyors had produced for Simeon De Witt, each of the 100 lots carefully numbered, the lakes, streams, and creeks drawn to scale and labeled. The book served as Watson's own guide to the territory—to which lands were valuable and likely to turn a profit and to those not worth bothering with. Lots 45 and 46 in Hannibal, for example, have "very good timber," he remarks, while "a large swamp runs through 44, 53–53, 64, 75, and 75. Lots 55 and 56 contain "very fine Indian clearings," and he singles out Lot 75 as having at least 300 acres-worth of good land. By contrast, "all lots on the Cayuga Outlet" in Brutus are "bad"—"except No. 47 this is good Land & Owasco outlet runs thro It. . . ." He distinguishes between land good for grass but poor for wheat, and translates each plot and its amenities into financial value, noting land that might fetch one dollar per acre and land that might fetch more.[56]

Watson was especially interested in Lot 100 in Brutus Township, along that stretch of the Seneca River that joins the Seneca and Cayuga lakes. Under the column "very good," he pronounces Lot 100 "capital."

On a second page he draws two versions of Lot 100. One, a small, rough sketch, shows a nearly blank parcel, except for a log house figured in the lower right corner. On its southern boundary, the Seneca River, he has drawn three somewhat equidistant oblongs, labeling the one furthest west "best mill site." The larger drawing shows that same plot developed, with mill seats and upper and lower landings indicated on either side of the river. Lot 100, now known as Seneca Falls and a once-key element of the canal system, is a compelling example of how Watson's transformation of space accompanies his own self-fashioning and role in the new republic.

Missing in Watson's narratives, however, is the repressed story Nye says runs counter to Second Creation stories in general and arguably to Watson's "grand desideratum" and "sublime plan" in particular: the story of how new lands were acquired by force, political legerdemain, fraud, and outright "legal trickery"; how new technologies—the grid itself, for example—in the process of transforming the landscape simultaneously undermined the existing community's way of life;[57] how lands of unequal value produced new social strains and inequities; and how a forest landscape and its "noxious" wild creatures were largely eradicated for an agricultural patchwork of selected crops and domesticated cattle, pigs, chickens, and sheep.[58]

CONCLUSION: READING THE LANDSCAPE OF PRIMITIVE ACCUMULATION

Frederic Jameson has argued for a "new spatial imagination" capable of "reading [the] less tangible secrets of the past off the templates of its spatial structures. . . ."[59] One reading of New York's spatial template turns out to be less a secret than a historically familiar, if denied or repressed, story: about taking land by force, enclosing it, expelling its population, and transforming the landscape into a system supportive of capitalist agriculture. Among the oldest of plots, its classic form is the English enclosure movement between the 15th through the 18th centuries. Marx called it primitive accumulation, capitalism's starting point in a series of thefts and appropriations that produced the agricultural base and transportation systems essential for industrial capitalism.[60] It is the process of taking land from those who would hold it in common and transforming it into capital. It is, in other words, a foundational violence whose memory we can bodily trace as we move through the landscape.

This, however, must not remain the whole story (as if there were such a thing), as boundaries in general and these in particular are potential resources for recovering a host of forgotten if interlocking and conflicting meanings: further memories of political and social exclusion and inclusion, of resistance and acquiescence, of displacement and reorganization, of identity and loss–all nested within a dizzying weave of these and other marks and traces left on the earth and awaiting decipherment. Awaiting re-membrance.

NOTES

1. Michel de Certeau, *The Practice of Everyday Life*, trans. Steven Rendall (Berkeley: University of California Press, 1988), 115.
2. Peter Brooks, *Reading for the Plot*, (Cambridge: Harvard University Press, 1992), 11–12.
3. R. H. Schein, "A Historical Geography of Central New York: Patterns and Processes of Colonization on the New Military Tract, 1782–1820" (PhD diss., Syracuse University, 1989), 81.
4. "Even housing developments" observation made by landscape archaeologist Kathryn Gleason, echoing Christopher Taylor, *Fields in the English Landscape* (Alan Sutton Publishing, 1987).
5. For Meinig and Ingold quotations, see Tim Ingold, "The Temporality of the Landscape," *World Archaeology* 25:2 (Routledge, 1993): 24–174. For brief overview of scholarship on landscape and memory, see Anna Bohlin, "Places of Longing and Belonging," in *Contested Landscapes: Movement, Exile, and Place*, ed. Barbara Bender and Margot Winer (Oxford: Berg, 2001), 274.
6. For "subterranean" and "boundedness," see Brooks, *Reading for the Plot*, 11–12.
7. Drawn from "Spatial Stories," de Certeau *The Practice of Everyday Life*, 115–30.
8. William Wyckoff, *The Developer's Frontier*, (New Haven: Yale University Press, 1988) 174.
9. Ibid., 173.
10. Ibid., 173–79.
11. Thanks to Kathryn Gleason for walking and deciphering the landscape with me.
12. John C. Fitzpatrick, "Instructions to Major General John Sullivan," in *The Writings of George Washington From the Original Manuscript Sources, 1745–1799*. Electronic Text Center, University of Virginia Library. http://etext.virginia.edu/etcbin/toccer-new2?id=WasFi15.xml&images=images/modeng&data=/texts/english/modeng/parsed&tag=public&part=165&division=div1. Retrieved on July 15, 2011.
13. Alan Taylor, *The Divided Ground: Indians, Settlers, and the Northern Borderland of the American Revolution* (New York: Random House, 2006), 102.
14. Martin Bruckner, *The Geographical Revolution in Early America: Maps, Literacy, and National Identity* (Omohundro Institute: University of North Carolina Press, 2006), 14.
15. "Washington's Instructions to Sullivan," in Frederick Cook, ed. General George Washington, *Journals of the Military Expedition of Major John Sullivan Against the Six Nations of Indians in 1779 with Records of Centennial Celebrations* (Auburn, NY: Knapp, Peck & Thompson, 1887), 382–83.
16. Barbara Graymont, *The Iroquois in the American Revolution*, (Syracuse: Syracuse University Press, 1972), 220.
17. See the introduction to Daniel K. Richter, *The Ordeal of the Longhouse*, (Chapel Hill: University of North Carolina Press, 1992).

18. Max M. Mintz, *Seeds of Empire* (New York: New York University Press, 1999), 1.
19. Journal of Reverend William Rogers, (Cook, 1887), 260.
20. Journal of Major John Burrowes, (Cook, 1887), 45.
21. Journal of Thomas Grant, (Cook, 1887), 140–41
22. Journal of Jeremiah Fogg, (Cook, 1887), 96–97
23. Journal of Thomas Grant, (Cook, 1887), 142.
24. Robert Erskine letter of August 1, 1777, to George Washington in Albert Heusser, *George Washington's Map Maker*, (New Brunswick, NJ: Rutgers University Press, 1928), 220.
25. Journal of Jeremiah Fogg, (Cook, 1887), 97.
26. de Certeau, *The Practice of Everyday Life*, 125.
27. DeWitt Family Papers [DFP], Box 7, Field Books Moses De Witt Townships, (Syracuse: New York, Arents Research Library), 1–25.
28. J. B. Harley, "Maps, Knowledge and Power," in Denis Cosgrove and Stephen Daniels, eds., *The Iconography of Landscape* (Cambridge: Cambridge University Press, 1988), 279.
29. Denis Cosgrove, *Mappings*, (London: Reaktion Books Ltd., 1999), 5.
30. J. B. Harley, *The New Nature of Maps*, ed. Paul Laxton (Baltimore and London: The Johns Hopkins University Press, 2001), 57.
31. Taylor, *Fields in the English Landscape,* 143.
32. Ibid., 166.
33. Richard Schein, "Framing the Frontier," *New York History* 74 (1993): 5–28.
34. Nye calls surveying "the essential precondition" to owning lands, building canals, and developing technological narratives leading to free-market landscapes. David E. Nye, *America as Second Creation* (Cambridge: MIT Press, 2004), 21–42.
35. Schein, "A Historical Geography of Central New York," 69–84.
36. DFP, Moses De Witt's Journal of 1789, Box 6.
37. Ibid.
38. P. L. Marks and Sana Gardescu, "Vegetation of the Central Finger Lakes Region of New York in the 1790s," in *Late Eighteenth Century Vegetation of Central and Western New York State on the Basis of Original Land Survey Records* (Albany: New York State Museum Bulletin No. 484), 3.
39. William Cooper, *A Guide in the Wilderness* (Rochester: G. P. Humphrey, 1879).
40. Schein, "A Historical Geography of Central New York," 103.
41. Ibid., 104–07.
42. Ibid., 58.
43. Ibid., 54.
44. DFP, "Moses De Witt 1794 Petition, Onondaga Reservation," Box 6.
45. Elkanah Watson, *Men and Times of the Revolution: or, Memoirs of Elkanah Watson*, ed. Winslow C. Watson (New York: D. Appleton & Co., 1861), 354.
46. Nye, *America as Second Creation*, 29. See chapters 1 and 2.
47. Schein's term.
48. Bruckner, *The Geographical Revolution in Early America.*
49. Elkanah Watson, *History of the Rise, Progress and Existing Condition of the Western Canals in the State of New York* (Albany: D. Steel, 1820), 11.
50. Ibid., 342.
51. Ibid., 345
52. Ibid., 346
53. Nye, 2004 *America as Second Creation*, 22

54. Ibid., 25

55. Elkanah Watson Papers, GB 13294, Box 22, "Journals and Letter Books" (Albany: Manuscripts and Special Collections, New York State Library).

56. EWP, GB 13294, Box 27, "Survey Field Notes—Military Tract."

57. Nye, 2004, *America as Second Creation*, 15.

58. For a detailed account of the transformation from a forested to an agricultural landscape, see Alan Taylor, "The Great Change Begins: Settling the Forest of Central New York," *New York History* 65:3 (July 1995): 265–90.

59. Quoted in Dolores Hayden, *The Power of Place* (Cambridge: MIT Press, 1997), 19.

60. For Karl Marx's discussion of primitive accumulation, begin with *Das Kapital*, vol. 1, part 8.

2 The Unexpected Encounter
Confronting Holocaust Memory in the Streets of Post-Wall Berlin

Margaret Ewing

Irina Liebmann's snapshots of East Berlin's Scheunenviertel district in the early 1980s convey something of the environment with which artists were confronted in the immediate years after the fall of the Berlin Wall in November 1989. They show the haphazard amalgamation of history, much of it in crumbling disrepair, typical of East Berlin's neighborhoods where practicality trumped calculation first during post-war recovery and later under the economic constraints of the East German economy.[1] Structures in various states of deterioration interspersed with empty lots reveal a pastiche of materials which, ranging from pre-war brick to post-war concrete, register the city's layers of historical accumulation. In the German Democratic Republic, pre-1945 history remained marginalized compared to the urgency of reconstruction—both physical and social—in the wake of wartime decimation and subsequent political division. Berlin's heterogeneous urban landscape circa 1989, with its endless traces of past events and communities, offered a fertile and provocative set of raw materials for artists seeking to interrogate the city's past and its impact on the present.

Among the artists drawn to Berlin in the early 1990s were three who inserted site-specific interventions into the spaces of everyday life with the intention of bringing to light local histories obscured by the city's post-war recovery and development. Berlin projects by Shimon Attie (b.1957, Los Angeles), Gunter Demnig (b.1947, Berlin), and Christian Boltanski (b.1945, Paris) in this period represent a strain of contemporary art practice devoted to historical recovery and public memorialization that was especially apt within the context of Berlin's densely layered histories and fast-paced post-Wall transformation. Attie's *The Writing on the Wall* series (1991–93) transformed pre-war photographs gleaned from city archives into life-sized installations in the streets, producing an early and incendiary reassertion of the Scheunenviertel's missing Jewish community. Operating on a comparatively intimate scale, Demnig's *Stolpersteine* project (1996–ongoing) marks the former homes of Holocaust victims with personalized memorial stones in the sidewalk, creating a trail of memory that extends across the city. Boltanski's *The Missing House* (1990), meanwhile, recovered the history of a single apartment building destroyed in the war through archival documents and plaques dedicated to the former residents. Using distinct strategies to bring these invisible histories into the city's contemporary visual landscape, each project demanded attention to individual narratives in danger of being buried in the city's rush toward reunification.

Site-specific installations signify that "this happened *here*" and, I argue, activate a visceral perception that operates on a non-linguistic and non-rational level. While visual cues offer the first indication of a site's significance, it is rather the phenomenological elements of the works—triggered by the visual interventions—that produce the critical psychological operations. In responding to the power of place, this genre of installation art harnesses the particular energy that is located at the site of traumatic history. It facilitates the integration of historical awareness into the viewer's own body through direct perception of the site. Counter-memory lies at the heart of these practices, which, as James Young explains, aims to interrupt official memory narratives, "resist the certainty of monumental forms," and complicate the memorial process.[2] In contrast to traditional memorials, which court obsolescence in their attempts to permanently fix memory, these projects seek "not to console but to provoke; not to remain fixed but to change; . . . not to be ignored by [their] passersby but to demand interaction. . ."[3] However, while counter-memory begins to explain the significance of these projects, their site-specificity makes them still more effective in provoking memory when compared to projects in more arbitrary locations. In this way, they offer a possible remedy to Pierre Nora's claim of a divergence between memory and history and the loss of embodied memory in the modern era.[4] Employing strategies that assimilate sites of memory into an integrated consciousness, these projects challenge Nora's assertion that sites of memory are now external to any instinctive relationship to the past. By situating the viewer in the very sites where these lives were lived, the installations trigger memorial operations in the mind, thereby facilitating a personal assimilation of history.

Attie, Demnig, and Boltanski make history discernible in this fundamental way through an exposition of space. The perception of the site shifts in the experience of the artists' interventions. The city now mingles with the city then, and leads to a deeper awareness of the historical layers that mark a place over time. The works demand recognition of a more expansive picture of a site and, with a sensitized awareness of history, the viewer may begin to reevaluate his or her own relationship to the Holocaust.

The site-specific nature of these installations—their identification of places where individual violent episodes occurred—enables a particular kind of viewing experience. In comparison to large-scale memorials typically subject to lengthy deliberation and compromise due to the attempt to represent huge numbers of victims or collective remorse, these independent projects center on the private narratives that comprise an otherwise incomprehensible history. While official memorials certainly contribute to keeping the Holocaust present in Berlin's physical landscape, visitors have a more distant relationship to history at those sites than they do at these smaller-scale installations. Standing in the very spaces where individuals lived before waves of violence ripped apart the patterns of everyday life, viewers access a more immediate connection to history than is available at non-site-specific memorials.

SHIMON ATTIE, *THE WRITING ON THE WALL*, 1991–93

The Scheunenviertel ("barn district") had been the center of Berlin's Eastern European Jewish community before the war. This history had been deemphasized, however, by the homogenizing efforts of an East German government committed to an idea of collective victimhood under the Nazi dictatorship and by 1991, scant visual trace of that population remained.[5] This divergence between the district's known historical reality and its present appearance precipitated Attie's project, as he sought to restore evidence of this population. Describing his own phenomenological response to the neighborhood, he writes, "I felt the presence of this lost community very strongly . . . I wanted to give this invisible past a voice, to bring it to light, if only for some brief moments."[6] With a succession of public installations, the project produced sites where viewers would be forced to confront the neighborhood's traumatic past through the visualized discord between the present uses of the buildings and the memory of their occupants before 1945.

In a piece stretched over one year beginning in September 1991, Attie projected black-and-white archival photographs of pre-war Jews and Jewish businesses onto buildings in the neighborhood—both pre-war and post—as well as provisional fences concealing empty lots.[7] Each projection existed for one or two nights, with Attie present to observe viewers' responses and make documentary photographs of the installations. While he attempted to match the locations of the photographs to the remaining buildings in the neighborhood, many had been destroyed and replaced by the sterile gray cement apartment buildings of post-war East Berlin. Observing that the pre-war architecture retained a historical resonance missing from these newer utilitarian constructions, Attie sometimes substituted other old buildings in cases where the original structures no longer existed. More interested in restoring the overall atmosphere of this formerly Jewish neighborhood than in historical precision, Attie privileged feeling over strict documentation.

Linienstraße 137 (*Police Raid on Jewish Residents, 1920*) is one of the twenty-seven twenty-by-twenty-four-inch richly colored photographs in the series. Eight anachronistically dressed figures line up along a building exterior, uniformed police officers blocking the entrance at the left and displaced residents grouped to the right. Within the series, this photograph stands out for its evidence of the building's current occupants. Framed within a brightly lit window just above the residents' heads, a pair of leafy houseplants stands in for an undisturbed domesticity of the present moment. Attie interrogates spaces where people still reside after former inhabitants were forced to leave, in most cases deported to concentration camps, and reveals the intrinsic conflict in continued use of sites of traumatic history. In contrast to other spaces in Berlin that have been sanctioned for memorialization, most domestic spaces remain in use, making it impossible to fully isolate past crimes and traumas from experiences and utilizations in the present.

Local archives were an integral element of *The Writing on the Wall*. Among the sources Attie mined was a private collection of photographs documenting the Scheunenviertel's pre-war community.[8] But while the projections originated from these source photographs, they were significantly transformed in Attie's installations. The *Police Raid* image, for example, was originally a daylight scene. In Attie's nighttime installation crafted through the bright beam of his projector, however, the figures assume a ghost-like presence. Further still, the installation undoes the fixed nature of the photograph with the dematerializing quality of projected light. This combination of physical space, projected history, and the ambient darkness transformed these streets into liminal spaces of intermingled present and past.

Figure 2.1   Shimon Attie, *Linienstraße 137 (Police Raid on Jewish Residents, 1920)*, 1991–93. Courtesy of Shimon Attie and Jack Shainman Gallery, New York.

Having conceived the project partly as a means to remedy the perceived absences in the city, Attie further intended *The Writing on the Wall* to be provocative. "By attempting to renegotiate the relationship between past and present events," he writes, "the aim of the project was to interrupt the collective processes of denial and forgetting."[9] Local reception to Attie's installations revealed the unease of residents forced to acknowledge the histories in which their homes were steeped by this visual reassertion of the past. One resident called the police, fearing these projected signs of Jewishness could lead his neighbors to think he was Jewish. Another threw a bucket of water at Attie and his equipment, and a third waged a verbal protest by defending his legitimate ownership of a formerly Jewish-owned property.[10]

Despite Attie's exclusion of figures from his photographic documentation of the project, he clearly intended for these projections to be seen. Each installation was a strident intervention into an otherwise dark and quiet neighborhood. He sought to give the people of these histories a space in the present, to compel the viewer to recognize the inherent absence in this district, and to become aware of those who had been here before and their traumas in these places. At the same time that East Berliners struggled with reintegration into a unified Germany, Attie's project challenged them to acknowledge the proximity of the Holocaust, which had been repressed in the GDR.[11] As an American appropriating the neighborhood for artistic intervention, Attie's project was not, it should be recognized, without greater political implications. Within the fraught circumstances of reunification, many East Germans were sensitive to claims from the West regarding how history should be articulated after 1989. Some of Attie's viewers conveyed this unease in their responses, such as one who shouted, "Wessie, go home!" Thus, his viewership comprised multiple constituencies and the work participated in larger questions about historical assimilation.[12]

The siting of Attie's project in the former East Berlin also implicitly critiques official attitudes toward the Holocaust in East Germany. While the Federal Republic had gone through a long and public struggle of incorporating this history into a national narrative, the government of the GDR had distanced its citizens and itself from the Third Reich, claiming victim status under fascism and denying all responsibility. With the fall of the Berlin Wall and the rise of artists' interrogations of this history within the spaces of the city itself, longtime residents of East Berlin were forced to reckon with the disjunction between what they had been told and the documentary evidence brought to light by those artists. The line between perpetrator and victim became increasingly blurred. Attie's confrontational installation challenged the understandable inclination of most East Germans to avoid direct confrontation with this aspect of German history.[13]

By merging images of pre-war Jewish society with buildings that had been stripped of their historical layers, Attie created moments of cognitive dissonance for viewers unprepared for a jarring confrontation with an unresolved past. Leaving the viewers little choice in an encounter with these images, Attie provoked a meditation on invisible histories. Wavering between presence and absence, these interventions, with their transformation of archival photographs into ghost-like apparitions, haunted a neighborhood still raw amidst the city's reunification.

Attie's mark on the city was temporary, but he meant it to have a lasting impact. He intended the memory of these projections to become a permanent part of one's experience of the city, and though only visible for a limited time, to open up one's awareness of the former existence of this lost community. As Thomas Crow argues, the temporality of site-specific art is central to its meaning and significance. Its very existence presents a challenge to the everyday experience of a site, transforming the way in which it is apprehended.[14] Beyond Attie's temporary installations, viewers' perceptions of the sites would have shifted, now incorporating the remembered images of the former residents he had reconnected with these local spaces.

GUNTER DEMNIG, *STOLPERSTEINE*, 1996–ONGOING

While Attie's project suffused a single neighborhood, Gunter Demnig's *Stolpersteine* extend across the city in an expansive claim on public space that helps to convey the pervasiveness of Nazi deportations. These "stumbling blocks," as their name translates, have a double reference: at once literally stones built into public sidewalks and at the same time disruptions of one's perception of the city. A network of four-inch-square memorial stones linking multiple city districts, the *Stolpersteine* document the lives of individual victims through these discrete memorials, each of which are engraved with the following: "Here lived [name, year of birth, date of deportation or death, place of imprisonment]." The stones are often installed as multiples to mark the deportation of family groups. Demnig's inclusivity with regard to who gets memorialized—not only Jews, but political resisters, Sinti-Roma, and others—further expands the bounds of many memorials that attend to distinct communities. At the same time, this articulation of Holocaust memory in terms of individual victims is an intentional move to reassert specific identities in contrast to the anonymizing tendencies of large-scale collective memorials.[15]

The *Stolpersteine* first developed out of Demnig's 1990 project *Roma-Sinti Trail* in Cologne, in which he retraced the path of deportation of members of this community with a white chalk line through the city to the main train station. Four years later, seeking a more permanent means of marking this chapter of local history, Demnig began to embed the memory of individual victims into city sidewalks with the installation of these brass-covered stones. The choice to mark public sidewalks rather than private buildings reflected Demnig's suspicion that, as Attie had found, individual residents might object to direct links between their

Figure 2.2   Gunter Demnig, *Stolpersteine*, Berlin, 1996–ongoing. Courtesy of Gunter Demnig. Photo by Margaret Ewing.

homes and Holocaust deportations. The project's siting on publicly-owned land made questions of public space and public process into integral components.

The first Berlin installation of the *Stolpersteine* was initiated as Demnig's contribution to the 1996 exhibition *Künstler forschen nach Auschwitz* (Artists Search for Auschwitz), organized by the Neue Gesellschaft für bildende Kunst (New Society for Visual Arts) in the former West Berlin's Kreuzberg district. Aware that the permit process would take longer than the exhibition's duration, Demnig acted without official permission.[16] The project provoked a response immediately. Three months after their installation, construction work necessitated their removal. Presuming them to be an official memorial, however, the workers refused to disrupt them. Indeed, although Demnig intends the stones to be walked upon, and suggests that the repeated wear of pedestrian traffic will help to keep the stones polished and their memory active, many viewers choose to step around them, treating them as sacrosanct markers of memory.[17] This instinct to protect the *Stolpersteine*, even in the absence of physical barriers, reflects accumulated experiences of memorialization through which viewers learn to defend memorials against desecration. Demnig, in integrating the stones into the spaces of daily life and impeding any separation between this past and the lived reality of the present, directly challenges this propensity for distancing.

Like Attie's installations that inhabited a whole neighborhood in successive installations, the *Stolpersteine* are distributed around large areas of Berlin, so that walking and one's own navigation of the city become part of the experience of the work. Not contained in a museum, nor even in a single site, the *Stolpersteine* pervade the whole city, integrating history into the spaces of everyday life. More than transforming a single historic site, they mark these larger territories with an expansive layer of Holocaust memory. Encountering a stone, an observant viewer will read the biographical details and then look up at the building before which they stand. The continuity of daily life, i.e. the way in which today's residents and passersby echo the presence of those no longer alive, generates a realm of memory through which the viewer moves closer to historical understanding.

Demnig recognizes the importance of public process to the work and, in contrast to Attie, enters into close involvement with local communities in the realization of his project. With each installation he confronts a new round of bureaucratic authorization. In some communities the permissions come quickly and easily, while in others they spark heated debates about the use of public space and the rights of current residents to determine how their homes are represented.[18] Each proposed installation activates the permission process anew, and reveals a community's relative degree of comfort with its own Holocaust history. In collaboration with individuals and groups, he and local residents use the archives of the Third Reich to match victims to former homes, marking the spaces with these stones. For most of those named, this will be their only memorial, and different from most Holocaust memorials which are organized around a victimhood of undifferentiated masses. Whereas elsewhere in Berlin, Daniel Liebeskind's Jewish Museum (1999) and Peter Eisenman's Memorial to the Murdered Jews of Europe (2005) speak to this overarching narrative, Demnig's project honors singular stories. Through these individual lives, it becomes possible to connect personally and emotionally to history.

One room in the underground documentation center at the Eisenman Memorial is dedicated to the stories of particular families told through pre-war photographs and biographical accounts. Here are people's stories before they became the victims, before the attacks on their individual identities when they were stripped of hair, belongings, and dignity, and visibly transformed into collective victimhood. In contrast to the danger of desensitization in response to repeated exposure to graphic images of victims after their deaths, this emphasis on the living reasserts individual humanity, allowing viewers to perceive them as not so unlike themselves. By refocusing the narrative on individuals and challenging the Nazi-construct of anonymity and worthlessness, both the exhibit at the Memorial and Demnig's stones shift perception into the human terms which alone make it more comprehensible.

Both the photography exhibit at the Memorial and the *Stolpersteine* transform the experience of memory. Like Attie, Demnig reconnects this history to its originating location. Rather than memorialize the victims at the places of their deaths, he links them to the places they lived. Indexing these events to the living spaces in the present, Demnig's project too becomes a lasting element in one's experience of Berlin. No trip through the city is insulated from the potential of an encounter with the bronze stones, and as the work continues it will permeate even further the fabric of the city. As Stefanie Endlich observes, this link between history and the local neighborhood frustrates any attempt to confine Holocaust crimes to distant sites of imprisonment and extermination.[19] Bringing the specificities of individual lives into the immediate environment, the artist demands acknowledgment of the past's proximity. As of early 2010, Demnig had installed approximately 23,000 stones in Berlin and other German and European cities, in a project that remains ongoing.[20]

CHRISTIAN BOLTANSKI, *THE MISSING HOUSE*, 1990

While Holocaust memory has certainly dominated approaches to working through the German past, a parallel inquiry into the question of German victimhood—of German civilians and Allied bombing raids—during the war has recently emerged as a rich site of investigation.[21] Boltanski's project did not initially set out to pursue these questions, but the unexpected contents of the archive pushed it into this new terrain. An artist long concerned with questions about Holocaust memory, he first sought to ascertain the biographical details linked to an evocative empty lot. Perhaps expecting the site to unravel a narrative of local Jewish history, Boltanski discovered a more tangled set of archival threads. For although it is located in the center of the Scheunenviertel, by the time the house was destroyed in 1945, all Jewish residents had long since been deported, their rooms occupied by a new group of residents.

On a May 1990 walk around the vicinity of the destroyed Oranienburger Strasse Synagogue in the heart of Berlin's former East, just months following the fall of the Wall, Boltanski became interested in this site where he recognized people had once lived, but of whom nearly all traces had vanished. With the assistance of two Berlin art students, he, like Attie, collected materials from local archives with which to reconstruct the history of the building and its occupants. This archival work was the basis for Boltanski's contribution to the September–October 1990 exhibition *Die Endlichkeit der Freiheit* (The Finitude of Freedom), a city-wide exhibition of public art, for which eleven artists were invited to explore the newly reunited city and to undertake site-specific projects in an examination of its division and subsequent reunification.[22] In a pair of installations, one at the empty lot at 15/16 Grosse Hamburger Strasse and the other near the Lehrte train station on the opposite side of the Wall, Boltanski presented his discoveries. On February 3, 1945, the middle section of this U-shaped apartment block was destroyed by Allied bombs. Because damage was confined to this one area, however, the dwellings on either side remained intact. By 1990, this center lot was empty and contrasted starkly with the fully occupied structures on either side.

At irregular intervals on the exposed walls of the neighboring buildings, Boltanski installed placards—simple presentations of black text on white ground—documenting name, occupation, and dates in residence of the occupants in 1945. This minimal material intervention is subtle. In contrast to the personal details revealed in the research—the photographs, interviews with surviving family members, a dead child's sketchbook—the plaques are cool and detached. There is no express emotion in Boltanski's installation. Its site-specific location, however, gives it an emotional charge.[23] Shifting the frame through which the space is perceived, it reconnects the site with the individuals who once lived here. The viewer's awareness of history's proximity becomes the substance of the piece, which is made possible by its site-specific location. Boltanski transforms this otherwise forgettable site into a mnemonic space where private histories re-emerge within the local landscape.

Figure 2.3   Christian Boltanski, *The Missing House*, 1990. Courtesy of Christian Boltanski. Photo by Margaret Ewing.

On the opposite side of the East-West divide, Boltanski installed an open-air exhibition in which copies of the archival documents were displayed in a series of ten rectangular vitrines. Suitably titled *The Museum*, this selection of family snapshots, a book of rent receipts, Nazi transport lists, and children's drawings supplemented the comparatively reserved information at *The Missing House*. A written narrative of the exhibition site was among the displayed materials, which outlined its initial function as an exhibition space for modern art in the late nineteenth century, its 1936 repurposing under Hermann Göring as the Reich Aviation Museum, and its bombing in the last year of the war.

Originally conceived as a temporary installation, one half of Boltanski's piece still exists due to the involvement of residents in the immediate vicinity of *The Missing House*, whose embrace of this recovery of pre-1945 history has made it an enduring piece of Berlin's post-Wall memorial landscape.[24] Indeed, this stretch of Grosse Hamburger Strasse counts among the city's most historically saturated blocks, existing in firm counterposition to the neighborhood's rapid revitalization since the early 1990s. Across the street from *The Missing House* lies a string of haunting remnants of the neighborhood's Jewish past, including Berlin's oldest Jewish cemetery (now a leveled park since the Nazis destroyed it, turning headstones into paving stones), another empty lot where a Jewish retirement home-turned Nazi collection center for Jews stood before also being destroyed by bombs, and a Jewish high school that later reopened in 1993. The neighbors' wish to maintain the installation as a permanent memorial suggests the power of this kind of specific archival discovery, and the potency of small-scale site-specific interventions within larger memorial endeavors such as Berlin's.

In its current state, there is no label at the site of *The Missing House*. It is a place that requires a personal introduction from someone who has seen it before, for although it can be seen from the street, it is so well-integrated into its setting that it is easily overlooked. Boltanski did not set out to make an "art object"; indeed, challenging assumptions about the definition of art is an inherent part of much of his work. He describes being more interested in art's potential as "a way to speak, a way to ask questions." In *The Missing House*, Boltanski bypasses the constructs of the museum or gallery, enabling a more direct connection between the viewer and the work. "I think [a viewer] can be touched . . . much more strong[ly] than if it was in a museum," he explains, "because in a museum they know it's modern art . . . it's something dangerous to them." But in the spaces of everyday life, there is not the same pressure to understand it as "art."[25] *The Missing House* frames this space with questions about its past and dares the viewer to consider them: Who lived here? Where did they go? How many analogous sites exist in this city, this country?

While *The Missing House* may be perceived on this direct level, it has additional implications as a critique of the limitations of the archive. Boltanski's declared interest in historical recovery is simultaneously frustrated by his own methodology. In relying on the archive for the reconstruction of the history of this building and its occupants, Boltanski reveals its inherent limitations. As Foucault formulated it, the archive—in this case, the collection of photographs, letters, oral histories, legal documents—delineates the limits of knowledge.[26] That is to say, the reconstruction of history is always already constrained by the fragments of information that have been preserved and the degrees to which they are accessible. In the case of Germany's wartime history, the surviving historical record is in large part a product of the Nazis' own documentation of their highly organized extermination campaigns. Among Boltanski's documentation, for example, were lists of possessions that Nazi authorities demanded of all Jews. Displaying these now as historical evidence problematizes the possibility of a "complete" historical account.

The Missing House is part of Boltanski's larger exploration of memory, loss, and history. An oeuvre known for its equivocation, frequently combining photographs and text to suggest traumatic histories that may or may not be historically factual, it tends to blur rather than elucidate. *The Missing House* is distinct within Boltanski's work for its site-specificity and focus on the history of an actual place. But while the apparent possibility of greater historical precision here might seem promising for the way in which it pins the project to a more verifiable truth, the reality of the archive is such that this too proves elusive. Boltanski's catalogue raisonné describes the artist's book from the project[27] as "the first publication by Boltanski where all the material is authentic,"[28] and this might be echoed in the viewer's initial perception of the installation. The documentary appearance of names and dates and its ensuing presumption of truth promises the chance to finally ground Boltanski's practice in verifiable evidence. But the uncertainty in his earlier works acts here as a caution, and both the fact that names and dates are never enough to reconstruct a full history as well as the fundamental resistance to clearly explain exactly what we are seeing, thwarts this expectation.

Despite this admitted impossibility of getting to a "truth," there is still a form of memory work operating at *The Missing House*. As curator Okwui Enwezor wrote for a recent exhibition on the manipulation of the archive in contemporary art, "it is also within the archive that acts of remembering and regeneration occur, where a suture between the past and present is performed, in the indeterminate zone between event and image, document and monument."[29] Boltanski complicates the viewer's access to history, offering bits of it, but ultimately frustrating it. The plaques reconnect this empty space with the past, but incompletely. The work's resistance of a prescribed memorial experience, in contrast to official memorial sites that present a clear narrative frame, leaves the viewer with an unfulfilled desire for a completeness which Boltanski's piece suggests is unattainable. At the site of *The Missing House*, one glimpses a fragment of this history, but full comprehension remains out of grasp.

Eschewing definitive statements in his work, Boltanski intentionally leaves space for the viewer's own experience, and sees this as a fundamental part of the production of meaning. For this reason, his work is ambiguous, which has led some scholars to criticize his lack of explicit moral stance as an irresponsible approach to treating the Holocaust.[30] The clear value in such an approach, however, is to stimulate independent thought. Rather than provoking a purely emotional response in the viewer, *The Missing House* opens onto a more gradual and deeper effect as a space for reflection through the stimulation of desire for more information about what this piece is and why it is here. Boltanski asserts that a successful memorial to the Holocaust is one that demands the continued attention of the viewer. It should be fragile. Traditional bronze monuments are complete unto themselves and don't require the viewer's participation; this makes their meaning easy to forget. Boltanski's memorial has to be constructed and reconstructed continually by the viewer.[31] With the limited amount of text at the site, there is not a lot for the viewer to do; there is little to distract from the effect of being in this particular space. The experience of *The Missing House* is not based on what one sees, but rather on what one comes to understand.

These projects by Attie, Demnig, and Boltanski are, of course, situated within the broader memorial landscape in Berlin, and the contrast between their localized attention and the larger sites of memory further suggests ways in which they activate a particular kind of memory work. The Holocaust Memorial and the Topography of Terror form, along with the Jewish Museum, the post-1989 "memory district,"[32] which is located in the center of the city and grounds it in historical consciousness.

The siting of the Holocaust Memorial between the Brandenburg Gate and Potsdamer Platz was a symbolic choice about the central position of this history in the German present. But although it is close to the seat of government and occupies a large and valuable piece of real estate, the fact that relatively few Holocaust victims were murdered in Berlin itself indicates a lack of historical specificity for this site, making it less of a visceral experience for the visitor. Eisenman's memorial, with its sea of gravestone-like pillars, which many have observed suggest a cemetery devoid of bodies, is about the *idea* of the Holocaust. In contrast, the named individuals that lived in *this* particular building, who were forcibly removed from *here*, connect the work of Attie, Demnig, and Boltanski—and as a result, this history—more directly to the viewer.

Marking the site of the Gestapo prison and administrative headquarters, the Topography of Terror has a more direct connection to history than the Holocaust Memorial, but it too fails to elicit the depth of these artworks.[33] Like them, it is based on historical documentation. But it lacks the poetry of individual experience. While the creation of a "memory district" in the city center is an important national symbol, the less grand and more targeted work of these artists succeeds far better in impacting the individual viewer on a deep level. Notably, Liebeskind's Jewish Museum, with its overwhelming architectural language, does create this kind of emotional experience, which is exceptional among large-scale memorials. Carefully controlling one's perception of space, through jagged corridors and other sharply defined rooms, Liebeskind successfully triggers an emotional response in many viewers. Unfortunately, however, the superfluous addition of wall texts replete with didactic instructions for the interpretation of the space undoes much of the direct experience provoked by the building alone.

While created in the early aftermath of 1989, these projects and the motives behind them have lasting implications for the definition of the city's public spaces now and into the future. They made an immediate impact on the viewers at the time, but simultaneously staked claims for the observance of the city's traumatic history in the midst of competing voices in the new realities of reunification. Inserted into the city's public spaces, these artists' interventions integrate the processes of memory into the present experience of Berlin. *The Missing House* and the *Stolpersteine* are now part of the greater memorial landscape of the city. As the city and country persevere in grappling with the social and economic conflicts produced by reunification, these sites mark the urban landscape with visual reminders of the lives and deaths of the city's former residents. The drive to mark these pasts that was so keen just after 1989 continues to keep both residents and visitors conscious of the past as they move through the spaces of the present.

NOTES

1. Irina Liebmann, *Stille Mitte von Berlin: Eine Recherche rund um den Hackeschen Markt* (Berlin: Nicolaische Verlagsbuchhandlung, 2002).
2. James E. Young, *At Memory's Edge: After-Images of the Holocaust in Contemporary Art and Architecture* (New Haven: Yale University Press, 2000), 7.
3. James E. Young, "The Counter-Monument: Memory against Itself in Germany Today," *Critical Inquiry,* 18 (Winter 1992): 277.
4. Pierre Nora, "Between Memory and History: Les Lieux de Mémoire," *Representations* 26 (Spring 1989): 7–24.
5. While not the focus of this essay, it is important to acknowledge the reliance of parts of Attie's project on stereotypical representations of Jews. Attie was aware of this, explaining that when he used images of "assimilated" German Jews, that is, those who blended in easily with the general German population, viewers did not understand the terms of the work. He turned, then, to images of more recent immigrants from Eastern Europe, whose appearances are easily identified as "Jewish."
6. Shimon Attie, "The Writing on the Wall Project," in Shimon Attie, Michael A. Bernstein, and Erwin Leiser, *The Writing on the Wall: Projections in Berlin's Jewish Quarter* (Heidelberg: Edition Braus, 1994), 9.
7. Ibid., 11.
8. Dora Apel, *Memory Effects: The Holocaust and the Art of Secondary Witnessing* (New Brunswick, NJ: Rutgers University Press, 2002), 48.
9. In Monica Bohm-Duchen, *After Auschwitz: Responses to the Holocaust in Contemporary Art*, exh. cat. (Sunderland, UK: Northern Centre for Contemporary Art, 1995), 147.

10. Attie, "The Writing on the Wall Project," 12.
11. See John Borneman, *After the Wall: East Meets West in the New Berlin* (New York: Basic Books, 1991).
12. Attie, "The Writing on the Wall Project," 12.
13. On the differences in Holocaust reception in East and West Germany see Jeffrey Herf, *Divided Memory: The Nazi Past in the Two Germanys* (Cambridge: Harvard University Press, 1997).
14. See Thomas Crow, "Site-Specific Art: The Strong and the Weak" in *Modern Art in the Common Culture* (New Haven: Yale University Press, 1992).
15. Gunter Demnig in conversation with Uta Franke, "Am treffendsten läßt sich meine Berufsbezeichnung mit Bildhauer umschreiben," in Demnig, *Stolpersteine: Für die von den Nazis ermordeten ehemaligen Nachbarn aus Friedrichshain und Kreuzberg: Dokumentation, Texte, Materialen* (Berlin: Vice-Versa, 2002), 13.
16. After the unauthorized installation, Demnig applied for official permission in 1997, which was finally granted in April 2000. Ibid., 14–15.
17. Ibid., 13–15.
18. Laura Katzman and Gabriella Paulix, "Against Forgetting: The Memorial Art of Gunter Demnig," *Art Papers* 29:6 (Nov–Dec 2005): 18.
19. Stefanie Endlich, "Ein 'dezentrales Monument'? Anmerkungen zu einem ungewöhnlichen Denkmalskonzept," in Demnig, *Stolpersteine*, 31.
20. Uta Franke, Stolpersteine Project Coordinator, e-mail message to author, March 19, 2010.
21. W. G. Sebald's essay "Air War and Literature," first delivered as a lecture in 1997, published in Germany in 1999, and translated into English in 2003, is frequently identified as the starting point of investigation into the question of German victimhood. In Sebald, *On the Natural History of Destruction* (New York: Random House, 2003).
22. Wulf Herzogenrath, Joachim Sartorius, and Christoph Tannert, *Die Endlichkeit der Freiheit Berlin 1990: Ein Ausstellungsprojekt in Ost und West*, exh. cat. (Berlin: Edition Hentrich, 1990).
23. This emphasis on the actual sites of history was in line with the construction of memorials in West Germany during the 1970s and 80s, which had also moved toward site-specificity with the aim of a stronger pedagogical effect. See Jennifer Jordan, *Structures of Memory: Understanding Urban Change in Berlin and Beyond* (Stanford: Stanford University Press, 2006), 44–45.
24. See Hans Dickel, "Frontiers of Freedom: Notes on die Endlichkeit der Freiheit," *Performance* (London) 63 (March 1991): 33.
25. Boltanski in conversation with Gerald Fox, *Christian Boltanski* (videorecording) (Chicago: Home Vision Arts, 1994).
26. Michel Foucault, *The Archaeology of Knowledge and the Discourse of Language* (New York: Pantheon Books, 1972), 129.
27. Christian Boltanski, Christiane Büchner, and Andreas Fischer, *La Maison Manquante: The Missing House* (Paris: La Hune, 1992).
28. Jennifer Flay, ed., *Christian Boltanski, Catalogue: Books, Printed Matter, Ephemera, 1966–1991* (Frankfurt am Main: Portikus, 1992), 207.
29. Okwui Enwezor, *Archive Fever: Uses of the Document in Contemporary Art* (New York: International Center of Photography, 2008), 47.
30. Abigail Solomon-Godeau, for example, writes, "The art of generic elegy, the melancholy acknowledgment of fatality, destiny, or mortality, is wholly inadequate to the historical, indeed to the ethical requirements of historical commemoration." Solomon-Godeau, "Mourning or Melancholia: Christian Boltanski's *Missing House*," *Oxford Art Journal* 21:2 (1998): 7.
31. Fox, *Christian Boltanski* (videorecording).

32. Karen E. Till, *The New Berlin: Memory, Politics, Place* (Minneapolis: The University of Minnesota Press, 2005), 7.

33. Discovered in the late 1970s, the site became the focus of early debates about how to treat places of Nazi persecution. The original exhibition (since redesigned in 2010) was the product of this first wave of memory work, in which West German citizen groups pushed to bring history to the fore of public consciousness. For a history of the site and its transformation into a permanent memorial space see Till, *The New Berlin*, chapter 3.

3   "A Disturbance of Memory"
Travel, Recollection, and the Experience of Place

Paul Duro

Lands with too little past may thrill the eye,
but not the memory.

—F. L. Lucas[1]

In 1788, Johann Wolfgang Goethe traveled to Italy and recorded his first impressions of Rome in a journal later published as *Italian Journey* (Figure 3.1). His unalloyed delight in being in the Eternal City is evident on every page. He writes that Rome had "come to life" before his eyes, confirming everything he expected to see, hear, and feel. In every way the city fulfills his hopes and substantiates long-held expectations:

> All the dreams of my youth have come to life; the first engravings I remember—my father hung views of Rome in the hall—I now see in reality, and everything I have known so long through paintings, drawings, etchings, woodcuts, plaster casts and cork models is now assembled before me.[2]

Faced with the reassuring reality, Goethe finally feels able to admit that "Now, at last, I can confess a secret mania of mine. For many years I did not dare to look into a Latin author or anything which evoked the image of Italy. If it happened by chance, I suffered agonies."[3]

Goethe's observation that the assembled reality of Rome is in some way a simulacrum of what he had long been familiar is not a function of an eighteenth century way of seeing. It is precisely echoed by the contemporary essayist and critic Clive James, whose first visit to Los Angeles in 1979 was less an arrival than a fulfillment of an already experienced encounter: "Los Angeles had been coming to me all my life, but this was the first time I had come to it . . . you are already living in it before you get there."[4] Tourists in Pisa line up to be photographed as if appearing to prop up the Leaning Tower, while those on Liberty Island in New York copy the pose of Lady Liberty. It goes without saying that not all these people independently and spontaneously think of the same visual joke; rather they reproduce a cliché with which they are already familiar. In each case the experience of

Figure 3.1   Johann Heinrich Tischbein the Elder, *Goethe in the Roman Campagna*, 1787. Courtesy of Bildarchiv Preussischer Kulturbesitz/Art Resource, New York.

place follows and depends upon these verbal/visual/textual sources, conditioning and coloring the eventual experience. In short, the experience is, as Chloe Chard has recognized in speaking of the European "Grand Tour," the result of "an imaginative topography to which various forms of representation, including travel narratives, attach themselves."[5]

These sentiments—of desire, longing, hope, fulfillment—are by no means unique to Goethe or James. Indeed, the confirmation, or contradiction, of travelers' expectations constitutes the dénouement of innumerable travel journals and memoirs. Expectation was the universal baggage tourists packed with their Baedekers. But the expectation was not spontaneous. As Robert Eisner remarks, writing about travel to nineteenth century Greece but equally applicable to eighteenth century Rome or twentieth century Los Angeles, "the travelers of yesteryear found in the Greek landscape and on the historical sites corroboration of their readings, whereas the mass of today's tourists usually learn about Greece, if at all, while actually there, from tour guides or handbooks."[6] François-René Chateaubriand prepared himself by reading some 200 books on travel to the Holy Land for his travel book *Itinéraire de Paris à Jérusalem* of 1811;[7] Thomas Watkins "arrived at the banks of the Rubicon, with Lucan in our hands," while Charles Sloane wrote from Rome in 1789 that "I have been for a good while past the constant companion of Livy, Virgil, Horace, etc."[8]

Under the circumstances, framing the experience of place through what I shall call anticipatory memory, a kind of pre-emptive nostalgia where the site or destination is prescriptively interpreted through the eyes of others, became the near-universal prophylactic against the potential for disappointment. Indeed, most travelers employed this kind of 'recollective memory' gleaned from travel journals, tourist guides, reproductive prints, photographs, snapshots, films, and videos and reproduced them in their own memoirs. That such memorialization remains part of the touristic experience is evidenced by the exponential growth of websites such as www.flickr.com on which tourists post the visual records of their travels to 'distant lands.'

The enthusiasm for travel to the "antique lands" of Italy and Greece often began with a classical education in boy or girl-hood. As Elizabeth Vassall, Lady Webster, expressed it early in the nineteenth century, "The first and strongest sensation one feels on entering Italy is the recollection of those historical events that from childhood are impressed on the mind,"[9] and Frederick, 6th Lord Baltimore, wrote of his tour of Greece and the Balkans: "what I saw in my travels recalled strongly to my remembrance the classical erudition I was happy to receive at *Eton College*."[10] The habit did not die out. In the late 1880s a young Norman Douglas wrote his grandmother, "I have been studying my Baedeker very diligently, and already *seem* to know my way around Naples quite well," and later noted before making a trip to Greece: 'I read one book on Greece every day, and will soon know the country and the language so intimately that it will be sheer waste of time and money going there.'[11] Early in the previous century Joseph Addison wrote that before he undertook his travels to Italy in 1701–1703 he "took care to refresh my memory among the *Classic* Authors, and to make such collections out of them as I might afterwards have occasion for," adding "the greatest pleasure I took in my journey from Rome to Naples was in seeing the fields, towns and rivers that had been described by so many classic authors, and have been the scenes of so many great actions," especially since the modern road is "extremely barren of curiosities."[12]

This rhetoric, evidenced through countless travel journals, memoirs, and recollections, in text, in image, or in sound, had to be learned, often against the run of tourists' initial impressions. Accounts of the sundry travails of cultural travel serve to illuminate the truth of the experience of place as encapsulated in Robert Louis Stevenson's oft-misquoted aphorism "to travel hopefully is a better thing than to arrive."[13] As Brian Musgrove has noted: "The travel text always supplements the insufficient act of 'witnessing' with epistemological reflection; a process which exposes fundamental morbidities in the ideologies of 'movement' and 'settlement.' In the end, this is a form of unresolved and unsatisfactory ascesis, whereby the attempt to revise and supplant a pre-existing culture

with the travelling-eye-view is not merely a partial but a complete evacu-
ation of self . . . the 'art of travel' . . . is underscored by an anxious sense
that to travel is to 'be nowhere.'"[14] Or at least nowhere the tourist recognizes as somewhere. Pretty much the same sentiments were expressed
on first contact with the artworks of antiquity and the masters of the
Italian Renaissance. In the 1840s the art critic Gustave Planche recounts
how a young painter, newly-arrived from Paris, hurried to the Vatican to
pay his respects to Raphael, at the time universally considered to be *the*
model of emulation. The young painter's disappointment was palpable,
and he came away saying, "If this is Raphael, he'll take some getting used
to."[15] Not only artworks, but also the landscape often disappointed; the
imaginary geography of Claude Lorrain's ideal landscapes had instilled
in the North European imagination the supposed beauties of the Roman
Campagna, yet few found the reality to be so sublime.[16] Charles Dupaty,
in *Lettres sur l'Italie en 1785*, expresses horror at finding the city of
Rome in a moribund state: "This city is not Rome; it is its corpse, and
the campagna is its tomb. Its populace, who swarm in its midst, are
the worms who devour it."[17] A typical reaction is that of the splenetic
Scottish novelist Tobias Smollett, whose disapproval of all things foreign (and generally unpleasant), began at Boulogne and hardly abated
during the entire voyage. He wrote in February 1765 with a degree of
aspersion, "the Campagna of Rome . . . is almost a desert. The view of
this country, in its present situation, cannot but produce emotions of
pity and indignation in the mind of every person who retains any idea
of its ancient cultivation and fertility. It is nothing but a naked withered
down, desolate and dreary, almost without enclosure, cornfield, hedge,
tree, shrub, house, hut, or habitation; exhibiting here and there the ruins
of an ancient castellum, tomb, or temple, and in some places the remains
of a Roman via."[18]

In this, guidebooks and memoirs played an indispensable role in whet-
ting the prospective tourists' appetite. The following, from the pen of
Guillet de Saint-Georges, is typical in many respects:

> At the first sight of [Athens] . . . I started immediately, and was taken
> with a universal shivering all over my Body. Nor was I singular in my
> commotion, we all of us stared, but could see nothing, our imagina-
> tions were too full of the Great Men which that City had produced.[19]

Born plain George Guillet in Thiers in the Auvergne in 1625, his guide
quickly ran to several editions and was translated into English the following year as *An Account of a Late Voyage to Athens* (1676). Guillet's
varied career had included journalism, a spell as designer for the theatri-
cal troupe of the Hôtel de Bourgone, and the post of historiographer to
the Académie royale de peinture et de sculpture. His first publication had
appeared in 1670, a book of etiquette, described as 'very interesting and

full of learning' and successful enough to run to five editions. Inspired by this success, he turned out a hasty translation of Machiavelli and then plunged into *Athènes ancienne and nouvelle* without ever having visited Greece. He attempted to avoid the inevitable criticism by excusing any faults such as might naturally occur in a work of the imagination by claiming he was merely transcribing the notes of his soldier brother, one "Guilletière" who, captured during the Hungarian Wars, had gained extensive knowledge of the Levant during enforced travels undertaken as a galley slave in a Tunisian privateer. Despite the improbability of his source, Guillet's book was hugely successful, although Châteaubriand complained it was no more factual than a novel.[20]

Whatever its shortcomings as an eyewitness account, such an ecstatic description is no more than a typical example of the benumbed traveler overcome by an almost physical malaise in the face of so much perceived splendor. No doubt only a minority of tourists experienced the *crise de nerfs* suffered by Marie-Henri Beyle, better known under the pen name Stendhal, who, after viewing Volterrano's *Sybils* in the church of Santa Croce in Florence, wrote that "my heart beat wildly . . . the life drained out of me, I walked in constant fear of collapse."[21] His experience was sufficiently memorable to be accorded, in the 1980s, the status of a medical condition—the Stendhal Syndrome—but he was far from unique.[22] As his contemporary, the playwright Auguste Creuzé de Lesser admitted, the mere contemplation of a visit to Italy brought on "an involuntary seizure, a vague kind of unease," that was cured only by undertaking the journey to the site of his anxiety.[23] The moment of encounter often stayed with the tourist for life:

> I do not know how to describe the agitation, the emotion, the distant sight of the Eternal City, in the middle of an immense, barren, and desolate plain, inspired in me . . . Everything in my eyes became grandiose, poetic, sublime.[24]

And Eugène-Emmanuel Amaury-Duval, who accompanied his teacher J.-A.-D. Ingres to Rome in 1835 recounts his experience on seeing the Vatican: "At last, St Peter's! A shiver ran through my body, and I was gripped by an emotion like no other I had experienced in my entire life."[25]

It would be easy, but misleading, to present these and other instances of culture shock as the overblown reactions of naïve tourists—the equivalent of learning, as a child, that Santa Claus doesn't live at the North Pole or that the Tooth Fairy isn't the one who leaves the quarter under your pillow. But historically, as today, tourists come in all shapes and sizes, and for each of those who evinced excitement, disappointment, or equanimity, just as many recognized the duality of perception, or what Robert Eisner has called the "double nature of place." As Percy Bysshe Shelley (1792–1822) observed, writing to a friend from Naples in 1818:

> There are two Italies ... one composed of the green earth and the transparent sea, and the mighty ruins of ancient time, and aerial mountains, and the warm and radiant atmosphere which is infused through all things. The other consists of the Italians of the present day, their works and ways. The one is the most sublime and lovely contemplation that can be conceived by the imagination of man; the other is the most degraded, disgusting and odious.[26]

What is remarkable about this passage is not Shelley's distinction between the timeless landscape and (we might suppose), equally timeless ruins and the "Italians of the present day"—that was a cliché long before Shelley's time—but the association of the former with the qualities of contemplation and imagination. It is the latter, an unlovely, unsublime present that William Makepeace Thackeray (1811–1863) presents in his *From Cornhill to Cairo* (1846):

> The truth is, then, that Athens is a disappointment, and I am angry that it should be so. To a skilled antiquarian, or an enthusiastic Greek scholar, the feeling created by the sight of the place of course will be different; but you who would be inspired by it must undergo a long preparation of reading, and possess too a particular feeling; both of which , I suspect, are uncommon in our busy newspaper-reading country.[27]

In fact, Thackeray had received an education in the classics, and therefore must be presumed to be speaking down to those unfamiliar with classical art and literature "in our busy newspaper-reading country." Even so, his point remains valid; a classical education, long preparation, and a sensibility for the past are all prerequisites for a successful visit to the sites of antiquity. As John Galt, an early biographer of Byron observes in his *Letters from the Levant* (1813): "The famous towns of Greece are, indeed, rather to be considered as places were recollections and trains of thought are excited, than as affording spectacles deserving of notice."[28]

Against this seemingly inevitable association the present-day is not afforded the privilege of any mediating lens. The sublimity of the image is confined to that which is already a memorialized. Reconstructive memory is at work in critic and historian Hippolyte Taine's astute observation after viewing the frescos in the Papal apartments in the Vatican in 1864:

> Without question nineteen out of twenty visitors are disappointed and stand there open mouthed, murmuring, "Is that it?" ... I too accepted that I understood nothing. It took me two or three visits to make the necessary abstractions and restorations.[29]

By "abstractions and restorations" it might be supposed that Taine is referring to the mental leap necessary to overcome the depredations of time all too evident in Raphael's frescos. But equally his remark may be interpreted as a leap of faith that the works displayed before his eyes really were equal to the reputation they enjoyed. Like many others before and since, Taine was in danger of substituting a priori memory for the presence of an original that was always already irretrievably lost.[30] George Carpenter, 1st Baron Carpenter of Killaghy, remarked that "I took a great deal of pleasure in comparing the descriptions that are given us by the ancient authors of particular places as rivers mountains etc. with what they are at present. I found that time had made such vast alterations in landscapes that it was not easy to know them by the descriptions."[31] It seems not to have occurred to Carpenter that it may well not be the landscape that is altered but his reliance on the accuracy of a written account—an ekphrastic solipsism that alienates the traveler intent on matching present-day geographical actuality with its textual/pictorial representation.

Wolfgang Ernst has pointed out that there is an "essential lack of primary presence" at the heart of the experience of place that distances the tourist from the *experience* of place.[32] It is no doubt to compensate for this loss that Marcel Proust has his Narrator in *Swann's Way* (the first volume of *Remembrance of Things Past*) lament the lack of guidance his perambulations on the Champs-Elysées afforded him.[33] The experience is bereft of meaning because no guide or memoir had adequately described the scene the better to designate it to his attention:

> If only Bergotte [a fictional character in *Remembrance of Things Past*] had described the place in one of his books, I should, no doubt, have longed to see it and to know it, like so many things else of which a simulacrum first found its way into my imagination.[34]

In other words, the meeting of place and event, in order to *be there* at all, had to be mediated through a commentary that would serve to reveal the truth of the experience. Without it, Proust's Narrator laments "there [is] nothing that attaches itself to my dreams." Experience is only validated when it is seen through the lens of prior representation. For Proust's Narrator to visit the Champs-Elysées without Bergotte's wished-for commentary is merely to be physically present, without hope of experiencing its essential presence. (Clive James, writing in 1980, remarks that he taught himself French by reading Proust, so much so that "Proust's Paris is between my mind and the real Paris.")[35]

In all such cases experience cannot be separated from recollection, rendering the actual event an always already memory that frames the way we experience the sense of place, as a short essay by Sigmund Freud attests. In September 1904, the psychoanalyst, then in his late forties, took his annual vacation in the company of his brother Alexander. While en route to Corfu, the brothers were persuaded by an acquaintance in Trieste to change their destination to Athens. This last-minute switch disturbed Freud, not least because he feared the renowned monuments of Greece could not live up to the reputation his boyhood teachers had instilled in him. Nevertheless, the pair booked tickets for the Greek capital that same afternoon. When, on arrival in Athens, Freud finally stood on the Acropolis he was assailed, like so many others before him, by a sense of unreality, in that what he saw with his own eyes was in some ways less tangible than what he had imagined in his expectations. Freud then notes, "a remarkable thought suddenly entered my mind: So all this really *does* exist, just as we learned at school!" At this point Freud imagines himself divided into two people:

> The first behaved as though he were obliged, under the impact of an unequivocal observation, to believe in something the reality of which had hitherto seemed doubtful. . . . The second person, on the other hand, was justifiably astonished, because he had been unaware that the real existence of Athens, the Acropolis, and the landscape around it had ever been objects of doubt.[36]

It was, in short, a "disturbance of memory"—the title Freud gives to his paper. No doubt his deliberations about the divided self and loss of reality were aided by his unparalleled understanding of the operation of the psyche, but otherwise his reactions seem largely typical in that, like so many before him, he had long wished to visit Athens, and having belatedly made the journey, found his expectations confounded by the peculiarly alienating effect that opposed anticipation and arrival. He is there, Athens is there, but the two refuse to cohere. As Freud recognizes, merely "being there" is not enough. In order for the experience to be meaningful, to be fully realized as an event, there must be an accord between expectation and arrival that his mere physical presence on the Acropolis cannot guarantee.[37] No amount of preparation, such as that provided by the classical education Freud received, or the assiduous study of guide books and recollections of earlier travelers, or even honest excitement at the anticipated journey, can ever adequately compensate for this loss.

Cultural geographer Tim Cresswell has argued that place is not just a thing, but also a way of experiencing the world. This observation has great importance for my argument, as it interprets place—which might seem to be little more than the location of where something is—as the means we bring to situate experience. "Place" in this sense is, as Creswell points out, a "way of seeing," a set of assumptions, attachments, and connections that we employ to create meaning in the world.[38] The philosopher J. E. Malpas has argued:

> Place is instead that within and with respect to which subjectivity is itself established—place is not founded *on* subjectivity, but it is rather that *on which* subjectivity is founded. Thus one does not first have a subject that apprehends certain features of the world in terms of

the idea of place; instead, the structure of subjectivity is given in and through the structure of place.[39]

And Edward S. Casey argues in *Remembering: a Phenomenological Study*, that the history of a place, and place as history, is a fundamental way in which we remember experiences:

> It is this stabilizing persistence of place as a container of experience that contributes so powerfully to its intrinsic memorability. An alert and alive memory connects spontaneously with place, find in it features that favor and parallel its own activities. We might even say that memory is naturally place-oriented or at least place-supported.[40]

This suggests that subjectivity and memory are inextricably linked, or at the very least that what we think of as our subjectivity has a memorial aspect. Furthermore, it detracts nothing from these observations to note that the memory may antedate the actual experience of place. In this sense, anticipatory memory may well be an even more powerful contributory factor to the "structure of subjectivity" than the actual face to face contact with the place in question.

One of the most sustained meditations on the role of memory in the experience of place is Martin Heidegger's recently translated travel journal *Sojourns*, which recounts his first visit to Greece, in Spring 1962, in the company of his wife, Elfride Petri, as a passenger on the cruise ship SS Yugoslavia.[41] Perhaps not since Kant has a philosopher had as much to say about the conditions under which the world is experienced and yet traveled so little in search of his material. Apart from five years at Marburg University and widely spaced visits to Provence, Rome, and Amsterdam, Heidegger traveled little beyond his home in the Black Forest. But this lack of peripatetic activity no more prevented Heidegger from inquiring into the nature of the experience of place than it stopped Kant from discoursing on the aesthetic properties of the distant lands he would never see.[42]

Heidegger begins *Sojourns* with what, for him, is the crucial problem that will haunt the rest of his visit—how to open up the experience of place to what he calls "the coming of god" so that "the vigil for the feast of his arrival can be prepared."[43] His language alone is warning enough that this will be no easy read. If this is travel writing then it is travel writing of a particularly difficult kind. Yet beyond the opacities and neologisms of the text it is clear that Heidegger is addressing fears—of loss, of displacement, of fragmentation, of origin—that have preoccupied travelers for a long as there has been travel. Even before he has out on his tour, Heidegger anxiously asks:

> I wonder of we are ever to find the region that we are seeking? And whether the finding will ever be given to us, if we visit the still existing

land of the Greeks and greet its earth, its sky, its sea and its islands, the abandoned temples and the sacred theaters?[44]

These are questions that clearly exceed the scope of most voyagers' anxieties about foreign travel (lost passports, strange food, missed connections), to embrace fundamental issues of time, place, and experience. Heidegger's text is not totally bereft of prosaic moments—at one point he notes fretfully that the view from his deck cabin "was blocked by the lifeboats," and at another describes the light meal taken "with other traveling groups in the hall of a hotel."[45] But for the most part the journal is rigorously philosophical. The accepted language of tourist literature is almost completely absent. There are no descriptions of picturesque ruins or charming taverns, no vignettes of local customs or beliefs, and no reference to the people he meets. Indeed, *Sojourns* is not, for the most part (if at all), a travel book or even a book about travel, but a philosophical treatise in the guise of an unassuming travel diary. The brevity of the book helps here. The translation runs to a mere fifty-seven pages, excluding introduction and notes, in small format. Furthermore, it indubitably deals with actual places—Corfu, Ithaca, Mycenae, Rhodes, Athens—that lend the journal an air of actuality. But its themes are those with which Heidegger was preoccupied throughout his life—being, world, time, origin, technology—ideas most pressingly introduced in the paradigm-shifting *Being and Time* of 1927. And in setting out to describe how thought, although preceded by existence, can never itself be in a position fully to grasp reality, he maps out the terrain of his inquiry in *Sojourns*:

> Thinking about all this is difficult, insofar as that which determined the world of Greece in its proper character remains concealed. Again and again the question arises: Where should we look for this proper character? Every visit to every place of its dwelling, work, and feast renders us more perplexed.[46]

Just as *Being and Time* acknowledges the impossibility of thought ever fully capturing existence, so then his visit to Mycenae can never adequately reinstate its lost ("proper" is Heidegger's preferred adjective) Greek character. In place of this lack Heidegger substitutes the landscape of anticipation, setting up an encounter with modern Greece that will satisfy or disappoint him to the degree that it meets long-held expectations.

The operation of this kind of imaginary recollection is close to what Heidegger calls "recollective thinking" in *Sojourns*. At several points in the narrative he uses the noun *Andenken*, as in "The thinking [*Andenken*] of the proper character of Greece is a world-alienating occupation."[47] But this "thinking" is not the analytic kind of "thinking through" that popularly characterizes the work of philosophy. The primary meanings of *Andenken* are "memory," "remembrance," "memento," "souvenir." For

Heidegger, thinking has the quality of recalling, remembering, a re-finding of an authentic Greece that is lost to the present day.

Beyond concerns whether modern travel would allow the tourist to experience the Greece of antiquity, Heidegger recognizes that his visit would take place both in the past and the future—in the past as part of his cultural memory, in the future because his journey has yet to take place:

> Who is to show us the path? What is to give us a hint about the field that we seek? This field lies behind us, not before us. What is of necessity is to look back and reflect on that which an ancient memory has preserved for us and yet, through all the things that we think we know and we possess, remains distorted.[48]

Sojourns, ostensibly written during the voyage, is no more an on-the-spot reflection on Heidegger's experiences in Greece than Stendhal's account of his collapse in Santa Croce, written years later in a hôtel on the rue Richelieu in Paris, is a contemporary account of his travels in Italy. Unlike Stendhal, however, who sought to communicate a sense of oneness with his subject, Heidegger's account is permeated with feelings of disconnection and doubt—about what he would find in Greece, about the nature of history, about the difficulty of reconciling expectation and event, doubt even about the wisdom of making the journey at all.

At several points in the journal Heidegger comments on the tourist experience—donkeys brought to the shore to carry the ship's passengers; colorful fabrics laid out along the path to tempt the tourist; taking snapshots; a performance of folk dances staged for visitors. While he does not call this inauthentic (it is after all authentic tourism), it is clear that he is unable to accept it as meaningful because the *that* which he seeks remains elusive. There exists a brief and fuzzy home movie of Heidegger, in the company of Elfride and sundry traveling companions, clambering around ruins, consulting a guide book, gazing out over the Mediterranean.[49] The movie reveals the reality of his situation—that to travel is willy-nilly to be a tourist—a perception, perhaps, that prompted him to comment, "it never crossed my mind, during the journey, to question the usefulness and the pleasure of such trips." But when he adds, "neither, though, did the thought leave my mind that what matters is not us and our experience of Greece, but Greece itself."[50] We might say that to travel, even hopefully, is not the same as arriving. But Heidegger does not believe that if these travelers suddenly disappeared he could have the experience he desires. "Should we wonder, then," he asks rhetorically, "if we take into account this matter, that presumably an ancient tradition in Plato's *Phaedrus* speaks of the 'field of unconcealment,' where everything that truthfully comes-to-presence is allowed to stay?"[51]

Leaving Venice, where Heidegger and his wife boarded ship, "it would be hard to imagine a more proper way of approaching the ever-distant island country," Heidegger notes with considerable satisfaction.[52] But his reaction to the SS Yugoslavia's first port-of-call, the island of Corfu, is one of disappointment:

> Early in the morning, after the journey's second night, the island of Corfu appeared, the ancient Cephallenia. Was this the land of the Phaeacians? The first impression would not agree with the picture that the poet gives in Book VI of the *Odyssey*.[53]

In one minor respect Heidegger is mistaken. Ancient Corfu was known as Corcyra, not Cephallenia, but the slip does nothing to alleviate his sense of displacement. As Wolfgang Ernst has remarked, when the philosopher arrived there was, "in the words of Gertrude Stein, no *there* there, just stones."[54] So great was his dis-ease at the hiatus between anticipation and arrival, that when the moment came to disembark he was unable to summon the requisite leap of faith and stayed on board. With beguiling frankness Heidegger notes: "What I had sensed and expected did not appear," and adds with disarming honesty, "maybe the notions that I had brought with me were exaggerated and misleading."[55]

The angst-ridden questions that prevented Heidegger from going ashore at Corfu were repeated with increased urgency as the ship reached the wooded coastline of Ithaca. Here Heidegger asks: "The home of Odysseus? Many things in this picture too would not fit in with the picture that I had from the days of my first reading Homer in the Gymnasium in Constance."[56] At this point, still early in his journey, Heidegger voices real despair: "Doubts remained whether we would ever be granted the experience of what is originarily [*anfänglich*] Greek; whether any such experience, as is already well known, would not be predetermined."[57] And again Heidegger asks himself whether "this essence [of Greece] long-cherished and often thought through, was a creature of fancy without any connection with what actually had been."[58] The ruins remain just that, ruins, and the stones just stones, fragments of an anticipated encounter that refuses to coalesce into reality.

Heidegger's search continues. At Olympia—"that place where once all of Greece gathered"—Heidegger is again disappointed. He comments discontentedly on the nearby village disfigured by modern, and still unfinished, hotels "for the American tourists," seemingly forgetting for the moment his own inescapably touristic persona. At Olympia he exclaims incredulously: 'What is even more unthinkable is that this very landscape . . . was established as *the* place of Greek festival and in accordance with them, the reckoning of time in Olympiads.[59] The comment is anticipated by Herman Melville on visiting Patmos in 1857, "Again afflicted with the great curse of modern travel—skepticism. Could no more realize that St. John had ever had revelations here, than when off Juan Fernandez, could believe in Robinson Crusoe according to DeFoe."[60] Happily, Heidegger finds a more "proper" Greece in the nearby Temple of Hera and the stadium in which the games took place, but notes, referring the opening lines of Pindar's "Olympian Ode":[61] "What would all these be without the song that praises, without the word which first, through the vibrating-articulated tone, reveals and veils that which has been here."[62]

What Heidegger seeks is an originary, primordial, Greece. This is not merely the Greece of the ancients, but the essence of the Greek character from which the historical Greece had sprung. In seeking out this Greek beginning Heidegger voices doubts about whether such effort "to return to the origin [*Anfang*]" could only remain vain and ineffective, and whether pursuing such an impossible quarry "would not ruin the immediate experience of the journey."[63] Doubtless Heidegger was thinking of this yet-to-be visited Greece when he lamented in "The Origin of the Work of Art," an essay written in 1935 but not published until 1950:

> World-withdrawal and world-decay can never be undone. The works are no longer the works they were. It is they themselves, to be sure, that we encounter there, but they themselves are gone by.[64]

Heidegger's unease continues to the next port-of-call at Rhodes. Once again he declines to disembark, just as he stays on board the next day when the ship berths at Kos and Patmos. He explains that it is neither his "stubborn will" nor fatigue that holds him back, but "the insistent call of the question regarding the proper character of the Greek Dasein and its world."[65] Heidegger's formulation of Dasein (*da*—here/there; *sein*—to be), meaning "to be here/there," "to be present," "to exist," and "to dwell," has much to offer for a better understanding of Heidegger's motivations in *Sojourns*. His repeated questioning of the meaning of experience revolves around a sense of place. Merely to be there is not *being* there in the Heideggerian sense. Place is not simply to be visited or not according to the whims of the traveler or the schedules of a cruise ship. Rather the journey is one of longed-for consummation, whereby the traveler is a supplicant before the spirit of the encounter.

As the ship steamed toward Athens, Heidegger, addressing concerns familiar to Walter Benjamin, again poses the question whether the modern world will erase all sense of distance, of the "homeless-ness" that allows for the possibility of a journey, resulting in a situation where "modern man feels everywhere at home?"[66] Approaching Athens, where "the haze over the modern metropolis was covering everything Greek," Heidegger remarks forlornly:

> Neither despair nor alienated comparison between the today and that which-once-was gave rise to my thoughts. But rather a singular question confronted the mind: whether man would be granted another familiar sojourn, as it was once given to Hellenism, an inceptive and

great sojourn, rich and yet moderate? But that had its time and was suddenly dismantled.[67]

While his situation as a tourist clearly troubled Heidegger, he believed that by far the greatest hurdle to the realization of the still hoped-for sojourn was the oppressive character of modern technological society. At the Acropolis, which his party had at first experienced in the comparative quiet of early morning, Heidegger becomes annoyed at the swelling crowds, not because they obstruct access to the temples, but for their zealous "toing and fro-ing, in which one was, without being aware, included, as it threatened to degrade what was just now the element of our experience into an object ready-at-hand for the viewer."[68] Sojourn, the long sought-after experience of the "Greek Dasein" that was Heidegger's reason for traveling in the first place, was being held at arm's length by sightseers and "the functioning of cameras and film recorders." Heidegger laments: "[Visitors] throw their memories in the technically produced picture. They abandon without clue the feast of thinking that they ignore."[69] The avatars of the present—modern transportation, the media, industrial society—all conspire to render what was once remote as immediate, and in doing so, deprive the traveler of the experience of the encounter.

Above all, it is in "The Origin of the Work of Art" that Heidegger poses questions that offer an insight into travelers' anxieties about the experience of place. What is at the origin of the work of art? What are the conditions of its coming into presence? And perhaps most important of all: What kind of experience does the work bring into being? David Farrell Krell has related these concerns to Heidegger's important, and counter-intuitive, concept of truth (*Alētheia*) as an "uncovering" or "unconcealment (*Entborgenheit*)", suggesting that it is art's emergence from hidden-ness that denotes its essence at the origin of the Heideggerian world (*Welt*)—itself a concept that provides the space, and *place*, for the human. No doubt the "thingly" character of the work of art (like the place-ness of place) must be present in order for art to be manifest, but it is not the essence of art—or place—to be the work; rather the "work" of the work of art/place is to open up a world hitherto concealed, surrounded as it is by its "earthy" nature. Heidegger seems to be thinking of the Greece that in 1935 he was still decades away from visiting:

> The temple, in its standing there, first gives to things their look and to men their outlook on themselves. This view remains open as long as the work is a work, as long as the god has not fled from it.[70]

The observation could have come straight from *Sojourns*. And in a sentence that has particular meaning in relation to his later visit to Greece, "In a world's worldling is gathered that spaciousness out of which the protective grace of the gods is granted or withheld."[71] We have come a long way from Smollet.

The relationship between concealment and unconcealment, an opening up of experience to presence, the locating of the "Greek Dasein," finally occurs at Delos: "At once [the island] laid a claim totally unique that we had nowhere felt before up to that point. Through everything a veiled great beginning [*Anfangs*] was expressed that once was."[72] Heidegger is unable to contain his satisfaction:

> Δῆλος is the name of the island: the manifest, the visible, the one that gathers every thing in its open, every thing to which she offers shelter through her appearing she gathers into *one* present . . . Δῆλος, the manifest, the signifying one, shows that she—the insignificant and humble center in the circle of islands—hides what is sacred and protects against the profane crush. One barely begins to think enough what the name of the island contains, that which calls the entirety of the Greek people to celebrate the festival that grants them the grace of divine favor and demands from the mortals the reticence of awe.[73]

It is perhaps not surprising that Heidegger should finally accede to a sense of place most strongly at Delos (the name of which literally means "Revelation"). According to legend this tiny island was the birthplace of Artemis and Apollo, who once had an oracle there. For Heidegger, travel was not merely a going-there, or even a getting-there, but an encounter, a supplication to a hidden god. And he makes it clear that such an encounter most closely resembles a religious experience, something akin to a pilgrimage, when he speaks of the sojourn being found "in the antechamber of the holy."[74] The pages Heidegger devotes to Delos are replete with references to hallowed ground, to festivals and sacred rites. In experiencing this revelation, what had hitherto been no more than a journey had become a sojourn.

At the end of the cruise Heidegger visits Delphi, high in a valley at the foot of Mt. Parnassus. The village was filled with modern hotels, "[bringing] a cacophony to the harmony of my thought," Heidegger laments. But by the time his party reached the Castalian spring "a shimmer of sacredness had again fallen over the place":

> Under a lofty sky, in the clear air of which the eagle, Zeus's bird, was flying in circles, the region revealed itself as *the* temple of the place. The place itself before anything else unveiled for the mortals the hidden mystery of this location where it was allowed to erect their dedications—and first among them, as fits its rank and dignity, the Doric temple of Apollo.[75]

The Delphic experience was short-lived. The new hotels, the museum, the crowds of visitors all compromise the experience of place. Yet despite the humdrum nature of this last contact, the journey to Greece ends in triumph. As the SS Yugoslavia sails back up the Adriatic toward Venice, Heidegger concludes with satisfaction:

The entirety of ancient Greece was transformed into a single island, enclosed from all the rest of the worlds, known and unknown. The departure from it became its arrival. What had arrived and brought the assurance of its stay was the sojourn of the flown gods that opens itself to recollective thinking.[76]

"Recollective thinking." Heidegger's remark suggest that, finally, the visit offered itself as a mediation through which notions of reality and truth, of rightness, and a sense of place, to say nothing of his anticipatory memories, were given a seeming coherence. Yet it is hard not to feel that the destination, any destination, will be forever denied, our chosen site of travel glimpsed, but never fully attained. It will always be a little further ahead, just around the next bend in the road, over the next hill. The experience of place, and place of experience, withdraws at the very moment it seems to offer itself for our taking.

NOTES

1. F. L. Lucas, "The Literature of Greek Travel," *Transactions of the Royal Society of Literature of the UK*, 17 (1930): 17–45 (17).
2. Johann Wolfgang Goethe, *Italian Journey*, trans. W. H. Auden and Elizabeth Mayer (Harmondsworth: Penguin, 1982), 129.
3. Goethe in March 1788; cited in this translation in Richard Wrigley's wide-ranging and informative "Infectious Enthusiasms: Influence, Contagion, and the Experience of Rome," in *Transports: Travel, Pleasure, and Imaginative Geography, 1600–1830*, ed. Chloe Chard and Helen Langdon, 'Studies in British Art', vol. 3 (New Haven and London: Yale University Press, 1996), 75–116 (78).
4. Clive James, "Postcard from Los Angeles: I 'No Stopping at Any Time,'" in *Flying Visits: Postcards from the Observer 1976–83* (New York: W.W. Norton & Company, 1984), 82.
5. Chard and Langdon, *Transports*, 11.
6. Robert Eisner, *Travelers to an Antique Land: The History and Literature of Travel to Greece* (Ann Arbor: University of Michigan Press, 1991), 130.
7. Eisner, *Travelers to an Antique Land*, 96.
8. Jeremy Black, *The British Abroad: the Grand Tour in the Eighteenth Century* (Stroud, Gloucestershire: Sutton Publishing, 2003), 308.
9. Brian Dolan, *Ladies of the Grand Tour* (London: Harper Collins, 2001), 6.
10. Black, *The British Abroad*, 307.
11. Paul Fussell, *Abroad: British Literary Traveling between the Wars* (Oxford: Oxford University Press, 1980), 122.
12. Elizabeth A. Bohls and Ian Duncan, eds., *Travel Writing 1700–1830: An Anthology* (Oxford: Oxford University Press, 2005), 5, 7.
13. Robert Louis Stevenson, "El Dorado," *Virginibus Puerisque and Other Papers* (New York: C. Scribner's Sons, 1905).
14. Brian Musgrove, "Travel and Unsettlement," in *Travel Writing and Empire: Postcolonial Theory in Transit*, ed. Steve Clark (London: Zed Books, 1999), 31–44 (32).
15. Gustave Planche, "De l'éducation et de l'avenir des artistes," *Revue des deux-mondes* (1848), 608–29 (624).

16. See Helen Langdon, "The Imaginative Geographies of Claude Lorrain," in *Transports,* ed. Chard and Langdon, 151–78.
17. Charles Dupaty, *Lettres sur l'Italie, en 1785* (Paris: Desenne, 1792), 149. My translation.
18. Paul Fussell, ed., *The Norton Book of Travel* (New York and London: W. W. Norton & Company, 1987), 218.
19. Eisner, *Travelers to an Antique Land,* 59.
20. Paul Duro, *The Academy and the Limits of Painting in Seventeenth-Century France* (New York: Cambridge University Press, 1997), 144–45.
21. Stendhal, *Rome, Naples et Florence* (Paris: Gallimard, 1987), 272. My translation. I would like to thank Cynthia Foo for drawing this passage to my attention.
22. For a study of the Stendhal Syndrome by the psychologist who named it, see Graziella Magherini, *La Sindrome di Stendhal* (Florence: Ponte alle Grazie, 1989).
23. Auguste Creuzé de Lesser, *Voyage en Italie et en Sicile fait en 1801 et 1802* (Paris: P. Didot, 1806). My translation. Cited in the original French in Wrigley, "Infectious Enthusiasms," 78.
24. Hector Berlioz, *Mémoires,* vol. 1 (Paris: Garnier-Flammarion, 1966), 195. My translation. Cited in the original French in Wrigley, "Infectious Enthusiasms," 79.
25. Eugène-Emmanuel Amaury-Duval, *l'Atelier d'Ingres* (Paris: Charpentier, 1878).
26. Percy Bysshe Shelley, *Letters,* vol. 2, ed. by Frederick L. Jones (Oxford: Clarendon Press, 1964), 489.
27. Eisner, *Travelers to an Antique Land,* 147.
28. John Galt, *Letters from the Levant* (London: Cadell and Davies, 1813), cited in C. W. J. Elliot, "John Galt's View of Greece," *Omphalos* 1 (1972): 42–57 (47–48).
29. Hippolyte Taine, *Voyage en Italie,* vol. 1 (Paris: Hachette, 1884), 171.
30. Wolfgang Ernst, "Framing the Fragment: Archaeology, Art, Museum," in *The Rhetoric of the Frame: Essays on the Boundaries of the Artwork,* ed. Paul Duro (New York: Cambridge University Press, 1996), 111–35 (125).
31. Black, *The British Abroad,* 306.
32. Ernst, "Framing the Fragment," 124.
33. For the idea of a "mediator" see René Girard, *Deceit, Desire, and the Novel: The Self and Other in Literary Structure,* trans. Yvonne Freccero (Baltimore: Johns Hopkins University Press, 1965), 31.
34. Marcel Proust, *Remembrance of Things Past* [*Swann's Way*], vol. 2, trans. C. K. Scott Moncrieff (New York: Random House, 1934) 301.
35. James, *Flying Visits,* 115.
36. Sigmund Freud, "A Disturbance of Memory on the Acropolis," *Collected Papers,* vol. 5, ed. James Strachey (New York: Basic Books, 1959), 302–12 (304).
37. For further analysis of Freud's essay see Musgrove, "Travel and Unsettlement," esp. 41–44.
38. Tim Cresswell, *Place; A Short Introduction* (London: Blackwell Publishing, 2004), 11.
39. J. E. Malpas, *Place and Experience: A Philosophical Topography* (Cambridge: Cambridge University Press, 1999), 35; quoted in Creswell, *Place,* 31–32.
40. Edward S. Casey, *Remembering: A Phenomenological Study* (Bloomington: Indiana University Press, 1987), 186–87; quoted in Creswell, *Place,* 86.
41. Martin Heidegger, *Sojourns: the Journey to Greece,* trans. John Panteleimon Manoussakis, foreword by John Sallis (New York: State University of New York Press, 2005).

42. Kant's references include St. Peter's in Rome, the pyramids of Egypt, and the beauties of the island of Sumatra. See Immanuel Kant, *Critique of Judgment*, translated with an introduction by Werner S. Pluhar (Indianapolis: Hackett Publishing Company, 1987), § 26 (108); § 22 (93–94).
43. Heidegger, *Sojourns*, 2.
44. Ibid., 4.
45. Ibid., 7, 55.
46. Ibid., 22.
47. Ibid., 26.
48. Ibid., 3.
49. Heidegger home movie. Retrieved February 13, 2007 from http://www.youtube.com/watch?v=BqGPGRXx8gw.
50. Heidegger, *Sojourns*, 9.
51. Ibid., 11, 33.
52. Ibid., 5.
53. Ibid., 7–8.
54. Ernst, "Framing the Fragment," 124. See Gertrude Stein, referring to Oakland, California, in *Everybody's Autobiography* (New York: Vintage Books 1973 [1937]), 289.
55. Heidegger, *Sojourns*, 7–8.
56. Ibid., 10.
57. Ibid., 8.
58. Ibid., 12–13.
59. Ibid., 13.
60. Herman Melville, *Journal of a Visit to Europe and the Levant*, ed. Howard Horsford (Princeton: Princeton University Press, 1955), 166.
61. The poem celebrates the victory of Hieron, king of Syracuse, in a horse race that took place during the Olympic games of 478 BCE. *Sojourns*, 15 and 67 (n.11).
62. Heidegger, *Sojourns*, 14–15.
63. Ibid., 9.
64. Martin Heidegger, "The Origin of the Work of Art," in *Basic Writings*, ed. David Farrell Kress (San Francisco: Harper Collins, 1993), 143–203 (166).
65. Heidegger, *Sojourns*, 25, 29.
66. Ibid., 36–37.
67. Ibid., 38–39.
68. Ibid., 41–42.
69. Ibid., 54.
70. Heidegger, "Origin," 140.
71. Heidegger, "Origin," 140, 168–70. See also Simon Glendinning, "Heidegger," in *The Routledge Companion to Aesthetics*, ed. Berys Gaut and Dominic McIver Lopes (London and New York: Routledge, 2003), 107–18
72. Heidegger, *Sojourns*, 30.
73. Ibid., 31–32.
74. Ibid., 45.
75. Ibid., 51.
76. Ibid., 56.

4 Woodland Cemetery
Modernism and Memory

Malcolm Woollen

Many scholars have classified displays of death as summations of distinctive worldviews. These have been designed to deliver messages of comfort and discomfort while also strengthening solidarity and excluding outsiders. Some nineteenth century American cemeteries, for example, have sought to portray landscapes of desire, originally conceived by French painters and later realized in English estates and public parks. Another distinctive tradition, reflected in large public monuments in Washington D.C., attempts to confront death with the memory of a heroic life.[1] Amidst these traditions, Stockholm's Woodland Cemetery presents a unique case study. Unlike a cemetery like Mount Auburn in Cambridge, the Woodland Cemetery is not a portrait of one time and one worldview. Instead, it reveals a transitional view of a changing country, struggling with modernity and memory. In this process, it shows intent to be inclusive by artful rhetorical consolidation of pre-Christian, Christian, and Vitalist traditions. Lastly, it serves as a demonstration that modernism has the capacity to embrace these traditions and offer diverse meanings.

The changing ethos that underlies this creation was partly a product of a history largely unscathed by famine, war, or revolution in the past two centuries. This was due in large part to a consensus based on industry, neutrality, and a rejection of class conflict. Simultaneously drawing on the culture of the peasant and modern industrial values, Swedes used this consensus to develop an uncommon form of nationalism in the late nineteenth and early twentieth centuries. They did this with a moral imperative that rarely isolated problems; aesthetics, health, landscape, housing, and economic development were invariably thought of as one national cause. This new way of thinking, according to Arne Ruth, "retained significant elements of the tradition it was superseding. Swedish national culture would once more serve as a liberating force in the world. Sweden would build a new spiritual empire as the native land of modern values."[2] This new mission, however, had an inherent contradiction with deep-seated values. Because the national ambition to be modern meant rapid urbanization, there was a massive displacement of the rural population in the early twentieth century and widespread anxiety about the disappearance of rural culture and landscape.

Collective memory under these circumstances was not a matter of national storytelling about tragedies and heroic victories. Instead, beginning in the nineteenth century, Swedes began to find a new ethos in the everyday: caring for the family in a beautiful and efficient home and appreciating a unique landscape. Just as home and landscape were united in life, the displays of death likewise offered the opportunity to comfort the bereaved by reminding them of the binding ties between family, culture, and landscape. The more difficult challenge was to claim that modern values—clarity, efficiency, and socialism—were not incompatible with an appreciation of family, culture, and landscape. The architects of the Woodland Cemetery, Gunnar Asplund and Sigurd Lewerentz, responded to this challenge and proposed a resolution of this perceived conflict.

To explain how this happened, it is best to begin with the essential qualities of the Swedish landscape. First, the quality of light is distinctive: "In relation to misty Mediterranean horizons and the flat sky," writes Thorbjorn Andersson, "the northern bowl of heaven really is a bowl and on land its light is apparent even in its long mild shadows."[3] Dawn and dusk are particularly long with colors of "dull nuances of greys, greens and blues."[4] Because of the cold climate, there are a limited number of plant species that reinforce a widely shared attitude about landscape. Finally, there is a consistent character to the landscape due to the glaciers 10,000 years ago. This caused a familiar pattern of concave and convex forms that varies little across Sweden.

Swedes have long enjoyed a comfort and identification with the essential character of this landscape. Andersson notes that unlike Middle Eastern countries, where gardens have become an expression of paradise very different from the arid landscape, Swedes have been content to find paradise in their existing environment.[5] Their sense of collective admiration of landscape is reflected in a code of shared rights of access called "allemansrätten," a social code that governs access to private property. According to these rules, people have the right to traverse or overnight in a tent on the land of another. There is also the right to pick flowers and berries, but not nuts or twigs. With this background, "Swedes have an understanding that the natural world plays a decisive role in people's striving after both physical and also spiritual well being."[6] This feeling for nature became a matter of nationalism in the late nineteenth century; "Pine, fir and birch were seen as indigenous trees and so in a way represented Sweden, in paintings as well as *in situ*. According to long tradition, Swedish men and women believe they are fonder of nature and the rural landscape than other peoples, that we have a certain feeling for Nature."[7] The Swedish version of nature, which translated into care for forests and open spaces, was the emotional currency that everyone shared and became the setting for all significant memories, including childhood play, courtship, work, and family holidays.

This national pride, however, was not always expressed in what was built. For much of their pre-industrial history, Swedes followed the example of their larger European neighbors in the design of public buildings and landscapes. Drottingholm Palace Garden was designed in the Baroque manner by Nicolas Tessin the Elder and Nicolas Tessin the Younger in the late seventeenth century. Haga Park in Stockholm was created by Frederic Magnus Piper in the style of the English Picturesque in the late eighteenth century.[8] The situation changed in the second half of the nineteenth century when there was a search for a new national style in landscape. The municipal government of Stockholm seized the initiative during the late 1860s by beginning a policy to buy up large estates on the periphery of the city to preserve natural areas and limit speculation. At this time, there was widespread anxiety about urban growth and a will to preserve the memory of the wilder landscape. This movement was guided by the Lindhagen Plan of 1866 that established a principle that "no resident of the capital should be without a park in the vicinity, in other words that access to green areas was a right for the city's inhabitants."[9] This forethought was providential because when city leaders took up the problem of scarce housing and cemetery space in the early twentieth century, they were in a strong position to intervene.[10] They could shape a city that could respond to a growing industrial economy and allay the fears of a population with profound discomfort with urbanism.

Although these leaders were committed to a program to expand public parks in Stockholm in the early twentieth century, there was not yet a consensus on the design of the parks. In reaction to overly formal and derivative designs, Rutger Sernander, a professor of Botany at Uppsala University, helped to form a new philosophy. He encouraged parks with "a stylized landscape of pastures and grove that integrated the features of the local landscape with plant materials sympathetic to the existing characteristics of the site."[11] In his book *Stockholms Natur*, he praises the unique beauty of Swedish trees and cites different ways in which they have been integrated into urban environments. He shows examples of specific venerable trees in Stockholm that are treated like landmarks, something like memorials in Rome. He also draws attention to the unique beauty of rocky highlands and shorelines, characteristic of the geography of Stockholm.[12] This appeal of rugged places can partly be explained by the rapid depopulation of rural areas. In 1850 more than 90% of the population lived in the country; by 1900, thanks to industrialization, this figure was reduced to 75%. Meanwhile, between 1845 and 1929, one million Swedes left for North America. With the departure of rural people, the typical Swedish landscape was slowly disappearing.[13] Given the emotional significance of rural places for Swedes, this trend amounted to a growing crisis, both spiritual and demographic.

This anxiety about a changing country is captured in an artistic movement called National Romanticism, a collective search for national identity that began in the late nineteenth century. Eva Eriksson explains how artists responded to the social upheaval of the 1880s by joining artist colonies on the Continent. After a number of years, many artists began to see their country with fresh eyes and returned home eager to define a Nordic identity. They found a country that, despite industrialization, still had a sense of itself: "The daily life of most people was closely allied to the conditions of nature and the changing seasons. A feeling for nature is also deeply rooted in Nordic tradition and has characterized myths and popular stories since time out of mind."[14] A group of artists called the Artists Association, formed in 1886, began to paint subjects featuring northern evenings, pine forests, and rural people in everyday activities.[15] Eriksson points out how the cultural dichotomy of the period was evident at the Stockholm Art and Industry Exhibit of 1897. On one hand, there were exhibits that expressed optimism about the future and technology. On the other, "it expressed an interest in nature, backward looks, and care about tradition, where change could imply a threat to essential values."[16] This expresses the fundamental tension that Gunnar Asplund and Sigurd Lewerentz confronted later with the design of the Woodland Cemetery.

This tense union between tradition and modernism also happened in development of the Swedish home. What began as an effort to sustain Swedish identity by preserving rural craft and architecture later inspired a movement that embraced beauty in the home as a force of social regeneration. This in turn had its impact on successive exhibitions and new progressive housing programs in the early twentieth century. Artur Hazelius, a linguist, began the movement by founding both the Nordic Museum (1873), dedicated to Nordic rural crafts, and Skansen (1891), a museum of rural architecture. At the same time, Carl Larsson gave this movement significance in the art world by moving his family to a farmhouse called Lilla Hyttnäs at Sundborn in Dalarna. Over many years, he and his wife Karin transformed this house with colors, textile, and furniture in a style that is both vernacular and original. He made many paintings, presented in his book *Et Hem,* which both document the spaces and family life. His example showed how beautiful domestic environments can be stimulating places to raise children. It is noteworthy that the Larssons began the tradition of painting eighteenth century Swedish chairs pearl white, a model for Asplund's chairs in the Woodland Chapel.

Larsson was fundamentally a conservative by instinct, but he inspired many thinkers who were decidedly progressive. Among the most important of them was Ellen Key, who became the advocate for this cult of the domestic. In a pamphlet called *Beauty for All* and a book called *Beauty in the Home,* she made a case for the close relationship between beauty and utility for furnishing and decorating the home. She wrote, "you work better, feel better, become friendlier and more joyful if you surround yourself in your home with beautiful shapes and colors."[17] She also insisted that beauty in the home was not a luxury only reserved for the wealthy; with educated taste, all classes could enjoy its' benefits.

Gregor Paulsson, an art historian and theorist, took inspiration from Ellen Key, and campaigned for a new approach to machine-made products for the home. As head of the Swedish Arts and Crafts Society, he organized the Home Exhibition of 1917 to introduce modern designs for the home. Addressing the extreme shortage of adequate homes for workers in urban areas, housing was the real motive for the show. Paulsson, like Key, wanted to demonstrate that the housing crisis was an aesthetic, social, and economic problem.[18] He later went on to organize the Stockholm Exhibition in 1931 with the purpose of promoting design innovation in housing and furnishings.

Because housing was at the core of Social Democratic ideology, spending on housing became the primary way to stimulate the economy during the 1930s.[19] Low-rise public housing blocks were built in Stockholm and other urban areas, many of them bordering public parks: "A midnineteenth century interest in homes grew into cooperation between non-profit-making organizations, big industry and the central government; this favored the growth of the home furnishing industry. Culminating in the 1950s, this long process uniquely combined research, ideology, practical knowledge, aesthetic ambitions and industrial production."[20] Homes, according to Wickham, were invested with the primary goals of Swedish culture, shaping children, fostering democratic values, and promoting beauty and high standards. This new consensus was not led by one visionary artist or architect. Instead, it was shaped by public officials, interest groups, scientists, poets, artists, and architects. It had a political dimension as well; they not only defined the desirable landscape and the beautiful home, but went on to declare that every Swede had a right to enjoy them.[21]

Because the Swedish urban home was invested with the national ambition to embrace modernity, memory had little presence here. Instead, it was lodged in Stockholm parks that preserved rugged and sweeping landscapes. A form of urbanism where modern housing blocks abut ragged, open spaces became the accepted approach for urban living. This pattern represents the union of the cult of the modern home with the memory of the rural landscape; everyday efficiency was bonded with an artifact of natural space once enjoyed by ancestors. Though these parks were places of amenity, they also spoke of natural cycles, decay and loss of a way of life. In this way death had a latent presence in the everyday.

Given this realignment of natural space and urban living in the early twentieth century, it is no coincidence that other progressive groups were campaigning for a new conception of the urban cemetery. Swedes at the time had the benefit of new thinking in Europe about the design of cemeteries, cremation, and death. After much reluctance on the part of the Swedish Lutheran Church, cremation had gained acceptance as hygienic and pragmatic.[22] Meanwhile, Hans Grassel, a municipal architect in Munich, designed the *Waldfriedhof* (1907), an influential cemetery sited in a forest and broken down into intimate units.[23] Finally, Maurice Maeterlink, a Belgian dramatist who wrote a book called *Death* in 1913, was particularly influential. He advocated a clearer conception of death, unencumbered by cultural mythology and instinct; "Here begins the open sea," he wrote, "here begins the wonderful adventure, the only one to be worthy of man's enquiring mind, the only one to raise itself as high as his highest yearning. May we become used to regarding death as a form of life, a form as yet we do not understand."[24] His book was widely read by advocates of cremation in Sweden and served for many as a foundation for a modern conception of death.

These influences all contributed to the cultural milieu when the Stockholm Cemetery Authority announced a competition for an addition to Sandsborg Cemetery in 1914. This competition was won by Sigurd Lewerentz and Gunnar Asplund in 1915 thanks to their intention to preserve the existing forest and a subdued approach to monumentality. In contrast to the other competitors, many from Germany, Asplund and Lewerentz were very much in tune with the Swedish appreciation of native landscape. The site was 120 acres in Enskede, a suburb to the south of the city's center; "The site, covered by a pine forest interspersed with spruce trees and various secondary growth, including birch, rowan, alder and willow trees, was dotted with boulders and scarred by gravel pits, the remnants of a sand and gravel quarry."[25] In their winning competition entry called "Tallum," they worked with the existing landscape, emphasizing the melancholy of graves in the dark forest, and terracing the contours of the former gravel pits. Pathways cut through the pine forest with names like the Way of the Cross and the Way of the Seven Wells allow processions of smaller ritualized sites.[26] This return to the dark forest, a setting for many Swedish folktales, was an appeal to the collective memory of Old Sweden and served to make all graves equal in its shadow.

Death in their conception becomes identified with the vanished rural landscape—the place of longing for recently urbanized Swedes. It can be considered an enhanced version of the public parks advocated by Sernander, the sacred places of the everyday, to the point where urban density is replaced by the density of the pine forest, allowing roads and small clearings to be carved. In this respect, it is a manifestation of Foucault's heterotopia, an "other" place where the rhetoric of the everyday is realigned; whereas "the good life" means dwelling at the edge of the forest, death means an eternity *in* the forest, a more perfect city.[27] It should be noted that the forest in Swedish lore is not considered a place of darkness and danger but rather a place of sustenance and dwelling. The root of the Swedish word for forest, *Skog*, means "shelter" in Old Icelandic, contrary to the more foreboding meanings in other languages.[28]

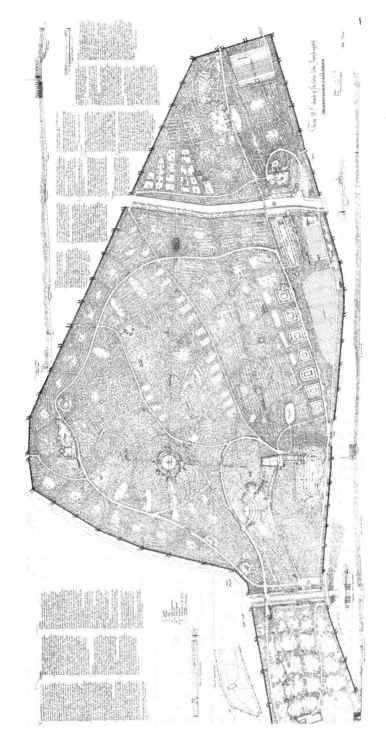

Figure 4.1   Tallum Competition Entry, Gunnar Asplund and Sigurd Lewerentz, 1915. Photo by Javier Beltran, The Stockholm Cemeteries Administration Archive.

Although their concept had wide appeal, the design was not fully executed all at once. Instead it evolved in stages over twenty-five years, reflecting the changes requested by the Cemetery Authority and a new sensibility about modernism and memory. The first chapel, intended to support these conservative values, was to be made of stone and sited at a prominent location. The Cemetery Authority, however, decided to relocate it in the forest and save money by building it in wood and stucco.[29] Asplund was given this commission in 1918 and the result is very effective at capturing the traditional Swedish themes of landscape and home, while also introducing more modern interpretations. The Woodland Chapel sits within a walled enclosure within the forest, reminiscent of a country churchyard.[30] The scale is modest and domestic, inspired by a Danish eighteenth century house called *Liselund*, a combination of vernacular and classical themes.[31] There is a deep low porch with rows of columns that relates to the columnar pines nearby. It also invites entry and serves as a preliminary gathering place (Figure 4.2). The interior is a startling contrast, evoking the cosmos with a skylight plaster dome—a miniature Pantheon.[32] This grand gesture is balanced by an intimate circle of chairs for the funeral party.

The contrast between the domestic exterior and the cosmic interior involves several layers of memory. First, because the structure is very small, only those most intimate with the deceased can attend. As a result, the deceased is remembered as a member of a family, rather than a public figure. The circle places them in relationship to each other, rather than an altar. This reflects the priorities popularized by Carl Larsson and Ellen Key where the family was of preeminent importance. On another level, the domestic scale speaks to how the dead were remembered in homes in rural Sweden. The dome of the Pantheon, however, introduces a new dimension of memory. It comes as a surprise to see an illusion of the sky, coming from the forest where the view of it is concealed. This gesture defies the memory of Christian design, dictating nave and sanctuary, and returns the bereaved to a pre-Christian concept of space and the cosmos. By doing this, it suggests that death can introduce an unexpected experience of time and space, a variation on Maeterlinck's idea of a journey to the unknown.

This pre-Christian sensibility suggests that while remembering the life of an individual, the bereaved should also be aware of a bond between body, earth, and sky. This is a variation on Heidegger's formula for dwelling—earth, sky, mortals, and the divinities.[33] The intended subtext is that this place is invested with enduring spirit; meanings that Swedes attribute to home and landscape are not new inventions but are related to the beliefs, if not the presence, of ancestors. In other words, the spirit of the individual is being returned to the eternal life all around them, not to some remote afterlife. The mound-like mortuary next to the chapel supports this interpretation; despite its shape and grass roof, it has a classical semi-circular window and chimney, suggesting that life continues within the earth. Elias Cornell has commented on Asplund's enduring interest in the sky as a cosmic theme, present in the Scandia Cinema and the Stockholm Public Library. The implication in Asplund's work is that all meanings that we give to interiors, particularly sacred ones, come from both the outdoors and the qualities of our own bodies.[34]

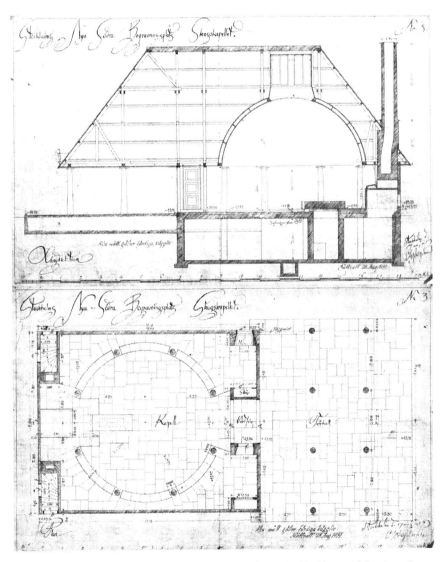

Figure 4.2 Woodland Chapel, Gunnar Asplund, 1918–20, Plan and Section. Courtesy of the Swedish Museum of Architecture.

This link between body and cosmos is also suggested by a small sculpture called *Angel of Death* (1921) by Carl Milles, perched on the roof of the Woodland Chapel. It functions as a quiet *momento mori*, but the message is not as explicit as those found in early American cemeteries. Though she has wings, this angel is nude in the mode of a Neolithic earth goddess with generous breasts, belly, and hips. A figure of the heavens, in other words, has been portrayed as a symbol of earthly fertility. Some visitors might miss this as a composite of two very different traditions. Others might appreciate the gentle irony. Finally, there are those who might see it as a promise of maternal care and rebirth beyond this life. In any case, it is not intended to inspire fear but to welcome all the bereaved with their different hopes, fears, and expectations. Instead of shunning all symbolism, an effort has been made to artfully consolidate traditions for spiritual solidarity in the face of death.

The earthly side of *The Angel of Death* can be described as a variation on Vitalism, a philosophical inquiry that goes back to Aristotle. It poses questions about whether life can be explained purely as a matter of mechanism or as a matter of a force animating that mechanism. In the early twentieth century, Henri Bergson's conception of the *élan vital* was the most noteworthy version of this branch of philosophy. Bergson explored in particular the finality of the parts and the whole of a given organism. If you trace any organism, or part, back to its origins, all are related to the same "protoplasmic jelly."[35] "In this sense each individual may be said to remain united with the totality of living beings by invisible bonds."[36]

It was an easy step for artists and poets in Sweden to extend this idea to a bond between humanity and landscape. In the 1890s, many artists left the cities to join colonies in the country in order to be closer to the natural world. Among them were J. A. G. Acke and Eugene Jansson who pioneered "Open-Air Vitalism" in painting between 1904 and 1910. Acke is notable for seascapes with nudes where the viewer is invited to appreciate the analogy between forces of nature and the latent power of the human body. He also painted landscapes where the analogy with the human body is unmistakable. Though he never wrote about it and was a professed agnostic, Asplund reveals a deep interest in the presence of the human form in projects spanning decades. His Snellman House, from 1917, features a womb room and the Lister County Courthouse has balusters with an unmistakable bulge.[37] In addition, his vacation house in Stennäs has a memorable swelling fireplace, positioned on a staircase. Though its presence is subdued in the early phases of the cemetery, Vitalism is the philosophical underpinning of the alternative spirituality expressed at the cemetery. Like Asplund's union of antiquity with Swedish vernacular at the Woodland Chapel, *The Angel of Death* demonstrates how Vitalist messages will be linked to other memorial forms in later phases of the cemetery.

These themes, however, were not sustained in the second phase of development of the cemetery (1923–30). For both landscaping and architecture, this phase was largely undertaken by Sigurd Lewerentz. The Resurrection Chapel, designed by Lewerentz in 1923, reveals a different approach. It receives an axis on the Path of the Seven Wells, taking a more public site than the Woodland Chapel. The intent is both ceremonial and quietly provocative. The scale of the entry porch and the chapel is increased to induce a sensation of insignificance in the face of death. Small details—the slight skew of the front porch, the deep reveal at the eave, the ghostly pilasters inside the chapel—prompt questions rather than offering reassurance. Although the chapel is possessed of thoughtful proportions and details, the scale of spaces does not speak to the domestic sensibility of Swedes nor does it offer any hint of an afterlife. Lewerentz's plan for the new crematorium and North Entry of 1922 takes a similar approach. He proposes a grand formal axis with a sophisticated spatial sequence concluding in the new crematorium. Another space shifts the axis to receive the existing Path of Seven Wells. Again, traditional architecture and planning have been manipulated without undermining their essential premises. Like the Resurrection Chapel, classicism is used as a reminder that the ancients accepted death with dignity but there are no hints about any spiritual beliefs that modern Swedes might share with them. Rules of classicism demand rigorous attention to the axis and its proper termination. As Versailles and countless other public buildings reveal, landscape is subject to domination rather than deference. Although antiquity has unique meanings in Nordic culture, the use of classicism also bears the weight of its memory as the architectural language of power. It was questionable whether these attributes were consistent with a culture that valued landscape highly and sought new social equity.

Lewerentz had a chance to correct these deficiencies when he designed a revised plan for the new crematorium and North Entry of 1931. This design evolved in the late 1920s and early 30s at a time when modernism was taking hold in Swedish culture and the country was undergoing dramatic political change. After a long period of coalition government and political stalemate in the 1920s, the Social Democrats took office after the election of 1932 in response to massive unemployment, lower wages, and labor conflict. To assume power, however, they formed a compromise with the Farmer's Party whereby the Social Democrats abandoned their commitment to nationalize the means of production and proposed an agricultural subsidy program. This allowed them to pass comprehensive legislation on social services, pensions, education, and health care. This became the basis of the *folkhemmet*, or society as a home for everyone, a term coined by the Social Democratic leader Per Albin Hansson. *Folkhemmet* was the foundation of the Swedish model in government, the so-called "The Third Way" popularized in America, and represented a brilliant use of political rhetoric to make the people comfortable with comprehensive change.[38] Here, politicians deftly combined rural memory with modern ambition in a package that appeared fundamentally Swedish.

The Stockholm Exhibition, planned and partly designed by Gunnar Asplund, also serves as example of the use of Swedish values to make people comfortable with change. This was Gregor Paulsson's opportunity to launch the new functionalist architecture in Sweden and market a plethora of Swedish products and homes of modern design. As a secular counterpart of the Woodland Cemetery, it could be called a temporary "landscape of desire" that prefigures the last phase of design. While casting a gentle spell in the summer of 1931 that foretold a modern future for Sweden, it proposed a non-monumental urbanism where buildings play a secondary role to the beauty of the lagoon. This pattern was fundamentally residential, having close kinship with new modern housing blocks in Stockholm. Despite the novelty of the design and the festive occasion, one intended message was that modern design could sustain Sweden's fundamental respect for wild natural space, following the lead of Rutger Sernander's philosophy of Stockholm parks. Instead of the grove or rocky hillock, however, it suggests large open spaces like the lagoon could be invested with sacred qualities as well.

Architects at the time, including Asplund, felt the need to follow up after the Stockholm Exhibition with a manifesto called *Acceptera,* meaning "accept," that would assert the relevance of the modern agenda in Sweden.[39] In it they explained the realities of "Europe A" that was industrialized and urban and "Europe B" that was agrarian and traditional.[40] They proclaimed the urgency to adopt a functionalist style that fit the agenda of "Europe A," but like good politicians, they realized that functionalism could only be accepted and understood by the people if it were presented in the terms of "Europe B." The underlying mission was to make functionalism inherently Swedish. For example, they explain that the quality of coziness need not be sacrificed; it simply needs to be understood as a functional outlook where "all things are in their proper place, that the home functions smoothly and this need not contradict at all the desire for psychological identification."[41] In this context, old and new can comfortably coexist, provided that both are true to their functions and made with care.

These polemical examples are necessary in order to understand how design, culture, and politics were closely intertwined in the 1930s when the North Entry and the Woodland Crematorium were built. Leaders wanted a compromise that was both progressive and respectful of cultural memory of all kinds. The first assertive statement of this new cultural agenda is the plan that Lewerentz designed with Asplund's participation for the North Entry. It features a remarkable open landscape where the focus is on a large knoll with a meditation grove on top (Figure 4.3). Stuart Wrede has written about this as a Freidrichian landscape that puts the design in the tradition of the German Romantic Movement.[42] It is more accurate to say that this landscape is deliberately ambiguous. It can be seen in the tradition of Swedish burial mounds such as those at

Gamla Uppsala that were erected on the burned remains of prominent individuals and kings, going back into prehistory.[43] Mores at the time dictated quite strictly that these earth forms were only for the elite. Fredric Magnus Piper followed in this tradition when he built Monument Hill at Drottingholm as the burial place for King Gustav III in 1797. Lewerentz and Asplund effectively appropriated this royal tradition for remembering one individual and reinterpreted it as a collective memorial; at a time when there was some lingering discomfort with cremation and the separation of grave and landscape, this served as a collective marker for all. It is noteworthy that this mound is distinctly asymmetrical with a cleft at the rear. These details suggest that this landform can also be understood as an evocation of a breast or swelling womb, again recalling the ambiguities of *The Angel of Death* and the theme of Vitalism in Asplund's work. While it could still be understood as a collective memorial, those with more modern inclinations were able to attribute a different meaning to it.

Just as there is choice in the interpretation of the landform, there is also choice in the selection of route and focus. Unlike the North Entry plan of 1922 with one route and one focus, the plan for the final version of the North Entry is distinctive in the selection the possible pathways.[44] Visitors have a choice between three paths, unlike the single route of the 1922 plan (Figure 4.4). First, there is a path that skirts along the edge of the crematorium and an allée of trees that ends at the Monument Hall. This is intended for the funeral parties who proceed directly to the chapels while viewing the larger landscape between the trees. Next there is the Way of the Cross that continues over the hill beyond the crematorium. Finally, there is a path on the right that connects to the Meditation Grove and the Way of the Seven Wells. This care in redirecting all routes to one side or the other ascribes monumentality to the landscape, without the coercion of one processional path. At the same time, it attends to the particular needs of visitors, allowing those going to or from the funeral chapels to take a more private route, separate from the Way of the Cross.

Choice is also present in other interpretations of the environment. Amid the multiple focal points in the open landscape, there is also a large cross, sited along the side of the Way of the Cross, which was intended to be seen in silhouette against the sky. Unlike a church, where the cross lies on axis with the processional route, this cross, though powerful, is one among many points of interest. Like *the Angel of Death*, which combines traditions, the cross is one of a number of statements in a complex landscape. Like their contemporaries in the Social Democratic Party, Asplund and Lewerentz performed an act of political dexterity. Thanks to its presence and the name the Way of the Cross, Christians are more likely to accept this environment as their own. By virtue of the dominating landscape, non-believers and believers alike are allowed to make

Figure 4.3 North Entry View with Way of the Cross and Meditation Grove. Photo by C.G. Rosenberg, 1962, Swedish Museum of Architecture.

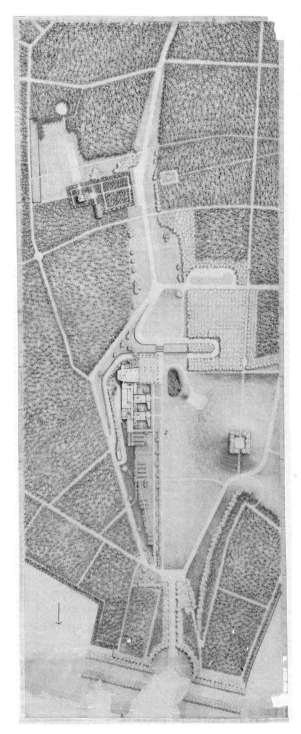

Figure 4.4 North Entry Site Plan, Gunnar Asplund, 1940. Courtesy of the Collection Centre Canadien d'Architecture/Canadian Center for Architecture, Montreal.

other emotional connections based on Swedish history, body analogies and rural and urban landscapes.

The preeminence given to the landscape was made possible by the decision to site the new crematorium along the edge of the Way of the Cross. This non-monumental approach also appears in Asplund's site plan for the Stockholm Exhibit of 1931, sited on a lagoon, east of the city's center. The Woodland Crematorium, like the buildings of the Stockholm Exhibition, is composed as a wall made of the Chapels of Faith and Hope and a larger one called Chapel of the Holy Cross (Figure 4.4). This is the first modern building at the cemetery, though references to classicism and the vernacular have not been completely erased. The complex has a network of intermediary outdoor courts and gardens to receive funeral parties and provide a space for post-funeral conversation. The large program is broken up both to diminish monumentality and to suggest urbanism. In fact, this pattern of courts facing an open landscape is the same that was used increasingly in the design of public housing projects in the 1930s. Though the occasion of death is extraordinary, the memory of an everyday pattern of dwelling gives quiet support.

The most significant of these spaces is a large structure called Monument Hall, sited at the top of the hill as the most immediate destination on the Way of the Cross and as the foyer for the Chapel of the Holy Cross. It has a compluvium, a wood roof on columns pitched to drain in the middle. This space is analogous in function to large porticos that receive people at the Woodland Chapel and the Resurrection Chapel and, like them, it is loosely based on a classical model. In this case, it is taken from the structure that encloses the court of a traditional Roman house. Asplund would have seen a house of this kind when he visited Pompeii as a young architect. At the Woodland Chapel, he succeeded in reinterpreting the dome of the Pantheon at a domestic scale. In this case, he does the reverse by taking an ancient domestic model and reinventing it at an institutional scale. Here, however, Asplund is able to relate the compluvium to a sublime landscape of his own creation. Again, the domestic is combined with landscape to create a sensation of transcendence and reassurance.

The compluvium is not the only ancient barrowing at the Crematorium. The Way of the Cross has a random stone paving, meant to resemble a street in Pompeii or the Via Appia.[45] The Chapel of the Holy Cross, likewise, has ancient roots, though concealed on the interior. The corners and ceiling are curved to suggest the dome of the sky and there is an architrave and classical columns that appear to float free of the ceiling (Figure 4.5). One possible reference is a ruin of a classical temple, set within a wider landscape.[46] This sense is reinforced by the mural behind the altar called *Life, Death, Life* by a Vitalist painter named Sven Erixson. Like the Woodland Chapel, the interior is designed as a cosmic reflection of the outside.

References to antiquity had different meanings in Nordic countries than those prevailing in Europe. Matti Klinge explains that, "in the Nordic countries, Ossian and pre-Christian European mythology, together with Greece and Homer, came to represent the primitive, uncorrupted, anti-industrial and anti-Latin trend. Like Roussseauism, they were against the cities, and against luxury, intrigue and sophistry."[47] Many Nordic poets of the nineteenth century were drawn to the ancient Greeks as "natural people with their own mythology and folklore."[48] For some this translated into a strong identification with the values of the peasantry and the poor." Erik Gustaf Geijer, a Swedish Romantic poet of the early nineteenth century, "believed that the folk constituted the past and the present; memories, customs and traditions are passed between *the folk* which unite the folk as a unit."[49] This attraction to the culture of common people is evident in the values of young architects like Asplund, who made the Grand Tour to Italy and Greece in the early twentieth century. They were not interested in the details of particular monuments like their French and English predecessors. Instead, they preferred to document houses of common people and streetscapes.[50]

References to antiquity, however, do more than indicate the values of common people. They also assist in allowing a unique view of space and time. Because the Stockholm Exhibition and the Woodland Cemetery are both enhanced and segregated versions of the everyday world with special purposes, they can be considered variations of Foucault's understanding of the heterotopia.[51] Both can also be classified as heterotopias of time where the Stockholm Exhibition embraces an ephemeral vision of the future while the Woodland Cemetery serves as a gateway to eternity. In the latter case, with its layered references to different eras and simulated artifacts, it also has much common with the library or museum, another heterotopia of time. Because of this encyclopedic quality, the experience of the bereaved can be a distinctive understanding of time and space. They have the chance of assuming the perspective that Freud discusses in *Civilization and its Discontents* where he attempts to explain the simultaneous existence of older and newer parts of human consciousness. Here, he portrays this coexistence as a vision of ancient Roman where all buildings are intact, but overlapping: "Now let us, by flight of imagination, suppose that Rome is not a human habitation but a psychical entity with a similarly long and copious past—an entity, that is to say, in which nothing that has once come into existence will have passed away and all the earlier phases of development continue to exist alongside the latest one."[52]

Asplund and Lewerentz perform this feat of simultaneity through facsimiles of ancient buildings within modern ones while also creating the illusion of infinite space. For example, the Greek Temple lies embedded in the Chapel of the Holy Cross and the Pantheon lies within the diminutive Woodland Chapel. They also accomplish this through overlapping references. The Neolithic burial mound, for example, lies within the swelling breast shape of the Meditation Grove and the earth goddess lies within *The Angel of Death*. Some might see this as an analogy with our own psyche; following Freud's theory of the coexistence of early and modern parts of our consciousness, just as the temple survives within the modern chapel, pantheistic religion survives within all of us. The implication is that the deceased enjoy oneness with human memory and the spirit of ancestors persists within the living.

This spiritual communion could have been some consolation for Swedes whose lives were very different from those of parents and grandparents. In the first four decades of the twentieth century, Sweden underwent astonishing change. In 1900, it was a backwater with a constitutional monarchy and limited franchise. By 1940 when the Woodland Crematorium was finished, it was a prosperous, industrialized state with a popular Socialist government. Because of this significant change in less than one generation, the majority of Swedes, formerly with strong rural roots, were adjusting to urban existence. The doctrine of the "Stockholm School" of landscape design, which brought together modern housing blocks and new parks, addressed this native discomfort with urban existence. The final phase of the Woodland Cemetery, with the Stockholm Exhibition as a prelude, attempted to embody this new urban ideal as a series of courtyards, on the edge of a wilder version of the English commons. In this respect, the sweeping open space at the Woodland Cemetery draws on the memory of agrarian space and the Stockholm park. The equilibrium in the everyday between memory and modernism was translated to a place of death.

This translation was largely accomplished through the use of modern design. It allowed Asplund and Lewerentz to reframe ancient concepts of body, landscape, and cosmos in modern terms. In the process, they left open a range of interpretation, thereby welcoming Swedes of different beliefs. It also made an appropriate setting for cremation, a method that could be efficient, hygienic, and culturally meaningful. Finally, it permitted a design that emphasizes landscape more than architecture, recalling the memory of rural landscape and sanctifying a modern way of dwelling. The versatility of this expression signified that modernism was not a fashion of the moment in Sweden. Instead, as a polemic, the last phase of the Woodland Cemetery is a built epilogue to the *Acceptera* manifesto and the Stockholm Exhibition. It proved that it could offer durable solutions to real problems, both cultural and technical, and speak of the present and the past. The bereaved, in other words, were quietly assisted in accepting their loss *and* they were helped in accepting the world around them.

On a broader level, beyond the circumstances of the success of modernism in Sweden, this case history demonstrates that visual forms that embody traditional memory are not the exclusive domain of conservative ideologies. Deft manipulation and recombination can successfully marry them to a progressive cause. In this process, visual forms can shift and broaden; an idea of home can become an idea of home *and* landscape. Meanwhile, fundamentally different ideas of spirituality and their visual counterparts can also coexist in a mutually supportive way, expressing both new ideas of diversity as well as time and space.

NOTES

1. Richard Morris, "Death on Display," in *Rhetorics of Display*, ed. Lawrence Prelli (Columbia: University of South Carolina Press, 2006), 204–24.
2. Arne Ruth, "The Second New Nation: The Mythology of Modern Sweden," *Daedalus* 113 (1984): 85.
3. Thorbjorn Andersson, "The Functionalism of Gardening Art," in *Sweden: Twentieth Century Architecture*, ed. Claes Calenby (Munich: Prestel, 1998), 230.
4. Ibid.
5. Ibid.
6. Ibid.
7. Catharina Nolin, "Stockholm's Urban Parks: Meeting Places and Social Contexts from 1860–1930," in *The European City and Greenspace*, ed. Peter Clark (Aldeshot: Ashgate, 2006), 125.
8. Thorbjorn Andersson, "Erik Glemme and the Stockhom Park System," in *Modern Landscape Architecture: A Critical Review*, ed. Marc Treib (Cambridge: MIT Press, 1993), 117.
9. Nolin, "Stockholm's Urban Parks," 118.
10. Lars Nilsson, "Stockholm and Green Space: An Introduction," in *The European City and Green Space*, ed. Peter Clark (Aldershot, UK: Ashgate, 2006), 102.
11. Andersson, "Erik Glemme and the Stockholm Park System," 118.
12. Rutger Sernander, *Stockholms Natur* (Uppsalla: Almqvist & Wiksells Forlag, 1926).
13. Sten Carlsson, "The Transformation of Swedish Society," in *Tradition and Modern Society*, ed. Sven Gustavsson (Stockholm: Almqvist & Wiksell, 1989).
14. Eva Eriksson, "International Impulses and the National Tradition," in *Sweden: Twentieth Century Architecture*, ed. Claes Caldenby, Joran Lindvall, and Wilfried Wang (Munich: Prestel, 1998), 19.
15. Ibid., 19.
16. Ibid., 20.
17. Ellen Kay, "Beauty in the Home," in *Modern Swedish Design: Three Founding Texts*, ed. Lucy Creagh, Helena Kaberg and Barbara Miller Lane (New York: MOMA, 2008), 55.
18. Helena Kaberg, "An Introduction to Gregor Paulsson's *Better Things for Everyday Life*," in *Modern Swedish Design: Three Founding Texts*, ed. Lucy Creagh, Helena Kaberg, and Barbara Miller Lane (New York: MOMA, 2008), 65.
19. Ibid., 94.
20. Kerstin Wickman, "Homes," in *Sweden: Twentieth Century Architecture*, ed. Claes Caldenby, Joran Lindvall, and Wilfried Wang (Munich: Prestel, 1998), 199.
21. Ibid., 125.
22. Caroline Constant, *The Woodland Cemetery: Towards a Spiritual Landscape* (Stockholm: Byggforlaget, 1994), 15.
23. Ibid., 14.
24. Bengt O. H. Johansson, *Tallum: Gunnar Asplund's and Sigurd Lewerentz's Woodland Cemetery in Stockholm* (Stockholm: Byggforlaget, 1996), 15.
25. Constant, *The Woodland Cemetery*, 29.
26. Ibid., 32.
27. Michel Foucault, *Le Corps Utopique: suivi de Les Hétérotopies* (Fécamp: Nouvelles Editions Lignes, 2009), 30.
28. Andersson, "The Functionalism of the Gardening Art," 230.

29. Ibid., 55.
30. Constant, *The Woodland Cemetery*, 63.
31. Johansson, *Tallum*, 61.
32. Elias Cornell, "The Sky as a Vault," in *Asplund*, ed. Claes Calenby (New York: Rizzoli, 1986), 23.
33. Martin Heidegger, "Building, Dwelling, Thinking," in *Poetry, Language, Thought*, trans. Albert Hofstradter (New York: Harper & Row, 1971).
34. Cornell, "The Sky as a Vault," 23–29.
35. Henri Bergson, *Creative Evolution* (New York: Henry Holt, 1911), 43.
36. Ibid.
37. Stuart Wrede, *The Architecture of Erik Gunnar Asplund* (Cambridge: MIT Press, 1980), 57–64.
38. Ingvar Andersson and Jorgen Weibull, *Swedish History in Brief* (Stockholm: The Swedish Institute, 1988), 55.
39. Peter Blundell-Jones, *Gunnar Asplund* (London: Phaidon, 2006), 145–46.
40. Helena Mattsson and Sven-Olov Wallenstein, *1930/1931 Swedish Modernism at the Crossroads* (Stockholm: Axl Books, 2009), 42.
41. Ibid., 46.
42. Stuart Wrede, "Landscape and Architecture: Classical and Vernacular by Erik Gunnar Asplund," in *Asplund*, ed. Claes Caldenby (New York: Rizolli, 1986), 42–43.
43. Constant, *The Woodland Cemetery*, 103–05.
44. Ibid., 80–84.
45. Wrede, "Landscape and Architecture," 43.
46. Cornell, "The Sky as a Vault," 33.
47. Matti Klinge, "The North, Nature and Poverty: Some Background on Nordic Identity," in *Dreams of a Summer Night*, ed. Carl Thomas Edam (London, Arts Council of Great Britain, 1986), 50.
48. Ibid., 51.
49. Christine Agius, *The Social Construction of Swedish Neutrality* (Manchester: Manchester University Press, 2006), 63.
50. Erikson,"International Impulses," 41.
51. Foucault, *Le Corps Utopique*
52. Sigmund Freud, *Civilization and its Discontents* (New York: W.W. Norton & Company, 1961), 17.

Part II
Monuments and Memorials

Eyes Wide Open Traveling Exhibit

Ekaterina V. Haskins

How does one commemorate an ongoing war, especially if this war is being waged under false pretenses and its military and civilian toll is kept out of public discussion?[1] This was precisely the challenge faced by groups and persons opposed to the U.S.-led invasion and occupation of Iraq. Frustrated by the apparent indifference of the government and mainstream media to the mounting casualty count, many communities, citizen groups, and individuals took matters into their own hands in order to make visible, and sometimes to protest, the human cost of the Iraq war. Their interventions often took a conspicuously non-monumental form and sprang up in locations far away from the Washington Mall.

This essay addresses one such commemoration, the touring exhibit *Eyes Wide Open*, in order to explore the dynamic possibilities of ephemeral grassroots memorializing. *Eyes Wide Open* is a visual reminder of "the human cost of the Iraq war" and a place for public mourning. Its major design feature is the juxtaposition of a field of combat boots, each pair standing in for an American soldier who died in Iraq, and a collection of civilian shoes to symbolize dead Iraqis. In addition to the boot and shoe display, the exhibit also includes a wall of remembrance depicting "Dreams and Nightmares" of the Iraqi people as well as video and other installations that document the war. Sponsored by the American Friends Service Committee (a Quaker organization), the exhibit made its first appearance in Chicago's Federal Plaza in January 2004, when the number of U.S. military casualties reached 500. By spring of 2007, it had been divided into state exhibits due to its growing size and popularity.

Eyes Wide Open is by no means a conventional war memorial. The most striking—and controversial—aspect of the exhibit is its insistence on commemorating casualties on both sides of the Iraq conflict, rather than honoring only the American lives lost. In so doing, *Eyes Wide Open* performs what Carole Blair calls "confrontation" by unsettling expectations about the proper way to honor the dead.[2] If "visitors typically go to memory sites expecting to be inspired by, grateful for, and more deeply connected to the accomplished virtues of their imagined community,"[3] this memorial asks its audiences to reconsider familiar notions of patriotism. Moreover, unlike traditional monuments made of stone and granite, this memorial relies on a simple visual vocabulary and spatial arrangement to attract visitors and make their contributions part of the exhibit. The memorial is also decidedly ephemeral, as it is not fixed in one location but instead evolves through time and space. Each new location furnishes a set of different rhetorical opportunities depending on its cultural and political peculiarities and the input from volunteers and visitors alike.

Because of its multi-dimensional character and relatively open authorship, *Eyes Wide Open* resists characterization along traditional lines of analysis. Scholars of public memory have long urged a reconsideration of an approach to memorials as representations of political values written in stone. Arguing that memorials by themselves "remain inert and amnesiac," James Young presses critics to go beyond the aesthetic dimension of monuments, memorials, and commemorative displays:

> Public memory and its meanings depend not just on the forms and figures in the monument itself but on the viewer's response to the monument, how it is used politically and religiously in the community, who sees it under what circumstances, how its figures enter other media and are recast in new surroundings.[4]

Scholars who study public memory from a rhetorical perspective have similarly noted the need to shift the interpretive focus from the intention of memorial artifacts to their function—from questions about their potential symbolic power to questions about their impact on actual audiences. Blair and Michel write, "rhetoric typically does not address the material presence or practices of audiences"; however, they warn, "If we fail to deal with audiences as real, material beings and their experiences as significant, we almost certainly will overlook differences that *make* a difference in how discourses are used, consumed, and redeployed."[5]

This essay's purpose is not to celebrate the aesthetic originality of *Eyes Wide Open* as a novel grassroots war memorial. Rather, what interests me is how the memorial's symbolism enables its multiple audiences to take on an active role in the commemorative process. *Eyes Wide Open* invites the viewer to inhabit "a perspective by incongruity"—a spectator position that involves seemingly contradictory attitudes of mourning and political awareness. The memorial's symbolism thus provokes reflection on the tension between patriotism and dissent, private grief and public outrage, and memory and political action. This argument develops in three stages. First, I examine the symbolic resources the exhibit deploys to create a space of mourning and contemplation and to encourage audience participation. In the second part of the essay, I turn to the spatio-temporal aspect of the memorial to show how it evolves through time and how each new destination on its tour provides a distinct context for memorial enactments by volunteers and visitors. Finally, I attend to the issue of mediation, as the spatial and interactive possibilities of the memorial undergo a transformation when it becomes an object of representation in other media.

VISUAL PERSPECTIVE BY INCONGRUITY

Instead of inventing new symbols to convey the growing cost of war, *Eyes Wide Open* appropriates display strategies that are already in use. The memorial invokes two distinct, even incompatible, traditions of mourning the dead: the tradition of national military cemeteries and the grassroots memorializing epitomized by the NAMES project AIDS quilt. The juxtaposition of these traditions within the space of the same memorial yields a "perspective by incongruity," a "vantage point from which to see the inaccuracies of a situation."[6] The display of U.S. military boots and civilian shoes invites the audience simultaneously to honor the soldiers' sacrifice and to mourn them as victims of the unjust war alongside Iraqi casualties. In so doing, the memorial promotes reflection on the proper way to remember the war dead, mediates between private grief and public advocacy, and affirms the connection between memory and political action.

At first sight, an orderly formation of military boots that greets visitors at the *Eyes Wide Open* display conjures the regularity and solemnity of American military cemeteries such as the Arlington National cemetery and the cemetery at Gettysburg, which were designed not only as sites of repose for the war dead but also as civic lessons for the living. As such, they were meant to convey patriotism, egalitarianism, and transcendence of faction in favor of a unifying national ideal. The shape and layout of gravestones at Gettysburg, for example, signaled the equality of sacrifices for the Union cause regardless of rank. In the words of Abraham Lincoln's address at the consecration of Gettysburg, these war dead "gave their last measure of devotion" in defense of "the proposition that all men are created equal."[7]

Furthermore, a national cemetery's environment separates visitors from the immediate concerns of the day and invites them to contemplate eternity. Modeled after Victorian rural cemeteries, both Gettysburg and Arlington cemeteries are set in picturesque and tranquil surroundings amid sloping lawns and shady groves.[8] Many contemporaries noted the transcendent quality of these cemeteries' landscape and its healing effect on the human psyche. A short story by Constance Woolson published in the *Christian Union* in 1879 offers a glimpse of such a reaction on visiting Arlington. The mourning ritual is performed, paradigmatically, by a female visitor, whose sorrow for the loss of young lives is mitigated and transcended by patriotic pride:

> I often came here at sunset; the quiet beauty of the place seemed to shed a soothing influence over the close of my day. The uniformity and regularity of the close, low ranks of the dead made their number more apparent. . . . I went slowly back . . . my mind full of thoughts of the dead, sad, yet

sweet; for I, too, had lost loved ones on the field of battle, and mourned for them, yet felt proud of them, also, through every fiber of my being."[9]

Similarly, a National Park Service walking tour guide at Gettysburg encourages the viewer to

> observe the simple elegance the National Cemetery planners had hoped for. . . . As you finish your walk to the Visitor Center and pass beneath the broad shade trees and along the neatly trimmed gravestones, take time to reflect upon the inscriptions around you. They remind us of the devotion to country and the payment in human life Americans have given, and may be called on to give, to insure the freedoms we enjoy today.[10]

The layout and setting of American military cemeteries thus promote the attitude of grateful acceptance of military sacrifices as a price of the nation's immortality.

However, prideful contemplation of patriotic sacrifice at the *Eyes Wide Open* exhibit is mitigated—if not denied—by the presence of civilian shoes. Seen together en masse, military and civilian footwear connotes mortal calamity rather than the nobility of warfare. By displaying the loss of both military and civilian lives as a collective tragedy, *Eyes Wide Open* quotes the tradition of ephemeral grassroots memorializing most famously represented by the NAMES Project Memorial Quilt. The NAMES quilt was created by thousands of people in response to the AIDS epidemic. Comprised of multiple individually crafted three-by-six foot panels, each memorializing a particular person who died of AIDS, the Quilt not only made the disease impossible to ignore but also turned "what was perceived to be a 'gay disease' into a shared national tragedy."[11]

Eyes Wide Open borrows from the NAMES project Memorial Quilt several display strategies; chief among them are the use of "found" materials and the incorporation of visitors' offerings into the texture of the exhibit. The Quilt is distinct from most public memorials in its "phenomenology" and "authorship."[12] Instead of a durable medium, it is made of fragile materials; instead of uniform catalogue of names, it describes each person individually through inscriptions and various images and objects sewn into the panels. This variability owes to the diversity of authorship—panels were made by lovers, friends, family members, and even complete strangers. The fact that anyone could contribute to the production of the Quilt made the project into more than a collection of multiple testimonies about lives lost to the epidemic. The Quilt works as an expression of grief and individual morning as well as "a sounding board about issues about AIDS: some panel makers use it to speak to specific audiences, both those who already understand and those who need to be taught."[13] The discourse of consolation implied by the Quilt's tactile quality and its cultural association with homey virtues of family craft traditions thus exist in a state of tension with political advocacy and protest.

Eyes Wide Open also echoes the Quilt's activist political stance. Many contributors indeed regarded the Quilt as a kind of war memorial, except it memorialized the war that was still being fought. The death toll of the AIDS epidemic was often compared to that of the Vietnam War, and the U.S. government, rather than the virus, was portrayed as the biggest enemy. As Sturken comments, "the AIDS Quilt intends to end the 'war' it memorializes. As such, the debate it produces is very different from that raised by the Vietnam Veterans Memorial: it is a debate not only about how to remember the dead but about how to effectively end the dying."[14] By taking on an explicitly political role in relation to the epidemic, the Quilt goes beyond the rhetoric of war memorials, even anti-heroic ones like the Vietnam Veterans Memorial.

Although the Vietnam Veterans Memorial can be seen as a screen for the projection of disparate memories of the war, its implied anti-war stance is muted because the memorial was joined by unequivocal representations of military sacrifice on the Mall. The Quilt, by contrast, is not fixed in one location, its mobility both a sign of the marginal status of the gay community and a reminder that political visibility is contingent on a continuing collective effort. It therefore "accuses more strongly than the Vietnam Veterans Memorial because it is not as easily subsumed into the nationalistic discourse of the Washington Mall."[15] When the Quilt did come to Washington, its organizers wished to turn the Mall into a site of protest, to "call attention to the nation's conscience" and "make an accusation, bringing the evidence of the disaster to the doorstep of the people responsible for it."[16]

The two traditions simultaneously deployed by the *Eyes Wide Open* exhibit, then, illustrate contrasting ways to pay tribute to the war dead. National military cemeteries present an orderly array of generic grave markers to emphasize patriotic sacrifice. They invite visitors to mourn the fallen individually in private and to praise them collectively in public. The cemeteries' scenic placement, away from the bustle of everyday life, renders them into sanctuaries of civil religion. By contrast, traveling grassroots memorials accent collective loss while bringing private, idiosyncratic memories into the public. Their mobility allows them take over existing public spaces and thereby to "summon citizens for public advocacy in the presence of others."[17]

By drawing on both traditions, *Eyes Wide Open* issues an invitation to mourn and honor the dead on both sides of the conflict collectively and individually, to ponder the meaning of patriotic sacrifice and to question the cost of war. The most distinctive design feature of the *Eyes Wide Open* exhibit is the juxtaposition of combat boots standing for dead American soldiers and civilian shoes to symbolize dead Iraqis. A tag listing the soldier's name, rank, age at the time of death, and home state is attached to each boot. Since names of the fallen military personnel are public information, organizers did not ask permission to put names on tags. But if someone's family objected, the name was removed at their request. Civilian shoes were added to the display on July 4, 2004 in Philadelphia, when the names of about 3,000 dead Iraqis became available.[18]

Figure 5.1   Eyes Wide Open display in Washington, D.C. Photo courtesy of the American Friends Service Committee.

The uniform rows of military boots—one for each soldier lost to the war in Iraq—recall the minimalist aesthetic and egalitarian ethos of national military cemeteries. Unlike grave stones, however, the boots do not mark the fallen soldiers' final resting place but instead invite the visitor to think of the men and women wearing them as if they were standing at attention. This somber and decorous display signifies respect for the soldiers' ultimate sacrifice. In contrast with iconoclastic anti-war protests of the Vietnam era, this memorial aspires to acknowledge the dedication of men and women who voluntarily signed up to defend their country. As Mary Zerkel, the AFSC spokesperson, admitted,

> the decision to arrange the boots this way may not have been a conscious strategy, but this arrangement made the display look respectful of the military, which was important especially early on, when public opinion largely supported the war. We did consider our audience—the "movable middle"—and wanted people from different ends of the spectrum to participate. We were not hiding from our [anti-war] position, but did not want to beat people over the head with the message.[19]

Foregrounding the rows of boots as the display's central feature, *Eyes Wide Open* upholds the decorum and solemnity of the tradition of mourning the war dead.

At the same time, empty boots are an unmistakable sign of loss—not only the current body count but also impending deaths. Like the panels of the NAMES Quilt, boots will continue to be added as long as U.S. troops remain in Iraq. The naming of the dead will go on. According to Mary Ellen McNish, then General Secretary of the American Friends Service Committee, *Eyes Wide Open* prompts a question: "How many more boots will be standing at silent attention before this war ends, before Iraqis and American soldiers are out of harm's way?"[20]

The sense of futility of this loss is highlighted by the collection of civilian shoes that represent dead Iraqis—men, women, and children. Because these dead were too numerous,[21] their fate was symbolized by a pile of random shoes donated by volunteers and visitors. Their varying size and color present a stark contrast to the orderliness and uniformity of meticulously tagged boots. In some locations, shoes were arranged in concentric circles around one pair of untagged boots to underscore the point that about 200 Iraqi civilians die for every one American military casualty. Beyond their statistical significance, the civilian shoes possess a strong emotional appeal because they conjure up the iconographic dossier of crimes against humanity—one immediately thinks of heaped shoes as a symbol of Nazi death camps. As such, they vividly challenged the Bush Administration's rhetoric of "Operation Iraqi Freedom" and the sanitized discourse of "collateral damage."

Figure 5.2   Civilian Shoes and "Dreams and Nightmares" exhibit. Photo courtesy of the American Friends Service Committee.

In 2006, for the exhibit's Washington, D.C. appearance, the organizers set up "Dreams and Nightmares: An Exhibit on Life and Death in Iraq" to educate the audience about the cost of war to the Iraqis. The exhibit consists of thirty-two eight-foot panels covered with images and text on both sides. The majority of this makeshift wall's surface is inscribed with the names of Iraqi civilians killed during the war. Interspersed with the names are stories of several people from the list of casualties, young and old alike. Photographs of grieving Iraqis—a young girl in tears, men and women weeping over dead bodies of their relatives, a sobbing father holding a dead child—reveal the anguish and suffering that cannot be captured by numbers alone. Finally, some panels invite the audience to imagine the consequences of the U.S.-led occupation of Iraq as though the war were waged on U.S. territory.[22]

The exhibit has been described by the media as "at once monumental and mundane."[23] Seen together, the boots and shoes overwhelm. On the other hand, a welcoming layout and intimate character of the boots and shoes encourage interaction and contributions from visitors. These contributions—in the form of photographs, mementos, letters, and other tokens of tribute, affection, and grief—personalize and break the uniformity of the rows of boots, while preserving the overall message of collective loss. Combat boots are among the artifacts most frequently left at the Vietnam Veterans Memorial in Washington, D.C. Here, they become miniature memorials in themselves, acting as magnets for visitors' offerings.

The artifacts left by family, friends, and strangers often illustrate the tension between the expression of conventional patriotism and the mourning of lives lost. Along with flowers and American flags, visitors frequently attach family and school photographs, letters, poems, and other intimate mementos. These tokens amplify the meaning of "the cost of war"—young lives interrupted, families grief stricken, dreams shattered. Some contributions advocate against the war: such is the message telegraphed by buttons that merge the yellow ribbon with the peace symbol and a logo "Support our troops—bring them home." Incidentally, these buttons are a prime example of perspective by incongruity themselves, as they blend the two ideologically incompatible signifiers—the yellow ribbon from the first Gulf War and the peace sign of the anti-war protests of the Vietnam era.

As distinct from similar artifacts left at the Vietnam Veterans Memorial—which are archived for posterity—those added to the *Eyes Wide Open* exhibit are shipped along with the boots and shoes to the next

Figure 5.3   Visitor Contributions. Photo courtesy of the American Friends Service Committee.

destination. This changes the status of these objects from private mementos to public testimony. Some items, originally taken from a public source, such as a clipped newspaper article, are transformed into a private message to the dead, and then, after their inclusion in the exhibit, assume a new public meaning. For example, a newspaper article was attached to the boots standing for Staff Sgt. Aaron Reese who drowned in the Tigris River. The article quoted an Army officer as saying his Ohio National Guard unit received life vests three days after Reese's drowning.[24] In the context of the display, this article becomes simultaneously a message of regret and sorrow addressed to the deceased and a public accusation of the authorities responsible for the sergeant's unnecessary death.

By drawing on the visual lexicon and spatial arrangement of both military cemeteries and mobile grassroots memorials, *Eyes Wide Open* sets up a space within which visitors may engage in a variety of memorial gestures. It is not a blank space, to be sure, for the "perspective by incongruity" frustrates one's desire to see the memorial only as a tribute to fallen soldiers or as an accusation of war mongers responsible for both military and civilian casualties. Rather, it invites visitors to confront their biases and blind spots, thus enabling "maximum consciousness."[25] And by traveling to multiple destinations, the exhibit can amplify its appeal to a variety of audiences. It is to this conjunction of space and time as a significant display strategy that we now turn.

TAKING (OVER) PLACE

All rhetoric is situational insofar as public discourse responds to a sociopolitical and cultural context. Permanent memorials, similarly, while commemorating past events, simultaneously reflect the historical conditions under which they were created. But what about those memorials that are not anchored in a particular site and are designed to adapt to a continuously evolving situation? As the preceding discussion of *Eyes Wide Open*'s design shows, the simplicity of the exhibit's conception translates into the relative ease of installation and travel. This, in turn, allows organizers and volunteers to adapt to changing political circumstances and to capitalize on the significance of various places and occasions to engage audiences.

The initial impetus for *Eyes Wide Open* was the lack of public acknowledgment of the human cost of the Iraq War. As one Quaker volunteer pointed out in 2005, there was "no disturbing press coverage of deceased military personnel returning home in flag-draped caskets" and "thousands of Iraqi deaths [were] reduced to vague statistics through the lens of the mass media."[26] When *Eyes Wide Open* was first shown in January 2004 in Chicago's Federal Plaza, the number of American casualties was 504. As the body count continued to rise despite President Bush's assurance of "mission accomplished," the number of combat boots multiplied. By May 2007, the exhibit was too large to tour nationally, so the organizers adopted a state-by-state approach, displaying the boots to signify casualties from a single state. Although some feared that showing fewer boots would dilute the power of the full exhibit, the strategy succeeded in bringing home the human cost of the Iraq War. Within one year, between June 2007 and June 2008, state exhibits were shown in forty-eight states, with an estimated attendance of over 220,000 and an estimated media audience of over 6.5 million.[27]

Despite the war's waning popularity, however, the Bush administration continued its policies without major opposition in Congress. To raise public awareness of the *economic* costs of war, the AFSC added a *Cost of War* exhibit to the familiar boots and shoes display. *Cost of War* consisted of a series of banners that listed the price tag of one day of the Iraq War—$720 million—and a question, "How would you spend it?"[28] Thus asking the audiences to draw a connection between the current war and other programs that could be funded instead, *Eyes Wide Open/Cost of War* encouraged visitors to move beyond mourning to advocacy.

The modification of the exhibit's contents to reflect the growing costs of war—both human and economic—is not the only persuasive strategy afforded by its mobility. What makes *Eyes Wide Open* a timely intervention into the national conversation on the War in Iraq is its appearance in places set aside for other purposes, some of them seemingly uncongenial to the exhibit's goals. Instead of a special sacred space postulated by Pierre Nora's notion of *lieu de memoire*, or site of memory, ephemeral memorials are not attached to a specific site.[29] Instead, they may temporarily occupy a variety of locations, some already imbued with sacredness, others more profane and prosaic. Historian Steve J. Stern offers a more flexible construct—a "memory knot"—to account for interventionist memory practices:

> Memory knots on the social body . . . force charged issues of memory and forgetfulness into a public domain. They make claims or cause problems that heighten attention and consciousness, thereby unsettling reflexive everyday habits and euphemisms that foster numbing.[30]

In order to "heighten attention and consciousness," ephemeral interventions require a felicitous conjunction of time and place that is likely to yield maximum audience exposure. *Eyes Wide Open* exhibits are often timed to political events and other anniversaries that draw public attention. For example, during the 2008 election cycle, the exhibit was shown in the vicinity of both Republican and Democratic National Conventions. In Minneapolis, where the RNC was held, the Minnesota volunteer group organized three *Eyes Wide Open* events with different degrees of success. The one near the Xcel Center, the RNC convention site, attracted very few visitors: "few conventioneers wandered out of the Xcel Center into it, most local folks avoided the areas populated by the thousands of riot police." In contrast, at *Eyes Wide Open* shown in conjunction with the Vets for Peace rally at the Minnesota State Capitol Mall, "hundreds of people took time to walk through the boots" and volunteers "spoke with a lot of media people, many from outside of the United States."[31]

Organizers of *Eyes Wide Open* in Denver, Colorado, the location of the Democratic National Convention, timed the exhibit to coincide with the Tent State Music Festival to End the War and used a lottery for free tickets to a Rage against the Machine concert as a device to draw visitors. As a result, Colorado coordinator Sarah Gill reports, "15,000 Rage fans walked past our booth to register for tickets. I'm pretty certain of my assessment that many of these folks had never heard of AFSC before, and while they may have shared some of our convictions, we gave them a way to make those convictions known to others."[32]

In the course of its tour, *Eyes Wide Open* frequently capitalized on the symbolic significance of various locations. Tethering the exhibit to sites already imbued with symbolic history allowed its message to resonate differently in different places. For example, on the day of George W. Bush's second presidential Inauguration in 2005, *Eyes Wide Open* was displayed at the National Cathedral in Washington, D.C. In Memphis, *Eyes Wide Open* was shown next to the Lorraine Hotel, the site of Martin Luther King, Jr.'s assassination. Strawberry Fields in New York City's Central Park, immortalized by the Beatles song and now a memorial to John Lennon, also became host to the exhibit.

Not only iconic locales hosted the display. More often than not, the goal of organizers, in the words of AFSC spokesperson Mary Zerkel, was "to attract an accidental tourist," someone who was not planning to attend the exhibit. There have been some offbeat decisions about locations that turned out very successful, such as a Wal-Mart parking lot in Pennsylvania, where shoppers in search of cheap goods stumbled upon the exhibit. In Kansas City, volunteers used stretchers to make a mobile exhibit and carried it though a busy art fair.[33]

Organizers expected some locations to be friendlier to *Eyes Wide Open* than others. There was little doubt, for example, that Boston and San Francisco, both sites of massive demonstrations against the War in Iraq, would welcome the memorial. In 2007, the Massachusetts state exhibit formed a backdrop to an anti-war rally attended by nearly 10,000 people.[34] On the other end of the spectrum, the exhibit faced opposition by prominent members of local communities who lobbied their officials not to allow the display. In Largo, Florida, some residents objected to the showing of shoes representing Iraqi deaths as a "political" act inappropriate to the spirit of Memorial Day and asked the city to deny the organizers a permit. After negotiations, Largo officials agreed to display both boots and shoes as long as the sponsors promised not to make speeches, pass out literature, or wave signs.[35]

Especially in the early years of the war, when public opinion was still sharply divided on the subject of the U.S. invasion, organizers anticipated local opposition to the exhibit. An AFSC online guide for college campus volunteers, for example, instructed them to acknowledge those who disagree with the exhibit's anti-war message:

> Although Eyes Wide Open is a memorial to fallen service people, it does have an anti-war sentiment at its heart, which some people find objectionable. Handle counter demonstrations with respect, and let them know that you are willing to listen to their point of view. If possible, invite them to have a calm, reasonable conversation with you about their views. Do not turn Eyes Wide Open into a rally against any group. Remember that each pair of boots represents a real person who is no longer living. We must give them the utmost respect and not use their death for our own purposes.[36]

Asking volunteer "curators" to show sensitivity to local context and to practice openness to criticism and opposition, the exhibit's organizers acknowledged its audience's active role in memory work.

This approach paid off. A volunteer from Helena, Mountana, described how a fellow volunteer "spent half an hour engaging a well-known local right-wing commentator in conversation about the war at the exhibit, and in the end they found they agreed on everything—the war was a mess, we never should have started it in the first place, etc.—except that he believes in following orders from the commander-in-chief, and she believes in helping the commander-in-chief make the right orders."[37] At an exhibit in Hofstra University before the final Presidential Debate in 2008, a volunteer from New York State recalled how "a father showed up to remove his son's boots and name tag from the display. He was angered by the fact that AFSC would use his son's death in this way. . . . He argued with the AFSC coordinator about how we must kill the terrorists, and his son did not die in vain, and we had some nerve doing this, and then handed her a DVD of the latest right-wing garbage propaganda 'Obsession' detailing how 'all of Islam' wants us dead because of our 'freedoms.' The rest of us stood aside and let him rant, feeling his pain, anger, and frustration."[38] In some locations, however, "the anticipated resentment and anger never materialized." As a coordinator from Nevada, a swing state during the 2008 election, relates, "Displaying the [exhibit] gives me a different context for dialogue to engage people on a more heartfelt level than political races are able to touch. Emphasizing that we're non-partisan keeps people's attention, and holding both major parties accountable resonates with most folks."[39]

The temporary nature of the memorial is also part of its appeal. Because it will not be available for contemplation in perpetuity, its very existence depends on the labor of volunteers and the participation of audiences. Since most *Eyes Wide Open* displays are laid out outdoors, they have to be taken down for the night. The act of setting up and dismantling the exhibit is part of the performance of memory; volunteers and visitors become curators and guardians of memory. Occasionally, visitors were recruited as "accidental volunteers," as happened in Denver during the time of the Democratic National Convention. The exhibit's coordinator wrote in the AFSC newsletter:

> Mornings and evenings, we invited everyone at the exhibit or nearby to help us put up or take down the exhibit. If they agreed, I'd give them these instructions: As you pick up a pair of shoes or boots and place them in a bag, say the name of the person—out loud, or to yourself. . . . Many of these 'accidental volunteers' thanked me for offering them such a moving experience.[40]

The reading of names was envisioned by the exhibit's organizers as an integral part of the memorial; however, some volunteers took the practice a step further and added drama to the ritual of naming names. During the exhibit's sojourn on the Hofstra University campus, for example, visitors witnessed the "March of the Dead," a procession of students dressed in black with white face masks symbolizing the war dead from Iraq and Afghanistan.[41]

Volunteers also showed much ingenuity and spontaneity in adapting their display tactics to local circumstances. On August 7, 2007, New York State activists deployed the exhibit on Staten Island's Midland Beach, during the "National Night Out against Crime," an annual event sponsored by three police precincts and serving as a recruiting and public relations venue for law enforcement. As one of the organizers remarked, *Eyes Wide Open* expanded the theme of the evening to include "war crime."[42] Ironically, the booths sponsored by vendors at the National Night Out against Crime attracted young visitors by allowing them to hold weapons—grenades and firearms. When these visitors—quite a few of them youths contemplating signing up for military service—wandered through the *Eyes Wide Open* display, they witnessed the war's toll and encountered veterans who could explain to them the cost of war from a soldier's perspective.[43] In this case, then, the exhibit's pedagogical agenda received an improbable boost thanks to its proximity to a display whose agenda could not be more different.

The memorial exists as a series of unique enactments in space and time and as such relies on volunteers and visitors as well as specific locations for whatever persuasive effect it ultimately generates. Besides bringing home the human cost of war, the exhibit also reclaims public spaces and encourages strangers to enter a dialogue over the meaning of the memorial.

MEDIATING THE EPHEMERAL

Because it is ephemeral by design, *Eyes Wide Open* does not persist beyond the temporary installations. Unlike the NAMES Quilt, whose panels are unique and visually arresting aside from their function as a traveling memorial, *Eyes Wide Open*'s physical components are utterly prosaic. After the exhibit is taken down, it literally becomes a heap of plastic containers stuffed with boots and shoes. As I have argued so far, it is the performances of memory that they inspire that make a difference. At each location on its tour, the memorial takes on a distinct character, as volunteers arrange the rows of boots and shoes and visitors come to mourn, witness, and testify. I am not suggesting that the embodied experiences of the exhibit are unmediated—on the contrary, they are positioned vis-à-vis strategic spatio-temporal arrangements as well as spontaneous, contingent performances of others whom visitors encounter in and around the space of the display. However, these "spaces of attention," as Zagacki and Gallagher[44] would call them, do not retain their multi-modal and spontaneously interactive character once their contents are re-presented by a different medium. Therefore, while different forms of visual and discursive representation may aspire to capture the experience of the exhibit, they constitute a distinct performative modality, subject to a different set of narrative possibilities and technological constraints, not to mention institutional and political constraints of media organizations.

Perhaps due to its emphasis on quiet contemplation over dramatic protest, *Eyes Wide Open* scarcely appeared on national television. Designed to attract foot traffic and to encourage visitors to work through a perspective by incongruity created by the juxtaposition of military boots and civilian footwear, the exhibit did not offer itself as a camera-ready "image event."[45] For example, when the exhibit was set up near the Xcel Convention Center, the site of the 2008 Republican National Convention, "most media people sought out the clashes between the police and protestors. Quiet memorials were not in vogue."[46]

On the other hand, corporate media's lack of coverage may be attributed to the novelty of the concept of representing both sides of the Iraq conflict as casualties of war. Elaine Brower, volunteer from Staten Island, commented, "National media don't touch the anti-war stuff." The exhibit did receive favorable coverage from local and regional television stations, says Brower, but often their "positive spin rendered the memorial's chief message as that of 'honoring the sacrifice for our freedoms.' They ignored the fact that we had an Iraqi flag, a peace flag, and a globe flag next to the American flag there."[47]

To document the reception of the exhibit throughout the country, the website of the American Friends Service Committee keeps a log of its national tour through a selection of media stories, photographs, and narratives supplied by local coordinators and volunteers.[48] Not surprisingly, newspaper reporting, compared to television's episodic representation, is far more attentive to detail and context. Reporters relate the stories of local coordinators and sponsors, examine artifacts left at the exhibit, and interview visitors. Combined with accounts of tour managers, local volunteers, and coordinators, the archived coverage helps capture to some extent the ephemeral presence and impact of the memorial in its various destinations. However, maintaining such an archive electronically requires resources and labor. As of July 2009, several of the links to media coverage on the site did not function, and the list of locations had not been updated for at least a year.[49]

Outside of mainstream media, however, the exhibit was featured in numerous online publications and blogs, many of which combined still images of *Eyes Wide Open* with reporting and commentary. The profusion of coverage on the internet confirms the observation that today "everyone is a media outlet."[50] Unconstrained by considerations of neutrality espoused by corporate media, these independent reporters are free to editorialize on the perceived significance of the exhibit.

Eyes Wide Open originated as a Quaker project, and especially during its first year on the national tour Quaker volunteers were instrumental to its success. Although the AFSC did not use religiously-colored language in describing the project's goals, many sympathetic participants saw the exhibit through a religious lens. Inspired by the exhibit to meditate on Jesus' words, "count the cost," one Quaker blogger imagined how God might meditate on the display's message in "the Maker's Monologue":

> I see you have spent $155 billion of your children's and grandchildren's money making war in Iraq. You realize you could have invested exactly this amount of money doing any of the following?—fully funded world anti-hunger efforts for 6 years; fully funded world-wide AIDS programs for 15 years; ensured that every child in the world is given basic immunizations for 51 years. Any of these alternatives would be promoting life, making it literally more abundant as I intend, instead of inflicting death and grievous injury while *talking* about promoting life."[51]

This entry interprets the "cost of war" not only in terms of lives lost but also as a waste of resources and opportunities to support life.

To many of its supporters, the exhibit's value was in rallying a broad coalition of anti-war groups in an effort to end the War in Iraq. An independent online publication based in Staten Island, NY, *Next Left Notes*, which describes itself as "fiercely New Left and anti-authoritarian," covered a number of *Eyes Wide Open* events over several years. During its numerous appearances, the exhibit brought together members of local chapters of Veterans for Peace, Military Families Speak Out, and Movement for Democratic Society, among others. The Arlington New York State Exhibit—combining *Eyes Wide Open*'s boots and shoes with crosses similar to those erected by Veterans for Peace in Southern California— was a particularly poignant display of solidarity, as activists were joined by members of the clergy and local politicians. According to one of the organizers, the group of participants "could be the most diverse coalition Staten Island has ever seen—and is reflective of the country's waning enthusiasm for war, particularly in light of the economic disaster that is the U.S. economy."[52]

Eyes Wide Open also garnered recognition for its unconventional approach to commemorating the dead from an international online project called "The Polynational War Memorial," dedicated to conceptualizing and designing "a war memorial for all wars since World War II, which will include the names of more than 10 million killed soldiers and civilians."[53] A correspondent from Sweden noted the radical character of *Eyes Wide Open*'s effort to "memorialize all killed, regardless of their nationality, the side of the conflict they were participating on, and whether they were military personnel, civilians, aid workers or insurgents."[54] The author pointed out that even Maya Lin, the designer of the Vietnam Veterans Memorial, when asked in a recent interview about the appropriateness of including names of the Vietnamese killed in the war alongside the names of U.S. soldiers on the wall of the Vietnam Veterans Memorial, did not think Americans were ready for such a gesture either during the construction of the memorial or now.

Although negative responses to the exhibit online were few, their tenor seemed to demonstrate precisely the point made by Lin. A blogger who visited *Eyes Wide Open* in San Francisco in March 2005 argued against the display commemorating Iraqis on the grounds that it conflated "Iraqis" and "civilians." In this visitor's view, the U.S. "has gone to extremes to minimize civilian casualties," so "it seems fairly obvious that a substantial portion—I'd estimate 75% at least—of the casualties were (in order, from the start of the war) soldiers of Saddam Hussein's army, Republican guard troops, Ba'athist 'insurgents,' Sunni militia members, foreign jihadis, and all manner of thugs, fanatics, and killers." Incensed by this alleged display of "moral equivalence between the terrorists and those who fight terrorism," the blogger invoked the Manichean "us versus them" commonplace of the Bush administration's rhetoric: "Which side are you on, boys, which side are you on?"[55]

The wider impact of the exhibit is evident in the creative output it has generated in the form of still photography as well as amateur and professional films. Thanks to YouTube, it is now possible to share footage of the exhibit with the widest possible audience. The majority of YouTube videos featuring *Eyes Wide Open* simply record the exhibit's main features and actions of volunteers and participants, from setting up the boots to giving speeches at press conferences. Two films available on YouTube, however, stand out as artful interpretations of the memorial—independent producer Patricia Boiko's short "The Corporal's Boots" and blues musician Robert Cray's music video for "Twenty," the title song of his 2005 album.

"The Corporal's Boots" is a seven and a half-minute documentary narrated by a middle-aged woman, exhibit viewer Jeannie Graves.[56] Her point of view and emotional response to *Eyes Wide Open* resemble the Victorian female visitor's response to the Arlington national cemetery quoted earlier in this essay, with one exception: she is not comforted by the notion that the young soldiers gave their lives for a worthy cause. The first words uttered by the narrator testify to the memorial's ambiguity: "It's an interesting question whether the exhibit is anti-war or pro-war. Some people have taken it as an anti-war statement; some people have taken it as a tribute, a memorial to our fallen heroes." Rather than resolving this issue, she takes the audience on her journey through the boots and shoes before relating her encounter with one pair of boots—those standing for Corporal Jonathan Santos, who died in Iraq at the age of twenty-two. The narrator notices Jonathan's mother trying to attach a pendant to her son's boots. Her voice trembling, she describes how the mother "untied and retied the laces and tried to fix the boots so they were standing up straight . . . As I watched her, I thought: how many times does a mother tie her child's shoes?" A military mother herself (her son had served in Kosovo), the narrator easily identifies with Mrs. Santos: "My worst fears are what this woman was actually living through."

The film enacts cathartic witnessing and foregrounds empathy and consolation as the exhibit's chief rhetorical effects. Private grief is made public and publicly acknowledged via the narrator's testimony and the bereft mother's expression of gratitude for honoring her son. Although the film raises the question about the exhibit's meaning, it does not urge a single interpretation of it. This "strategic ambiguity" allows opposing interpretations of the display to coexist and converge in praise of the film.[57] Indeed, all of the comments posted on YouTube in response to the video lauded its emotional power, even though for some the film was about "our fallen heroes" and "sacrifice for freedom" while for others, it was a poignant reminder of "the cost of war" and a "must see for everyone including our politicians."

In contrast with the documentary's ambiguity, Robert Cray's "Twenty" passionately testifies against the ongoing war in Iraq.[58] It is a blues ballad that tells the story of a young American soldier who questions his military mission in Iraq, but is killed before his tour of duty is over. Cray wrote this "most explicitly political" of his songs[59] at the end of 2004, when *Eyes Wide Open* was completing the first year of its national tour. AFSC assisted Cray in setting up the exhibit in the rolling hills of a farm in New Hampshire.[60] The video uses the boots display as a framing device for the song's narrative, which at first appears to be a homecoming tale of a soldier returning from Iraq to a Northeastern town. Cray's refrain, "When you are used up, where do you go, soldier?" signals that this story is without a happy ending. As he is riding on a bus and gazing out the window at an idyllic autumn landscape, the young man is haunted by flashbacks of Iraq—soldiers in desert uniforms, explosions, dead Iraqi civilians. The soundtrack relates the soldier's inner thoughts: "Standing out here in the desert/Trying to protect an oil line/I'd really like to do my job but/This ain't the country that I had in mind/They call it a war on terror/I see a lot of civilians dying/Mothers, sons, fathers and daughters/Not to mention some friends of mine."

While the lyrics are silent on the connection between the war in Iraq and the trauma of Vietnam, the video makes it explicit: when the soldier steps off the bus, he offers a cigarette to a wheelchair-bound man holding a sign that says "Vietnam Vet." The parallel between the young soldier who has been "used up" and the disabled veteran of Vietnam hints at the uncertain future for those who do return home—even those whose bodies seem intact may, in fact, be psychologically damaged. As the video's final scenes make clear, however, the soldier is no longer among the living, and his homecoming is imagined by the artist. After his encounter with a Vietnam veteran, the young man continues on to a field outside of town, where the boots have been set up in neat rows. He walks among the boots and then, coming across a pair bearing a tag "Name not yet reported," he pulls the boots on. In the next scene, we see him clad in a desert uniform and standing at attention among the sea of boots and then vanishing as Cray sings his lament, "Late in 2004/Comes a knock at the door/It's no surprise/Mother dry your eyes."

The song stresses the soldier's integrity and dedication ("Mother dry your eyes/that's what I've signed up for") and presents his opposition to the conflict as a realization that he was "protecting the oil line" and thus "fighting the rich man's war." Casting the soldier as the war's primary victim along with Iraqi civilians, the artist exonerates the warrior while condemning the war. The story's authenticity is enhanced by the fact that the soldier is played by an actual Iraq War veteran—reservist Aidan Delgado, who became a conscientious objector while serving at Abu Ghraib.[61] Unlike Boiko's film, in which military mothers perform the act of cathartic remembrance, Cray's ballad does not offer the comfort of closure: although the soldier's guilt and shame no longer haunt him, the audience is made witness to his traumatic memory and therefore must come to terms with it.

Various forms of mediation of the *Eyes Wide Open* exhibit demonstrate both the limitations of mainstream media and the vitality of new and emerging media. In contrast with mainstream media's reluctance to cover unconventional war memorials, responses to the exhibit on the internet exemplify polemical possibilities of the online forums. Yet, while they are not facing institutional and ideological constraints of big media, they also tend to address their audiences as a collection of like-minded persons.[62] Unlike the actual spaces of encounter among strangers such as the one furnished by many locations of *Eyes Wide Open*, these forums lack the environmental possibilities of spectatorship in common. Even such evocative films as "The Corporal's Boots" and "Twenty" are unable to narrativize fully the display's representation of Iraqi casualties: in Boiko's documentary, civilian shoes remain in the background of the story as a depressing spectacle; in Cray's video, the shoes are not featured at all, and instead Iraqi deaths haunt the soldier's conscience.

CONCLUSION

The *Eyes Wide Open* exhibit is a plea for its own obsolescence. In contrast with most war memorials, it is erected while the war is still going on and is intended to hasten the war's end. As a reminder of the human cost of war,

the memorial invites its visitors not only to remember and mourn the casualties on both sides of the Iraq conflict, but also to question whether any war,
including the current one, can be considered just. While the latter is clearly the
belief shared by the Quakers and other groups who have actively supported
Eyes Wide Open throughout the country, the exhibit does not argue this—
instead, it allows audiences to derive their own conclusions from the spectacle
presented by the juxtaposition of military boots and civilian shoes.

But this is only part of the memorial's appeal, as the display also forms a
backdrop to a panoply of memorial gestures—from expressions of private
grief to conventional symbols of patriotism to explicit anti-war statements.
Because the memorial's visible surface is augmented by various contributions from visitors, it can be regarded as a product of collective authorship.
In addition to the memorial's artifacts, interaction among those present
at the exhibit is integral to its success as a space of mourning and advocacy. The work it performs by bringing together committed volunteers,
concerned visitors, and accidental tourists shifts the burden of meaning-
making to human agents. However, the memorial's ability to draw in visitors and make them part of the ongoing performance of memory is subject
to vicissitudes of time and place. Each occasion, then, becomes a unique
forum for mourning, witnessing, and argument.

The ephemeral spectacle provided by *Eyes Wide Open* temporarily
transformed random passersby into a community of people who were self-
consciously present to each other[63] at the time when the commemorated
events were still unfolding. The exhibit's rhetorical power stemmed not
only from the visually arresting presentation of the human cost of war but
also from the performances of memory prompted by the display. In this
way, the exhibit offered not closure but awareness, asking its visitors to
open their eyes to the realities of the war waged in the name of freedom
and thereby to transform their act of remembrance into a public testimony
in the presence of fellow citizens.

NOTES

1. Since the Persian Gulf War (1991), the media were banned from photographing flag-draped caskets of U.S. soldiers. The Obama Administration lifted
   the ban in February 2009.
2. Carole Blair, "Civil Rights/Civil Sites: '. . .Until Justice Rolls Down Like
   Waters,'" A Caroll C. Arnold Distinguished Lecture, National Communication Association Convention November 2006 (Boston: Pearson Education,
   2008), 6–9.
3. Ibid., 14.
4. James E. Young, *The Texture of Memory: Holocaust Memorials and Meaning* (New Haven and London: Yale University Press, 1993), xii–xiii.
5. Carole Blair and Neil Michel, "Commemorating in the Theme Park Zone:
   Reading the Astronauts Memorial," in *At the Intersection: Cultural Studies*

and Rhetorical Studies, ed. Thomas Rosteck (New York and London: the Guilford Press, 1999), 68.

6. Kenneth Burke, *Permanence and Change:An Anatomy of Purpose,* 3rd edition (Berkeley: University of California Press, 1984) and *Attitudes Toward History,* 3rd edition (Berkeley: University of California Press, 1984); Anne T. Demo, "The Guerilla Girls' Comic Politics of Subversion," *Women's Studies in Communication,* 23:2 (2000): 133–57.

7. On the symbolism of the Gettysburg National Cemetery, see especially Gary Wills, *Lincoln at Gettysburg: The Words that Remade America* (New York: Touchstone, 1992).

8. On Gettysburg's connection to the Victorian "culture of death," see ibid., 63–89.

9. Constance Woolson, "Mrs. Edward Pinckney," *The Christian Union* 20:6 (August 1879): 105–06.

10. *National Cemetery Walking Tour,* Gettysburg National Military Park, Pennsylvania. National Park Service. U.S. Department of Interior. n.d.

11. Peter Hawkins, "Naming Names: The Art of Memory and the NAMES Project AIDS Quilt," in *Thinking About Exhibitions,* ed. Reesa Greenberg, Bruce W. Ferguson, and Sandy Nairne (London: Routledge, 1996), 136.

12. Marita Sturken. *Tangled Memories: The Vietnam War, the AIDS Epidemic, and the Politics of Remembering* (Berkeley: University of California Press, 1997), 184.

13. Ibid., 189.

14. Ibid., 196.

15. Ibid., 195.

16. Quoted in ibid., 216.

17. Bradford Vivian, "Neoliberal Epideictic: Rhetorical Form and Commemorative Politics on September 11, 2002," *Quarterly Journal of Speech* 92:1 (2006): 16.

18. Mary Zerkel, Telephone Interview, July 17, 2008.

19. Ibid.

20. Mary Ellen McNish, "About the Exhibit," Retrieved July 15, 2009 from http://www.afsc.org/eyes/ht/d/sp/i/38782/pid/38782. "Many times when the exhibit was up," recalls Mary Zerkel, "casualties would be announced on the Department of Defense website and we would have to add boots to the exhibit. During the times of the heaviest casualties, we would have a board with moveable numbers, so that we could change the tally of casualties several times over the course of a few hours and announce the addition of another pair of boots to the crowd." Mary Zerkel, personal correspondence to the author. February 1, 2010.

21. In late 2006, the AFSC listed the number of Iraqi casualties at 655,000. The following quote on the website explains this estimate: "A study by Johns Hopkins University and Al Mustansiriya University researchers finds that between 420,000 and 790,000 Iraqis have died as a result of war and political violence since the beginning of the US invasion in March 2003. It was published in The Lancet medical journal on October 11, 2006." Retrieved July 15, 2009 from http://www.afsc.org/eyes/ht/display/ContentDetails/i/5098.

22. A pdf file of "Dreams and Nightmares"panels is available on the AFSC website. Retrieved July 15, 2009 from http://www.afsc.org/eyes/. This component of *Eyes Wide Open* was created in collaboration with Peaceful Tomorrows, an organization founded by family members of those killed on September 11, 2001.

23. Steven Winn, "Memorials Seek to Make Public Grief Personal," *San Francisco Chronicle*, (March 31, 2005), E1.
24. This contribution to the exhibit is described by Lindsey Millar, "The Shoes of the Soldiers. Iraq Exhibit at Statehouse Overwhelms," *Arkansas Times*, (February 2, 2005).
25. Kenneth Burke, *Attitudes Toward History*, 171.
26. Cindy Fowler, "Eyes Wide Open, Every Day: Bringing Home the Human Cost of War." *Friends Committee on Legislation Newsletter* 54:2 (February 2005): 1–2.
27. "Exhibition Report: the First Year." Retrieved July 15, 2009 from http://www.afsc.org/eyes/. Most state exhibits were also augmented by boots and shoes representing U.S. military and civilian casualties in Afghanistan. In October 2009, to mark the eighth anniversary of the war in Afghanistan, AFSC staged a display of over 800 boots in Washington, D.C., in front of the White House.
28. Kari Lydersen, "War Costing $720 Million Each Day, Group Says," *The Washington Post* (September 22, 2007), A11.
29. Pierre Nora, "Between Memory and History: *Les Lieux de Mémoire*," *Representations* 26 (1989): 7–12.
30. Steve J. Stern, *Remembering Pinochet's Chile: On the Eve of London 1998* (Durham: Duke University Press, 2006), 120.
31. Jeannette Raymond, "Cost of War and EWO: A Solemn Memorial Among Chaos or [sic] RNC." Retrieved July 15, 2009 from http://www.afsc.org/eyes/ht/display/ContentDetails/i/71048.
32. Sarah Gill, "Cost of War and EWO Colorado at DNC." Retrieved July 15, 2009 from http://www.afsc.org/eyes/ht/display/ContentDetails/i/71048.
33. Mary Zerkel, Telephone Interview, July 17, 2008.
34. Stephanie M. Peters, "10,000 in Boston Rally Against War—Part of Events Held Nationwide," *The Boston Globe* (October 28, 2007), B6.
35. Demorris A. Lee, "Boots, Shoes to Stand for War's Fallen," *St. Petersburg Times (Florida)* (May 25, 2008), Clearwater Times, 1.
36. "Eyes Wide Open College Organizing Toolkit." Retrieved July 15, 2009 from http://www.afsc.org/eyes/.
37. "Helena, Montana, 19–20, 2006," August 5, 2006. Retrieved July 15, 2009 from http://peace.chicago.blogspot.com.
38. Elaine Brower, "Prelude to the Debate: AFSC 'Eyes Wide Open' Exhibited on Hofstra Campus," October 16, 2008. Retrieved July 15, 2009 from http://radicalblogs.org/blog/2008/10/16/prelude-to-the-debate-afsc-"eyes-wide-open"-exhibited-on-hosftra-campus.
39. Jim Haber, "EWO Work Expands to Nevada." Retrieved July 15, 2009 from http://www.afsc.org/eyes/ht/display/ContentDetails/i/71048 .
40. Gill, "Cost of War"
41. Elaine Brower, "Prelude to the Debate."
42. Thomas Good, "Eyes Wide Open—at the National Night Out Against Crime," *Next Left Notes*, August 9, 2007. Retrieved July 15, 2009 from http://antiauthoritarian.net/NLN/index.php?s=eyes+wide+open .
43. Elaine Brower, Telephone Interview, August 4, 2009.
44. Kenneth S. Zagacki and Victoria J. Gallagher, "Rhetoric and Materiality in the Museum Park at the North Carolina Museum of Art," *Quarterly Journal of Speech* 95:2 (2009): 172.
45. See Kevin M. DeLuca, *Image Politics: The New Rhetoric of Environmental Activism* (New York: The Guilford Press, 1999) and Kevin M. DeLuca and Jennifer Peeples, "From Public Sphere to Public Screen: Democracy, Activism,

and the "Violence" of Seattle," *Critical Studies in Media Communication* 19:2 (2002): 125–51.

46. Raymond, "Cost of War and EWO"

47. Elaine Brower, Telephone Interview. August 4, 2009.

48. "See Where We've Been." Retrieved July 15, 2009 from http://www.afsc.org/eyes/ht/display/ContentDetails/i/5136.

49. Web enthusiasts are worried that digital data lacks durability. As historians Daniel Cohen and Roy Rosenzweig observe, "surprisingly few digital historians have thought about ensuring that what has been created today in digital formats will survive into the future. Digital materials are notoriously fragile and require special attention to withstand changing technologies and user demands." *Digital History: A Guide to Gathering, Preserving, and Presenting the Past on the Web* (Philadelphia: University of Pennsylvania Press, 2005), 16.

50. Clay Shirky, *Here Comes Everybody: The Power of Organizing Without Organizations* (New York: Penguin Press, 2008), 55.

51. "Maker Monologue (Eyes Wide Open and 'Counting the Cost')," *Mike's Weblog about Computing, Politics, and Faith (a Progressive View)* March 12, 2005. Retrieved July 15, 2009 from http://makimo.net/weblog/heeeres-yhwh.

52. Thomas Good, "Arlington New York State Returns on Memorial Day Weekend," *Next Left Notes* May 27, 2009 Retrieved July 15, 2009 from http://antiauthoritarian.net/NLN/index.php?s=arlington+new+york+state.

53. "A War Memorial for All Wars Since 1945," *The Polynational War Memorial*. Retrieved July 15, 2009 from http://www.war-memorial.net/index.asp.

54. Jon Brunberg, "Cross-National Commemoration in the Iraq War," *The Polynational War Memorial* December 28, 2004. Retrieved July 15, 2009 from http://www.warmemorial.net/news_details.asp?ID=34.

55. "Eyes Wide Open Anti-War Display." Retrieved July 15, 2009 from http://zombietime.com/eyes_wide_open/.

56. Patricia Boiko, producer, "The Corporal's Boots." Videorecording. Winning Pictures, LLC. (2005). Retrieved July 15, 2009 from http://www.youtube.com/watch?v=NolEYfzj0Vo.

57. On strategic ambiguity, see Leah Ceccarelli, "Polysemy: Multiple Meanings in Rhetorical Criticism," *Quarterly Journal of Speech* 84:4 (1998): 395–415.

58. Sue Turner-Cray, director, "Twenty." Music Video (2005). Retrieved July 15, 2009 from http://www.youtube.com/watch?v=hY4JlbC6wQE.

59. John Murphy. "Robert Cray—Twenty (Sanctuary)." *MusicOMH.* http://www.musicomh.com/albums/robert-cray.htm. Accessed July 27, 2009.

60. For an account of the AFSC involvement in the shooting of the video, see the American Friends Service Committee website, "New Music Video Features 'Eyes Wide Open' Boots." Retrieved July 15, 2009 from http://www.afsc.org/Iraq/ht/d/ContentDetails/i/2869.

61. Delgado was honorably discharged in April 2004. He published a biography, *The Sutras of Abu Ghraib* (Boston: Beacon Press, 2007) and was featured along with several other veterans in the documentary "Soldiers of Conscience" by Luna Productions, which was broadcast on the POV Series on PBS on October 16, 2008: http://www.pbs.org/pov/soldiersofconscience.

62. Scholars of political communication have noted that while the internet promotes a plurality of points of view on any given subject, it also abets political insularity and fragmentation. Many web users tend to focus narrowly on certain issues at the expense of a broad exposure to a spectrum of issues and opinions. See, for example, Bruce E. Gronbeck, "Citizen

Voices in Cyberpolitical Culture," in *Rhetorical Democracy: Discursive Practices of Civic Engagement,* ed. Gerard A. Hauser and Amy Grim (Mahwah, NJ: Lawrence Erlbaum, 2004); Gary W. Selnow, *Electronic Whistle Stops: The Impact of the Internet on American Politics* (Westport, CT: Praeger, 1998).

63. I am paraphrasing S. Michael Halloran, "Text and Performance in a Historical Pageant: Toward a Rhetoric of Spectacle," *Rhetoric Society Quarterly* 31 (2001): 5.

6   Patterns of Ambivalence
The Space between Memory and Form

Kingsley Baird

Remember winter, spring's welcome consolation[1]

—Jenny Bornhold

The ordinary response to atrocities is to banish them from consciousness. Certain violations of the social compact are too terrible to utter aloud: this is the meaning of the word *unspeakable*.[2]

—Judith Herman

What is true about the relations between invention, imagination and ideology in individual processes of remembering is of course also true of public, and communal memory. Nations put up public memorials to events that are part of a desired history. They construct history books for children. They prune and reinforce desiderated narratives.[3]

—A.S. Byatt

Since 2006, a stainless steel sculpture of a stylised traditional Maori cloak has stood in Nagasaki's Peace Park. The memorial sculpture, *The Cloak of Peace* (2006), was a gift of friendship from New Zealand to the people of Nagasaki. In this essay I discuss the integral roles of, and interface between, memory and visuality in the artist's conception and the public reception of the Cloak.[4] I describe how the Cloak's meaning is based largely upon a repository of personal childhood memories associated with Japan and analysis of an affecting and compelling photograph in the Hiroshima Peace Memorial Museum. These visual sources of inspiration are considered against a backdrop of an unresolved past: contested historical and cultural perceptions of Japan's role in World War II as perpetrator or victim.

Between a memorial artist's inspiration and the realization of ensuing ideas in material form can exist a space of diverse—even conflicting—memories. Such memories are often visual, selected according to the specific requirement of their recall, in this case study, to design a particular memorial. Responding to the words, "New Zealand peace memorial, Nagasaki,

Figure 6.1   Kingsley Baird, *The Cloak of Peace*. Stainless steel, 3 x 1.8 m. Nagasaki Peace Park, 2007. Photo by author.

Japan," the mind generates the data deemed relevant from a personal image library. The visual memories that inspired the Cloak sculpture ranged from the popular culture forms of comics, TV drama, and feature films to photography and fine art woodcut prints.

Once memory becomes an object (a memorial), the personal and public memories of those who experience it are added to the space containing the artist's memory. The artist can establish the aesthetic and material conditions to enable a negotiation of this amorphous space but not determine which memories will prevail over others and therefore comprise the memorial's meanings. For artist and viewer alike, the space and its contents are mutable; from time to time meaning may undergo change according to new experiences, insights, and the reconstitution of existing memories. Memories may be reinforced, made more complex, or even contested. Meaning is located between the artist's intention and the viewer's interpretation. In *The Cloak of Peace* project my intention is that the physical form of the memorial provide the opportunity for conflicting memories to be evoked by, and "bear witness" to, unresolved and "unspeakable" events. The challenge for memorial artists and the public is to reconcile the charged space between memory and its material expression.

Questions of intention and responsibility were paramount in formulating the concept and design of the Cloak. Public art, by its very nature, requires the negotiation of a complex social space. The commissioning process is often complicated by the existence of multiple agendas and the requirement that they be accommodated. This bicultural case included those of national and local governments, peace organizations from New Zealand and Japan, the authorities responsible for the peace park, and my own. My role was framed not only by a desire to support peace initiatives but also to disturb uncritical perspectives of an unresolved past. In attempting to achieve these goals, I set up conditions for the participation of members of the public visiting the park. Provided they are willing to accept the "terms of engagement," their comprehension of my intended meaning of the artwork is dependant upon knowledge of conflicting interpretations of historical events and particular imagery, and the imagination to connect these factors to their immediate experience of the sculpture.

Before I was commissioned to design *The Cloak of Peace*, Japan conjured up only a loose collection of autobiographical memories and experiences that were not entirely unstructured but were yet to be "polished, like objects taken out, burnished, and contemplated. . . ."[5] The Nagasaki project required that some of my images of Japan were edited out while others were selected, embellished with "the sentimental sheen that the remembered past so often acquires," and linked to form a coherent story of identity—both mine and Japan's.[6] I constructed a narrative based on *re*membering and *re*inventing.

Long before I visited Japan, in fact going back to my childhood, the country existed as a place in my imagination. I was raised with an appreciation of Japanese aesthetic sensibility. My mother was an enthusiastic amateur potter and Japanese pottery achieved a revered status in our household. However, on occasions she would echo what her father, stationed in the Pacific during World War II, had presumably said to her about *the* Japanese character: "They can be very cruel." This perception existed in her mind in a simultaneous binary opposition to cultured grace and aesthetic refinement.

As a child, I was drawn to the romance of a Japanese samurai TV drama that screened on New Zealand television in the 1960s.[7] Every week, Shintaro, the "cardboard cut-out" hero of the series, battled uneven odds to defeat the highly skilled but evil Ninja. The samurai's appeal to an eight-year-old was the conflation of martial arts skills and the Confucian code of honour and loyalty of bushido, "the way of the warrior." Contrary to these perceptions, and existing in parallel to the perceived noble attributes of samurai, was the representation of the demonized enemy: the cruel and fanatical Japanese soldier portrayed in British and American World War II comics and films I read and watched as a child. These comics often featured panels with a crazed Japanese officer, pistol in one hand and samurai sword in the other, leading his men in attack. His speech bubble shouted, "Banzai! For the Emperor and for Nippon!"

During the period of extreme nationalism and militarism that ended with Japan's defeat in 1945, the concept of loyalty was taken to excess and abused by those in command.[8] The actions of Colonel Saito, the Japanese prisoner of war camp commandant in David Lean's *The Bridge on the River Kwai* (1957), exemplify not only those of a bushido zealot, but also the attitude of many Japanese at the time, military and civilian. When the captive British Colonel Nicholson questions Saito's disregard for the Geneva Convention, the Japanese officer responds contemptuously: "You speak to me of code. What code? The coward's code. What do you know of the soldier's code of bushido? Nothing. You are unworthy of command."[9]

In April 2006, I visited Japan for the first time to undertake a site visit at the peace park where the sculpture I had designed would be located. Throughout the train journey from Tokyo to Nagasaki, the scenery outside conformed to my simplistic vision of Japan. Fujiyama, which has a reputation for shyness, was on full display, revealing its picturesque profile as in a woodcut print by Hiroshige. To compound the visual clichés, the sakura was in bloom.

Late in the afternoon, the Shinkansen stopped at Hiroshima and I alighted to visit the Peace Memorial Museum. There, I came across a color photograph of a woman sitting with her back to the photographer (and the viewer).[10] Her blue kimono has been slipped off her right shoulder to reveal skin "branded" with a cross-hatch pattern on the right side of her back, shoulder, and arm. When the atomic bomb was dropped on August 6, 1945, the resultant heat rays burnt onto her skin the dark parts of the pattern of the kimono she was wearing on that shocking day.

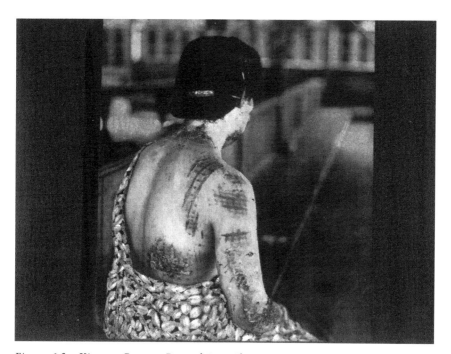

Figure 6.2 Kimono Pattern Burned into Skin (Ujina Branch of Hiroshima First Army Hospital/around August 15, 1945). Photo by Gonichi Kimura. Photo courtesy of Hiroshima Peace Memorial Museum.

Among so many awful and distressing images and artefacts in the museum, this metaphorically rich photograph had the most profound and revelatory affect on me.

Why did this image stand out amongst all the horror? It was as if all my knowledge and experience of Japan merged together in it. The subject is simultaneously an individual person and the representative of an entire nation. The photo evokes something of the stereotype of old and cultured Japan as well as its apparent antithesis, the fanatical and brutal military power of the 1930s and 1940s. Fundamentally, it is an image of defeated Japan. Umberto Eco could have been describing this image when he wrote:

> It has surpassed the individual circumstance that produced it; it no longer speaks of the single character or of those characters, but expresses concepts. It is unique, but at the same time it refers to other images that preceded it or that, in imitation, have followed it.[11]

The photographer has portrayed his subject, unintentionally or otherwise, in a way that suggests pictorial references broader than the apparent mere recording of the effects of the atomic bomb. Despite the primary focus of the photo being the woman's obvious injuries, an aesthetic interpretation is also possible. It can be read according to subject and compositional conventions of both Western and Japanese art. While apparently alluding to *Ukiyo-e*, pictures of the Floating World, the image is also ironically reminiscent of Western artworks influenced by Japanese models.[12] In addition, there are the polarized interpretations of modesty and dignity on one hand and objectification on the other. The latter including sexualised, Western male fantasies and clichés of the East: the submissive woman, demure, graceful, exotic, and "other." In Susan Sontag's words, the subject has been "symbolically possessed."[13]

When considered with her injuries, these readings could reinforce the ascription of her victim status. Does the woman's victimhood extend to her inclusion as the image's subject? Was she persuaded or pressured to take part? Is the photograph a scientific record of the effects of the bomb or one of a series measuring the progress of her treatment? If she had refused to comply, would she have been denied medical attention? Sontag argues that the act of taking a photograph is not merely the outcome of an encounter between an event and a photographer, but "an event in itself" in which the photographer is freed from moral responsibility "to interfere with, to invade, or to ignore whatever is going on."[14] What were the Japanese photographer's intentions and the nature of his relationship to his subject? Was it one of predation, violation, possession, humiliation, cooperation, complicity, sympathy, or detachment; one based on trust, or one of power? If the latter, whose power? Was he directed to take the photo, to compose and light it? Were the subject's motives altruistic? Did she see herself as a martyr to a future anti-bomb campaign? Whatever the subject's role in the image-making, as Paul Williams points out, "most photographs are taken without regard for what eventually became their historical consequence."[15]

Sontag proposes that "photographs are used to stimulate the moral impulse," to "mobilize conscience."[16] Recently, I showed the photograph of the Hiroshima bomb victim to a group of fine arts and design undergraduate students and asked them to describe the status of the female subject. My first intention was to observe how they would "read" the image based on their current experiences; and, secondly, to see how the meaning they attributed to the image might be modified according to new information (experiences) with which they were provided. The students had no knowledge of the subject's circumstances other than the visual information revealed in the image. Most thought that the marks on the woman's back were injuries sustained from an act of violence or in a fire. The overwhelming reading of the subject's status was that she was a victim. Such a response could fit E. Ann Kaplan's definition of "empty" empathy, which is "elicited by images of suffering provided without any context or background knowledge."[17]

I then described how the woman had received her injuries following the dropping of the atomic bomb on Hiroshima. Photographs were shown of the devastation caused by the bombs in Hiroshima and Nagasaki, including some that were very graphic and grisly, illustrating the effects of heat and radiation on humans, both survivors and those who died in the blast. After seeing these images, the students' response was more compassionate and they were emphatic that the woman was a victim. With an understanding of the immediate context—that is, the destruction caused by the bombs—their formerly detached curiosity was replaced by empathy. However, the focus of their sympathy was confined to individual experience—the state of the female subject—rather than such wider concerns as: Why did the U.S. drop atomic bombs on Hiroshima and Nagasaki? Were these actions justified? Why were the U.S. and Japan at war?

The group was then shown photographs of atrocities perpetrated by the Japanese army following their capture of the Chinese city of Nanjing in 1937. I provided limited descriptive information from a number of sources (including *The Rape of Nanking* by Iris Chang) to put the events portrayed in these images in an historical context.[18] I also explained that the views of the events I was presenting to them are at odds with alternative histories proposed by some Japanese nationalists.

Judith Herman asserts that witnesses to traumatic events resulting from human action, are "caught in the conflict between victim and perpetrator," unable to morally remain neutral.[19] This proved to be the case with the students: the images related to the massacre and the supporting information now elicited different responses. For some she was still a victim, regardless of any wider context. Others had been swayed by the Nanjing information and their reaction was along the lines of "she got what she deserved" for the treatment the Japanese had exacted on others during the war. She was no longer an individual but an emblem for an entire nation, "a comprehensible totality," and, for some at least, worthy of retribution.[20]

To a degree the trial of student responses to the photo, carried out some years after the peace park commission, mirrored my own experience in developing a concept for the artwork. Prior to the project my knowledge and understanding of Japanese culture and history was superficial and often based on stereotypes, both positive and negative. Following consideration of taking on the commission, my engagement deepened, particularly in regard to those events related to the war, including the dropping of the bomb and its aftermath. With each new experience, including meeting Japanese peace workers and visiting the peace museums and parks in Nagasaki and Hiroshima, came a reassessment of ideas and attitudes and, gradually, a realization that a simplistic expression of peaceful intent would not suffice. Through the sculpture I would attempt to express the complexity and contradictions of events and values—and therefore, ambivalence—to which my research had led me.

While the superficial "experiment" revealed for the students how perspectives can be revised (manipulated), no image—no matter how shocking—can convey the trauma of the woman (or other casualties of the bomb). She was a victim on two counts: firstly, of the effects of the bomb, and secondly, as the object of the viewer's gaze. This iconic photograph, which is publicly displayed in Hiroshima's Peace Memorial Museum, printed in at least one of the museum's publications, and viewable on various websites, could well be considered "offensive, disrespectful and [to have] transgressed the integrity of the human subject."[21]

How deep can our affinity be? Does cultural, geographic, and temporal distance from this and other shocking images in the Hiroshima and Nagasaki museums color one's response? Of course, distance will vary depending on each individual's "memory" in relation to what is witnessed. According to Georges Bataille, if we are remote from an event then our response will necessarily be one of "reflection" (distance) rather than "feeling" (empathy).[22] Bataille reminds us that "remoteness"—from the humanity of victims—is also experienced by those close to traumatic events. From John Hersey's *Hiroshima*, he recounts Tanimoto Kiyoshi's rescue attempt of about twenty victims of the blast, trapped on a sandbar in the Ota River. As he carried the "slimy living bodies" up the slope away from the tide, Tanimoto had to remind himself of his fellow citizens' humanity: "He had to keep consciously repeating to himself, 'These are human beings.'"[23] This notion of remoteness from the event, and therefore the image, could be extended to the number of occasions on which viewers are exposed to the photo. Indeed, Sontag argues that the "ethical content of photographs is fragile" and so repeated exposure dilutes their capacity to evoke an emotional response.[24] In regard to this image, I would dispute that contention; today, this "memory freeze-frame" remains as compelling and shocking as it did on my first viewing.[25]

There is an ethical dimension to *showing* as well as *looking*. Visitors to the two peace museums would expect to be confronted with visually shocking objects. Such exhibits are integral to a memorial museum's apparent *raison d'être*, "to illuminate, commemorate, and educate about a particular bounded and vivid historical event."[26] At the Nagasaki Atomic Bomb Museum, visitors encounter the ubiquitous clock whose frozen hands record the time of the blast; damaged personal effects; melted coins and bottles; and photos of blackened, burnt corpses, close ups of *hibaksha* injuries, and the devastated urban landscape devoid of all but the ruins of buildings and ghostly survivors. These "terrible byproducts" are affecting because they have undergone or record physical transformation.[27] The meaning we attach to these exhibits has also been transformed. They have acquired an "emotional and historic weight" that has elevated them from their ordinary, everyday, pre-bomb status to symbolic objects.[28] The gravitas attached to them has been compounded by their selection for display in the memorial museum's narrative.

The authenticity of such exhibits underpins the museum's authority. They are incontrovertible proof that the story the museum relates actually happened. Why it happened is less clear. Just as the "woman in a kimono" photograph and other exhibits in the Hiroshima and Nagasaki museums have been selected from a range of possible artifacts, some accounts of the events surrounding the dropping of the atomic bombs have been privileged over others. Williams asserts that an "uneasy conceptual coexistence of reverent remembrance and critical interpretation" exists in memorial museums.[29] Whereas data concerned with the technical aspects of the bombs and the physical impact of the explosions on people and buildings is detailed and explicit, issues concerned with blame and responsibility (who were the victims and perpetrators?) are avoided or treated in an obfuscatory manner. While the Nagasaki museum's fervent appeal for world peace is indisputably laudable, material related to events leading up to war suffers from physical marginalisation (being located on the periphery of the exhibition space), a lack of detail, and euphemistic or ambiguous language ("The people of other Asian nations were also dragged into the conflict and victimised in various ways").[30]

In contrast to the museum's equivocation, many of the artworks in the peace park are apparently straightforward in their meaning. For example, the figurative mother and child sculptures gifted by a number of former Eastern Bloc countries express solidarity with the bomb victims in a direct manner. Their denotative meaning is clear but the message behind their forms requires more scrutiny than most visitors to the park might be prepared to offer. For the ideology behind these works, such a lack of reflective engagement is not problematic, on the contrary, it is desirable. By not overtly expressing intent—either through subject or interpretive signage—an artist runs the risk of not being understood, or even, misunderstood. The success of the work in communicating the desired message relies on the knowledge and understanding visitors bring to the experience. If they comprehend the intended meaning on their own accord ultimately the artwork is more affecting.

冬を胸に　春は希望に満ちる

Figure 6.3 Kingsley Baird, *The Cloak of Peace* (detail), Japanese translation of "Remember winter, spring's welcome consolation." Photo by author.

Memorial museums are "politically loaded spaces," possibly none less so than the Yushukan "war museum" at Yasukuni Shrine in Tokyo.[31] It is the museum's perspective—one at odds with my own experience—that drew me to visit the shrine in 2006. In recent years, Japan's neighbours have voiced outrage about textbooks that promote alternative histories concerning the Asia-Pacific War to those commonly accepted outside of Japan. Prime ministerial visits to Yasukuni Shrine have met with similar condemnation. The Shinto shrine, dedicated to the spirits of the soldiers and others who died in the service of the Emperor, is a "deeply flawed" sacred ritual site, according to John Breen.[32] Included in the shrine's "Book of Souls" are over 1,000 people convicted of war crimes by the post-World War II International Military Tribunal for the Far East. On the Shrine's website they are described as "martyrs of Showa who were cruelly and unjustly tried as war criminals by the sham-like tribunal of the Allied forces."[33]

At Yasukuni, these war criminals are venerated as *kami* or the apotheosized war dead. Eighty of them, convicted of Class A war crimes, were described by IMTFE Chief Prosecutor Joseph Keenan as "plain, ordinary murderers."[34] John Breen argues, "while honouring and mourning the war dead is a noble undertaking, Yasukuni in its present guise runs the risk of appropriating the war dead for other purposes."[35] How does one honour the dead without becoming embroiled in the attendant ideological debates and controversies that surround a memory site such as Yasukuni?

Yushukan contains accounts of Japan's actions in the Asia-Pacific War, which are considered revisionist by many Western historians, including Breen. According to Williams, the painful history of this "unmastered past" could eventually re-emerge in "politically catastrophic ways."[36] Japanese scholar Takahashi Tetsuya, is concerned that the "revisionist politics" of the ruling Liberal Democratic Party—including the possible intention to amend legislation separating state and religious institutions—"will usher in a new kind of pre-war situation."[37] He believes there is a risk that Japan will return to the "triadic base" of the former Japanese Empire and its militaristic state: patriotic education, a revival of the Japanese military, and state support for religious entities such as Yasukuni.

Rather than Japan's attack on the U.S. naval base at Pearl Harbor being seen as an act of aggression, the museum argues that Japan was forced to do so by American policies, effectively giving President Franklin Roosevelt the opportunity he needed to enter the war. In addition, Yushukan highlights the West's colonial exploitation of Asia, the destruction of the Allies' fire bombing of Tokyo and the devastation of the atomic bombings of Hiroshima and Nagasaki. As Williams observes, "The perpetrator's arguments prove irresistible when the bystander faces them in isolation."[38] Even the Nanjing Incident (as the "Nanjing Massacre" is called in the Yushukan) is described in terms of a heavy defeat for the Chinese army that enabled the residents of Nanjing to "live their lives in peace."[39]

Despite its overtly revisionist rhetoric, the museum is justified in asserting that the Allies were not blameless in committing atrocities in World War II. Although not involved in the decision to use atomic weapons against Japan, my country is guilty by association, having fought alongside those who dropped the atomic bombs and who continue to defend that action on the grounds of saving Allied lives. The question remains, "was the bomb militarily necessary or was it used primarily for political/diplomatic reasons that had more to do with impressing the Soviets than winning the war against Japan?"[40]

Both victor and vanquished are guilty of complicity in promoting silence or forgetting. But this is more than withdrawing from a past that was painful for both sides; it was a post-war, Cold War reality. "Atrocities, however, refuse to be buried. Equally as powerful as the desire to deny atrocities is the conviction that denial does not work."[41] Now that geopolitical conditions have changed, the trauma that has been necessarily deferred in the establishment of a democratic, prosperous, and peaceful Japan, and the U.S.' need to defeat Communism, remains to be addressed. For Japan, argues Williams, assuming the role of victim has been beneficial in the construction of its post-war national identity and economy. Even the atomic bomb victims have been conscripted as "martyrs who sacrificed their lives for the prosperity of the post-war nation."[42]

However, the lack of historical resolution in which the roles of victim and perpetrator from World War II are still contested is an impediment to reconciliation between remembering and forgetting. This is compounded by the apparent erasure of memories from the consciousness of people on both sides of the conflict. Is it possible to rescue memories from oblivion, to resurrect and restore them? Certainly, the repression of memory by historical foes is not the solution to assuaging the trauma of past events and achieving reconciliation. "Remembering," according to A. S. Byatt, "is the only way to achieve benign forgetting."[43] Confronting the past will achieve a kind of closure.

Since the establishment of the Nagasaki Peace Park in 1955 near the hypocenter of the explosion, fifteen countries and cities—including New Zealand—have responded to an invitation to donate monuments. As an expression of consolation, protection, and solidarity for the inhabitants of Nagasaki, *The Cloak of Peace* presumably represents Byatt's "desired history" for both Japan and New Zealand. However, the intention behind the Cloak is not to draw a line under historical events; by embodying memory we are not relieved of the duty to remember, and memorials can play a constructive role in interpreting and re-presenting conflicting views of the past.[44]

In addition to its straightforward meaning, the Cloak is also intended to express—through its visual form and potential corporeal experience—complexity and contradictory historical and cultural viewpoints. While it is a reflection of my personal memories, it also aims to establish the conditions for the evocation and mediation of viewers' memories. Receiving the artist's intended meaning is dependent on the viewers' ability to orchestrate a variety of social, cultural, and visual experiences.[45] Sighting the visual and material culture in the Nagasaki Atomic Bomb Museum and having an awareness of the "weight" of the park's proximity to Ground Zero—a site of profound trauma—viewers may be primed to interpret the visually-encoded Cloak as intended by the artist. However, a lack of prescribed meaning leaves the Cloak open to misinterpretation and an acute reliance on the viewers' capacity to comprehend the intended meaning is risky. Moreover, to achieve the circumstances enabling the reception of the artist's full meaning, a coincidence of conditions is required: physical engagement by the viewer, sunlight, and a mind open to visual perception and the ability to make connections between a variety of memory sources.

The Cloak's curved form "invites" visitors to engage with the sculpture. Its surface is covered with a perforated pattern of native New Zealand kowhai flowers and when visitors stand within its "embrace," the sun's rays project the pattern of the flower motif onto their bodies. The experience of the projected light pattern is not intended to be vicarious, to put one in the position of a bomb victim. The Cloak is not mimetic: it "does not reproduce the visible; rather it makes visible."[46] As Guerin and Hallas state, "no representation can even begin to communicate the truth of the traumatic experience."[47] It does, however, have a mnemonic role in "bearing witness" to unresolved events of the past by allowing for the absent (contested or suppressed memories) to be present. By constructing a space between memory and form, the Cloak creates patterns of ambivalence. The ensuing unease—a disruption of complacency and a contemplation of the "unspeakable"—may provoke in the visitor the retrieval of forgotten memories.

Figure 6.4   Kingsley Baird, *The Cloak of Peace* (detail), Nagasaki Peace Park, 2007. Photo by Catherine O'Connell.

NOTES

1. The text of this poem appears on *The Cloak of Peace's* collar and contributes both to the meaning and the materiality of the work. I wanted the sculpture to express ambivalence not only through the projection of light but also by the use of text. Eminent New Zealand poet, Jenny Bornholdt, was commissioned to write a poem that was required to be short and convey ambivalence. Its brevity was necessary because the poem appears as a band of text around the collar in English along with Japanese and Maori translations.
2. Judith Herman, *Trauma and Recovery: The Aftermath of Violence—from Domestic Abuse to Political Terror* (New York: Basic Books, 1997), 1.
3. Harriet Harvey Wood and A. S. Byatt, eds., *Memory: An Anthology* (London: Chatto & Windus, 2008), xviii.
4. I am using the term "visuality" defined as "vision socialised" by the authors in John A. Walker and Sarah Chaplin, *Visual Culture: An Introduction* (Manchester: Manchester University Press, 1997), 22.
5. Wood and Byatt, *Memory*, xii.
6. Malcolm Bowie, "Remembering the Future," in *Memory: An Anthology*, eds., Harriet Harvey Wood and A. S. Byatt (London: Chatto & Windus, 2008), 14.

7. *The Samurai* (*Onmitsu kenshi*) was a Japanese television historical drama series made by Senkosha Productions running in Japan from 1962 until 1965. I have been unable to find any commentary on the program's reception in New Zealand but the following website provides some information about the Australian response. According to the website, the series had a significant impact on teen and pre-teen children in Australia: "The popularity of the series in Australia can perhaps be partially explained by Australia's fascination with its former enemy Japan (the show screened less than twenty years after the end of World War II); even so, the level of popularity it attained is remarkable given there was still much resentment of Japan in Australia at the time." Wikipedia, "The Samurai (TV series)," Last modified on February 12, 2011. Retrieved September 22, 2008 from http://en.wikipedia.org/wiki/The_Samurai_(TV_series).

8. Roger J. Davies and Osamu Ikeno, *The Japanese Mind: Understanding Contemporary Japanese Culture* (North Clarendon, VT: Tuttle Publishing, 2002), 47.

9. David Lean, director, *The Bridge on the River Kwai*, (Culver City, CA: Columbia Tristar Home Video, 2005 [1957]).

10. The caption of the photo reads "Kimono Pattern Burned into Skin (Photographed at the Ujina Branch of Hiroshima First Army Hospital/around August 15, 1945)." The photographer, Gonichi Kimura, was a member of the Japanese Army Photographers' Team.

11. Umberto Eco quoted in Paul Williams, *Memorial Museums: The Global Rush to Commemorate Atrocities* (New York: Berg, 2007), 54. Originally published in Umberto Eco, "A Photograph," in *Travels in Hyperreality*, trans. William Weaver (New York: Harcourt Brace Jovanovitch, 1986), 216.

12. *Ukiyo-e*, "pictures of the Floating World," describes the popular genre of Japanese woodblock prints and paintings of the seventeenth to the nineteenth century, a period of profound cultural and social change in Japan. *Ukiyo-e* subject matter is characterized by the notion of living only for the moment and depicts the pleasures of life, beauty, and celebrity. Themes and subjects are geishas and life in the pleasure quarter of Edo (now Tokyo), the theater and kabuki actors, landscapes, historical epics, and traditional tales. Leading exponents include Hokusai, Hiroshige, and Utamaro. From the mid- to late nineteenth century *Ukiyo-e* prints came to the attention of avant-garde artists in Europe. Mary Cassatt was inspired by the color woodblocks she saw in the Japanese art exhibition at the Ecole des Beaux-Arts in Paris in 1890, see Marc Rosen and Susan Pinsky, *Mary Cassatt: Prints and Drawings from the Artist's Studio*, (Princeton: Princeton University Press), 8. I find Gonichi Kimura's photograph reminiscent of two images, in particular, from Cassatt's set of ten drypoint and acquatint color prints inspired by the Paris exhibition: *Woman Bathing* (*La Toilette*) and *The Coiffure* (*Etude*), both 1890–1891.

13. Susan Sontag, *On Photography* (London: Penguin, 1979), 14.

14. Ibid., 11.

15. Williams, *Memorial Museums*, 62.

16. Sontag, *On Photography*, 16–17.

17. E. Ann Kaplan, *Trauma Culture: The Politics of Terror and Loss in Media and Literature* (New Brunswick, NJ: Rutgers University Press, 2005), 93.

18. Iris Chang, *The Rape of Nanking: The Forgotten Holocaust of World War II* (New York: Penguin Books, 1997). Chang's book frames the actions of the Japanese army in the city as an atrocity in which more than 300,000 Chinese combatants and civilians were brutally and systematically killed in late 1937 and early 1938.

19. Judith Herman, *Trauma and Recovery: The Aftermath of Violence—from Domestic Abuse to Political Terror* (New York: Basic Books, 1997), 7.
20. Sontag, *On Photography*, 65.
21. Frances Guerin and Roger Hallas, eds., *The Image and the Witness: Trauma, Memory and Visual Culture* (London: Wallflower Press, 2007), 6. Guerin and Hallas discuss the morality of the photos taken by the U.S. Army of survivors in German concentration camps which they conclude amount to the "erasure of the humanity and integrity of both the survivors and the dead."
22. Georges Bataille, "Concerning the Accounts Given by the Residents of Hiroshima," in *Trauma: Explorations in Memory*, ed. Cathy Caruth (Baltimore and London: The John Hopkins University Press, 1995), 223.
23. John Hersey, *Hiroshima* (London: Penguin Books, 1946), 60–61.
24. Sontag, *On Photography*, 21.
25. Susan Sontag, *Regarding the Pain of Others* (New York: Picador, 2003), 22.
26. Williams, *Memorial Museums*, 25.
27. Ibid., 27.
28. Ibid., 28.
29. Ibid., 8.
30. Nagasaki Atomic Bomb Museum exhibition material as of my last visit in May 2007. Paul Williams recounts that in March 1996 Nagasaki's mayor ordered the museum "to remove text and graphic photographs that made reference, although minimally, to the [Nanjing] massacre." 121–122. In contrast, the Hiroshima Peace Memorial Museum describes the Chinese inhabitants as being "slaughtered" by the Japanese army and quotes the Chinese government's figure of 300,000 killed.
31. Williams, *Memorial Museums*, 22.
32. John Breen, ed., *Yasukuni, the War Dead and the Struggle for Japan's Past* (Singapore: Horizon Books, 2007), xiii.
33. Yasukuni Shrine. Retrieved September 22, 2008 from http://www.yasukuni.or.jp/english/yushukan/index.html. The tenor of the website is now more moderate than when accessed in 2008 and refers to those "who were labeled war criminals and executed after having been tried by the Allies." Retrieved February 14, 2011 from http://www.yasukuni.or.jp/english/about/deities.html.
34. Tim Maga, *Judgment at Tokyo: The Japanese War Crimes Trials* (Lexington: The University Press of Kentucky, 2001), ix. The defendants included four former premiers (Tojo, Hiranuma, Hirota, and Koiso), three foreign ministers (Matsuoka, Shigemitsu, and Tojo), three economic and financial leaders (Hoshino, Kaya, and Suzuki), one imperial advisor (Kido), two ambassadors (Oshima and Shiratori), four war ministers (Araki, Hata, Itagaki, and Minami), two navy ministers (Nagano and Shimada), six former generals (Koihara, Kimura, Matsui, Muto, Sato, and Umezu), and numerous senior military officers.
35. Breen, *Yasukuni*, xiii.
36. Williams, *Memorial Museums*, 121.
37. Takahashi Tetsuya, "Legacies of Empire: the Yasukuni shrine controversy," in *Yasukuni, the War Dead and the Struggle for Japan's Past*, ed. John Breen (Singapore: Horizon Books, 2007), 105.
38. Williams, *Memorial Museums*, 8.
39. Yushukan exhibition material (October, 2006).

40. Samuel Walker, *Prompt and Utter Destruction: Truman and the Use of Atomic Bombs against Japan* (Chapel Hill and London: The University of North Carolina Press, revised edition 2004), xii.
41. Herman, *Trauma and Recovery*, 1.
42. Williams, *Memorial Museums*, 136.
43. Wood and Byatt, *Memory*, 7.
44. James E. Young, "Memory and Counter-Memory: The End of the Monument in Germany," *Harvard Design Magazine* 9 (Fall, 1999): 6.
45. See Norman Bryson's elaboration of "visuality" in Walker and Chaplin, *Visual Culture*, 22.
46. I am paraphrasing of Paul Klee's statement: "Art does not reproduce the visible; rather it makes visible" in Walker and Chaplin, *Visual Culture*, 23. Originally published in Paul Klee, "Creative Credo" (1920), *The Inward Vision: Watercolors, Drawings and Writings by Paul Klee*, (New York: Abrams, 1959), 5.
47. Guerin and Hallas, *The Image and the Witness*, 2.

7 Denying Denial
Trauma, Memory, and Automobility at Roadside Car Crash Shrines

Robert M. Bednar

In an interview with Sylvère Lotringer, Paul Virilio proposes building what he calls a "Museum of Accidents" to demonstrate that accidents are intrinsic to contemporary technological systems of social organization.[1] Virilio says that "Each invention creates the possibility of a specific failure": the train creates the derailment; the ship creates the shipwreck; the airplane creates the plane crash; and the car creates the car crash.[2] As Virilio sees it, the problem is that these accidents are coded as anomalies in an otherwise functioning system, which has the effect of containing the accident as an aberration—an abject disruption of the system instead of part of the system itself—"something that shouldn't have happened and would take everyone by surprise."[3] The Museum of Accidents would not only commemorate accidents as "integral" to a technological society but also be organized experientially so that visitors to the museum would have to *perform* the accident in some sense as they move through the museum. Virilio argues that a Museum of Accidents is necessary because "the accident has to be *exposed*, to play on words: exposing oneself to accident or exposing the accident. The major accident is the Medusa of modernity. To look Medusa in the face, you have to use a mirror. Its face has to be turned around, and this is the aim of the Museum of Accidents."[4] If such a Museum were created, Virilio says, the accident might begin "to have a place in history, through its memory"; it might begin "to have a place not simply as an accident, but as an element that runs parallel to positivity."[5]

I would like to suggest that a version of Virilio's Museum of Accidents already exists, but not exactly in the form he articulates. The Museum is not located in a singular place that archives and curates displays of accidents to the public through some institutional apparatus officially designated with the power to do so. Instead, the Museum is radically dispersed and collectively authored. Like Virilio's Museum, it hails visitors through complex dynamics of mirroring and distancing that expose the accident to viewers and expose the connections between the viewer and the accident. Most important, it is even more "experiential" than Virilio's vision of a Museum, taking the "museum" to visitors out there on the roads and streets of the automotive landscape where car accidents themselves occur, emplacing it in such a way as to make accidents visible right next to cars and drivers going about the business of automobility, where people encounter evidence of the "negative" fatal accident while performing the "positive" of autonomous mobility.

I am speaking of roadside car crash shrines, vernacular memorial assemblages built by private individuals at sites where family and friends have died in automobile accidents, either while driving cars or motorcycles or being hit by cars as pedestrians, bicyclists, or motorcyclists. Prevalent for decades in Latin America and in the American Southwest, roadside car crash shrines are now seen throughout the U.S. and around the world. Some are simply small white crosses, almost silent markers of deathsites; others are elaborate collections of objects, texts, and materials from all over the map culturally and physically, all significantly brought together not in the home or in a cemetery but on the roadside, in drivable public space, a space of what Raymond Williams has called "mobile privatization": a public space where private individuals perform private identities, together.[6]

Every year in the U.S., around 40,000 people die and over two million people are injured in some of the more than six million car crashes reported to the police. The numbers have trended downwards for the last thirty years, with a peak of nearly 55,000 reached in 1973.[7] Even with the

Figure 7.1 Soledad Canyon Road, South of Palmdale, California, 2006. Photo by author.

downward trend, though, those are enormous numbers. Indeed, the car crash haunts automobility—with its spectral presence hiding in the light, embedded throughout automobile culture—and car crash shrines are only one of its ghosts.[8] The car as ruin is encoded into its very form: we see the end game of the car crash inscribed into cars in the form of bumpers, seat belts, air bags, etc., and in the roadscape in the form of crash barriers. Unable to prevent car crashes, the culture is focused instead on minimizing their impact.

But while both a car's bumper and its chassis are designed to absorb and distribute the energy of the crash, and crash barriers are designed to do the same, there is no institutionally legitimated cultural technology to do the same thing for the people involved in car crashes—and no large-scale cultural practice of memorializing car crash deaths, no means of generalizing the trauma, no way of "translating the energy" of the crash into a politically significant process of public memory. Instead, the cultural work of remembering people killed in and by cars is left to individuals—sometimes individuals working within state-sponsored memorial programs, but more likely individuals constructing roadside shrines on their own.[9]

Perhaps it is fitting that the car crash, the spectacular end to a life of radically individual automobility, is figured individually as well, but the result is that as a form of cultural memory, roadside shrines are so idiosyncratic, so dispersed, and so diffused that they are difficult to perceive as a collectivity. Embedded as they are in someone else's territory, unable to police their own boundaries, heavily regulated and actually illegal in many states, and unable to make themselves officially known as public memories, they each fight their way into the collective consciousness, one by one.

The purpose of this chapter is to "collect" roadside car crash shrines by situating them within a dynamic of interlocking contemporary discourses— trauma, memory, automobility—where the dispersed and individual acts of road trauma, memorializing road trauma, *and* experiencing other people's acts of memorializing road trauma all mirror each other as they intersect on the road. My work here is based on mobile fieldwork I have been conducting for the last eight years, where I have been visiting this "museum" by traveling throughout the American Southwest looking for shrines, photographing them, and writing about their importance in contemporary U.S. culture.[10] Most of the work by other scholars studying roadside shrines has worked to show what roadside shrines mean to the people who build, maintain, and use them, establishing that the primary function of roadside shrines is to create a both a performative space for memory and mourning and a potential warning to other drivers to pay attention to the shrines to avoid their fate.[11] But I am more interested here in how roadside shrines work as collective memory forms for the rest of us—the drivers who drive past the shrines, for whom these deaths are anonymous and for whom the wrenching stories of traumatic loss, grief, and mourning are invisible. We "know" there *is* a story, but we do not "remember" the story itself. What we have instead are the shrines themselves: a collection of dispersed visual, material, and spatial forms we encounter on the roadside.

I argue that roadside car crash shrines remember trauma through a visual/material form that, like trauma itself, intrudes upon the everyday spaces in which they are located. As crash shrines memorialize private individuals in public space, they embody both a refusal to accept car crash deaths as collateral damage within automobility and an affective reminder to other drivers that the everyday traumas of automobility are not only individual traumas, but part of a collective trauma. The best way to see this spatially-defined dynamic operating is to place roadside car crash shrines not only within the discourses of trauma, memory, and memorialization, but also within the discourse of automobility. There, it becomes clear that when the family and friends of crash victims build shrines in the public right-of-way to help them work through their own traumas, these shrines also form a kind of vicarious trauma witnessed by other drivers. Passing drivers may not know what happened at the site, but seeing the shrine, they will clearly know that a death occurred, making space for a quiet but palpable recognition that the everyday traumas experienced within automobility are not a by-product of automobility but are instead central to its functioning.[12]

As spatially anchored stories of loss and defiance that transform a personal trauma into a public trauma, roadside shrines to car accident victims give visual, material, and spatial form to private memories that would otherwise be lost, ignored, or invisible. As such, they constitute a distinctive kind of memory with a distinctive kind of collective, and my analysis of them will contribute to the ongoing work of scholars of visual culture, material culture, and critical cultural geography engaged in understanding spatially anchored visual and material public memory forms. In performing and embodying memory visually and materially, shrines work against the personal and cultural acts of denial that allow drivers to step into their cars every day *knowing* that they could die at any moment but *believing* that it would never happen to them. In short, they deny denial. And seen this way, roadside car crash shrines start to look a lot like Virilio's Museum of Accidents.

ROAD TRAUMA AND CULTURAL MEMORY

The dominant model of trauma in trauma studies, derived from the work of Freud and associated with contemporary theorists such as Cathy Caruth, Bessel Van Der Kolk, and Onno Van Der Hart, emphasizes dissociation. Trauma separates the self from the conscious cognitive experience of and thus the memory of a traumatic event, which makes traumatic memory function outside narrative, living in the affective realm, where it is primarily experienced in belated, latent, intrusive repetition.[13] As Roger Luckhurst argues, the traumatic subject, both individual and cultural, is "dispersed 'horizontally' in various forms of dissociation. It cannot remember itself to itself; it has no cohesive narrative."[14] Consequently, as Ann Kaplan writes, because trauma does not produce narrative memory and "because the traumatic experience has not been given meaning, the subject is continually haunted by it in dreams, flashbacks, and hallucinations."[15] The goal of trauma therapy is then to "work-through" trauma to bridge that gap of dissociation so that the subject can not only "remember itself to itself," but also communicate that memory to others.

This understanding of trauma originated in psychoanalytic theory and practice, where it was first applied in individual psychotherapy. But trauma scholars also have applied this model to understand collective forms of trauma such as war, genocide, forced migration, and natural disasters as well, developing a body of work particularly concerned with the role of collective trauma in both the need for and struggle over cultural memory.[16] The question here is: if a group of people experiences trauma, does it produce a similar dissociative process that shapes how that trauma is remembered and communicated? Does the memory of large-scale cultural trauma take the form of intrusive "dreams, flashbacks, and hallucinations" as well? More recently, scholars analyzing the news media coverage of events like September 11th also have argued that the *mediated* collective experience of trauma takes similar forms as it is incorporated into cultural memory. For example, Alison Landsberg characterizes the shared memory of mediated events as a form of "prosthetic memory."[17] Similarly, Ann Kaplan applies the terms "secondary trauma" and "vicarious trauma"—terms originally used by psychotherapists to describe the traumas therapists experience as they help their clients work through trauma—to contemporary media audiences' experiences of trauma through television, film, and photojournalism. [18]

My work on shrines seeks to bring together these two strands within trauma studies—the study of direct individual experiences of large-scale trauma and the study of vicarious witnessing of trauma—to theorize roadside shrines as isolated, individual material forms of vicarious trauma memories of an otherwise large-scale trauma dispersed throughout the material and cultural landscape. A single car crash is immensely traumatic to the people directly involved, and friends and family members who build shrines create a shared space for mourning through the shrine. But what about for those of us driving by? How is road trauma shared publicly, and what kind of collective is formed though that sharing? How is it similar to and different from other forms of traumatic collective memory?

When individual traumatic memories of road deaths are shared in public, the act of sharing them opens up a potential space for connection through the experience of vicarious trauma. In this, they are like other "public" traumas. For instance, Roger Luckhurst argues that when traumatic subjects form a collective, it is a potentially intense but always also contingent, fragile, and effervescent public, built on what he calls "temporary communalities."[19] However, the trauma represented by roadside shrines is both unlike the sustained, collective, and catastrophic trauma of war, genocide, or forced migration *and* unlike the equally dispersed but more distanced experience of audiencing trauma through media technologies.

The kind of memory performed at roadside shrines could be seen as a form of intrusive familial remembrance of transgenerational knowledge of trauma at a cultural scale, the kind that has been theorized as "post-memory" in Holocaust studies and as "re-memory" in diaspora studies. Marianne Hirsch uses the term "post-memory" to describe the ways that the transgenerational memory of the Holocaust is lived as an embodied memory for the descendents of Holocaust victims.[20] Ann Kaplan notes that "in transgenerational trauma subjects are haunted by tragedies affecting their parents, grandparents, or ancestors from far back without conscious knowledge. In a sense, transgenerational trauma is a kind of unconscious vicarious trauma."[21] Likewise, Divya Tolia-Kelly, writing about the domestic shrines of British Asian women, calls such embodied experiences of diffused private/public memories "re-memories."[22] Tolia-Kelly defines re-memory as "a form of synthesized embodied heritage" that is stimulated by material sights, sounds, scents and textures and felt as "an intimate resonance with past narratives of others' not known"—a visceral personal memory even for people without direct personal experience of the people, places, and things the memory represents.[23]

Road traumas can certainly generate transgenerational post-memories and re-memories as their stories are translated through family stories and family rituals, but for strangers it would work differently. Roadside shrines establish this same kind of diffused, indirect relationship between the traumas they represent and the people driving by them who witness them, but ultimately, the public trauma represented in car crash shrines is most like the kinds of "everyday traumas" recently engaged in the recent work of Ann Cvetkovich and Kathleen Stewart. Cvetkovich has collected an analysis of lesbian "sites of trauma" into "an archive of feelings," which allowed her to identify and explore "a sense of trauma connected to the textures of everyday experience," where "affective experience can provide the basis for new cultures."[24] Cvetkovich shows how trauma texts—*and* the act of collecting dispersed trauma texts—can create temporary affective affiliations that can be used to both break through existing collectives and form new collectives. Likewise, Kathleen Stewart collects everyday acts that seek to create at least a temporary "we-feeling." Such an "ordinary affect . . . permeates politics of all kinds with the demand that some kind of intimate public of onlookers recognize something in a space of shared impact. If only for a minute."[25]

A roadside shrine is just such a momentary "space of shared impact," where drivers speeding by a shrine are presented with intrusive cultural flashbacks of vicarious traumas that pertain directly to the activity they are presently embarked upon: driving a car through the spaces of automobility.

Shrines form a dispersed material "archive" of traumatic experiences within the public right of way that, as Stewart puts it, "demand that some kind of intimate public of onlookers recognize something."[26] Like the affiliations focused on everyday trauma that Cvetkovich studies, shrines are mediations of trauma that themselves take the form of traumatic memory—intrusive, affective, visual, material—and do so not just for the people who knew and loved those who died at the site, but also for the rest of us who drive past them. If the shrines were not located on the roadside, they would not work the same way at all, for as Elizabeth Hallam and Jenny Hockey write, when a site of accidental death is actively performed and commemorated in public space, the site "materializes memories," and the original space of the trauma itself plays a critical role in the process.[27]

Roadside shrines are an intrusive presence in the roadscape, an affective reminder of the everyday traumas of automobility. But they are also affective reminders that we are living in denial because we appear to *need* denial about the prevalence and immanence of automobile deaths. There they sit, these silent witnesses to another reality that won't go away, no matter what we may wish, reminding us to remember that we forget. As individual shrine builders heal through repeating their encounter with the affective memory embodied in the shrine site, they bring the trauma to the rest of us, giving us an intrusive traumatic memory for us to work through in a different way. Together, they comprise an embodied, material refusal to either ignore car crash deaths or accept car crash deaths as a matter of course. Together, they deny denial by performing a "Museum of Accidents" on the roadside, where drivers driving by them are forced to experience them as something intimately connected with their own mobility.

TRAUMA, MEMORY, AND AUTOMOBILITY

Roadside car crash shrines are part of a wider worldwide phenomenon: something that folklorist Jack Santino calls "spontaneous shrines."[28] With roots reaching deeply and widely through many different cultural traditions, shrines to people who die suddenly in car accidents, murders, and political violence have proliferated in recent years. Consider Oklahoma City, Princess Diana, the Space Shuttle Columbia, Columbine, September 11th, and others. All spontaneous shrines aim to "make sense of senseless deaths"—deaths made surprising in a socio-cultural context where we "have gained such control over death that we now expect to die only of old age."[29] Spontaneous shrines memorialize "unanticipated violent deaths of people who do not fit into categories of those we expect to die, who may be engaging in routine activities in which there is a reasonable expectation of safety." [30]

Like roadside shrines, all spontaneous shrines are located not in cemeteries but within those spaces of everyday life where the unexpected deaths occurred—on roadside rights-of-way, sidewalks, fences, buildings, etc. Jack Santino argues that spontaneous shrines "insert and insist upon the presence of absent people"—they "place deceased individuals back into the fabric of society, into the middle of areas of commerce and travel, into everyday life as it is being lived."[31] Indeed, Santino calls them "performative commemoratives," and argues that because they occur in the public sphere, spontaneous shrines are both commemorative (dedicated to sustaining the memory of individuals and events) and performative (meant to "make something happen"—to materially transform the space of the event, the significance of an event, and anyone who interacts with the site).[32] The clearest example of this is when a spontaneous shrine performatively commemorates a singular violent event with manifest (though not monolithic) cultural significance, such as the World Trade Center explosions, which produced a "Ground Zero" serving as the locus for negotiating cultural memory.[33] The question then is what role space plays in more dispersed traumas such as the car crash, which works on an entirely different scale.

If the spatial anchorage of all spontaneous shrines is inseparable from what they do and how they do it, the space where roadside car crash spontaneous shrines exist is particularly important. Instead of being contained in a finite time and space where it can be celebrated, suppressed, managed, or ignored, affective traumatic memory intrudes upon consciousness, demanding an embodied experience of trauma right there, right then, all over again. And this is just like a roadside shrine, which is not only a materialization of the trauma of the individuals involved in that specific shrine, but a materialization of the larger *social* and *cultural* trauma associated with cars and car culture—the trauma of unassimilated, abject deaths with nowhere to go. Roadside car crash shrines can be consciously or unconsciously ignored, but once they do register with drivers, they work to represent and perform vicarious trauma—an intrusive, repetitive reminder of the trauma of others that simultaneously *speaks to* and *speaks of* automobility as it *speaks out of* automobility.

Here I am drawing on Jill Bennett's distinction between affective memory and narrative memory. Where narrative memory works in and through linguistic representation to be *about* a memory, affective memory is where "affective experience is not simply referenced, but activated or staged in some sense" by a process of "registering and producing affect," which produces "not so much a *speaking of* but *speaking out of* a particular memory or experience."[34] In this moment of contact between bodies that feel memories, even strangers potentially can feel another's pain as their own, not in an act of colonization of the other or even of projection of sameness, but just the opposite: feeling another's pain as a wound that ruptures the subject/object split instead of as the distanced pain of a contained other; it is "the point at which one both feels and knows feeling to be the property of an other."[35] Roadside shrines create memory spaces that can work on strangers as they work for intimates, and their location on the side of the road, where they can speak of and speak from automobility at the same time, opens a space not only for memory, but for recognition.

In this case, recognition is necessary to both revealing *and* mitigating structural forgetting. Erika Doss argues that spontaneous memorials are part of a larger contemporary "memorial mania" in the U.S.—a kind of "manic" and "excessive" compulsion to memorialize ordinary life in "visibly public contexts" that reveals a culture with an anxious relationship to time, history, and memory.[36] This is a point Marita Sturken also makes in *Tourists of History*, where she argues that the "surprise" of events like the Oklahoma City bombing and the 9/11 terrorist attacks is in part attributable to the prevailing attitude towards history and public memory in the contemporary U.S.[37] However, while I also see roadside car crash shrines representing these larger contemporary cultural discourses about trauma, death, and memory, I think it is even more important to locate shrines specifically and concretely within the discourse of automobility, which produces an additional layer of structural forgetting of everyday trauma in the U.S.

Part of this structural forgetting is due to the nature of road deaths themselves. Roadside car crash shrines are distinguished not only by their intimate spatial connection to automobility but also in the fact that they often memorialize local deaths of relatively unknown people—the kinds of deaths that hardly make the local papers, much less around-the-clock cable news coverage. Where some violent deaths can be made meaningful as cultural sacrifices by using spontaneous shrines to recuperate private deaths within discourses of nation and citizenship, the deaths of ordinary people who die in car crashes resist sense-making at the national, global, or even local scale. As Gregory Ulmer argues, this is because "traffic fatalities are fundamentally 'abject'": if they perform a cultural sacrifice on behalf of some larger cultural value, that value "remains inarticulate, within the bodies and behaviors of individuals in the private sphere, untransformed, nontranscendent, unredeemed."[38] In the absence of some larger public apparatus designed to shift each act of memory from "the sphere of one-at-a-time individual personal loss to the public sphere of collective identity," individual mourners remembering road deaths are left to take matters into their own hands.[39] But it is more than that. The very feature that gives a roadside shrine its material affect—its unique spatial relationship to a site of trauma—is the thing that keeps car crash memorial practices dispersed, and thus mitigates seeing them as a collective. Shrine builders consistently maintain that the site of death is central to the practice of building car crash shrines, mostly because shrine builders tend to see the sites not as death sites, but as "last alive" sites.[40] Moving the memorial elsewhere would negate the shrine's function as a spatially unique portal between the living and the dead, where mourning intervenes in the site of trauma.

Ubiquitous but dispersed, roadside shrines do not cohere in time or space to seem like anything more than a statistical (as opposed to a cultural) collective. One of the purposes of my larger study of car crash shrines, then, has been to build my own archive—to perform my own act of collective witnessing of road trauma so that I can then share it with others, as I am doing in this chapter. This is a goal I share with Jennifer Clark, who takes a similar approach in her study of roadside shrines in Australia and New Zealand. Clark argues that roadside shrines represent "the only way to register and put into public debate repeated road death as the disturbing outcome of automobility"; and even then, they exist as "an accumulation of small crashes" that have "the numbers" but not "the purpose" to elevate them or collect them into a palpable group.[41] Learning to see shrines "can challenge us to broaden our idea of motoring heritage" to include the "dark side" of the cultural history of the automobile and car culture into a collective heritage, or cultural memory, of both the benefits and costs of automobile-centered mobility.[42]

As a form of memory, car crash shrines are as quiet as they are ubiquitous. Experienced as they are by most people as small features of a striated landscape flying by outside the windshield or window, they can't hope to "say" much beyond their materiality. Compared to other more official and elaborate forms of cultural memory such as statuary, historical markers, named buildings, streets, etc., a roadside shrine is particularly mute. But it does carry a certain power—the power of "spatially anchored" material self-evidence.[43] Indeed, the material situatedness of a roadside shrine—its location at or near the location where someone died on the road—is its primary claim for authority, forming the foundation of the self-evident material appeal to undeniability it makes upon passers-by: here, right where the shrine is, something terrible happened, and this shrine simultaneously represents and performs that fact. This material self-evident appeal carries with it other implicit appeals: This should not have happened; I do not accept this as a matter of course; I will not allow you to ignore it either; by building this shrine where I have, I am making my personal story public; I refuse to forget, and I refuse to let you forget either. In short, in addition to their explicit communication, they "say": don't let *this* happen to you or someone who loves you or someone you love—where "this" is not only the crash and the death but also the materially present grief and anguish that drives the construction of the shrine itself. And this is exactly where the memory politics of roadside shrines are located. For if they demand recognition of private loss in public, they also attempt to make their own grief public, to demonstrate their own attempts at sighting memory.

But in actively working to sight memory, roadside shrines are a material reminder not only of memory but of a structured forgetting. Kenneth Foote argues that the American landscape is "shadowed ground," repeatedly inscribed, erased, and re-inscribed with acts of violence and tragedy, some of which are remembered extensively and many others which are forgotten—either through intentional suppression or by the slow erosion of neglect.[44] The unspoken, invisible past traumas of car crashes haunt the landscape of roadside America and the people who drive through it. Sometimes the materializations of these "shadows" are faint and easy to ignore, as in the ubiquitous but barely visible figures of the dented guardrail and the tree scar throughout the roadscape, or in the material history of past crashes inscribed in the dented bodies of vehicles driving alongside you on the road. When there is not a shrine to materially perform a memory of a death to passers-by, the roadscape can sometimes still remember the crash—contained in these even more subtle material reminders. The sites carry their memories more like a large-gauge wire is said to have a tensile memory: as a material representation and performance of its traumatic reshaping, with only limited access for passers-by to narratives about how or why the reshaping has occurred.

When these materializations of past crashes are incorporated into a larger shrine site—especially when they are accompanied by other material traces of the crash itself, such as burn patterns, skid marks, police outlines, and the ruins of crashed cars—tree scars, bent guardrails, and smashed car parts become spatial anchors that further materialize the traumatic content and form of a roadside shrine by *speaking out of* the material of the crash itself instead of *speaking of* the crash. Then, the shrine site becomes what Pierre Nora calls a *"lieu de memoire"*—a particular space where memory

Figure 7.2   US Highway 64, Carson National Forest, West of Tres Piedras, New Mexico, 2003. Photo by author.

both "crystallizes and secretes itself" in material form through multiple visual, material, and spatial means.[45] However, unlike Nora's sites, shrine sites do not appear to be always already *national* sites. They remember citizens without a clearly collective identity in a space that by itself makes no apparent claim to collectivity as well.

Jörg Beckmann argues that "automobility 'works,' *because its accidents are denied*. Collective denial enables individual mobility."[46] In a system where drivers' rights to autonomous mobility are not structured as conscious choices but are experienced as naturalized, taken-for-granted citizenship rights, the naturalizing of automobility in general and driving as a performative practice is dependent on denying the risks to self and others implied in the system from the beginning. Beckmann reasons that "if it wasn't the subject of denial, the wreck would simply be left in the ditch, as a testament to the dangerous aspects of driving along that particular stretch of road"—as a kind of *memento mori* displaying the risks of driving to discipline its drivers.[47] Each time an accident scene is "cleansed" by police, EMS, and road crews, the evidence of the risk of driving is materially denied. By rendering evidence of the lack of safety invisible, the crash clean-up not only reasserts the discourse of safety but facilitates the discourse of automobility by reinforcing the structured forgetting of the everyday traumas embedded in automobility.[48]

However, this "cleansing" of road crashes does leave its own traces in the roadscape. At some shrine sites, the deathsite is not only represented by a shrine but also by markings on the road and roadside placed there by police investigators: spray-painted outlines of vehicles where they came to rest, spray-painted skid paths, and the resonant letters "POI," or Point of Impact. One day these markings will fade, but their presence is a clear reminder not only that a car crash happened, but also that it was significant enough to mobilize the state apparatus around building a theory of cause, effect, and blame. They remind us that an investigated car crash encodes a different kind of public memory: the official determination of personal responsibility and innocence represented in the police report, which, along with parallel insurance company investigations, seeks to render a public interpretation of the crash— especially when there are criminal and civil charges at stake. But this is not the kind of public I have in mind when I say that car crashes have the potential to form new collective memories. Indeed, the process of officially determining or denying responsibility is the most forceful neoliberal form of re-privatizing of death that can happen in the case of a car crash: whether through absolution or conviction of individual drivers, the official determination of cause always lets the culture off the hook.

PRESENTING MEMORY

Roadside shrines are places where strangers visually and materially encounter an "intimate resonance" of the person who died *and* the people who build and maintain the shrines.[49] Whatever else you know, you know that they were here, right where you drive by or where you stand—that they died here or they constructed a shrine here. The shrine provides material evidence of both. In this way, roadside shrines, *by their very presence in the public right of way* (and even more by their form and their content), inscribe the past in the present, the sacred in the profane, the private in the public. As they do, they bring the politics of affect into the discourse of automobility, challenging drivers to remember that the risks of automobility are inscribed into the apparatus itself.

Given this inscription, it is important to recognize that a car crash reveals both the breakdown *and* the apotheoisis of automotive sociality—the collision of simultaneity that demands exchange, a crash of previously dispersed individual realities colliding into one another, a breakdown of one system and a breakthrough of another. And a shrine speaks of, to and from this dynamic, registering both a belief in and a betrayal by automobility: their location on the roadside presupposes that people in automobiles will see them in roadspace, which itself presupposes continuing automobility. As such, roadside shrines inscribe the landscape with affective, traumatic memory sites where memories intrude on our lives as drivers of public space unexpectedly, without us asking for them to do so, and they come in an evocative form, a visual/material/spatial form that shares with the language of dreams an iconicity that communicates visually and materially in excess of their explicit messages. Roadside car crash shrines take the "Museum of Accidents" to the accident sites themselves. They remind us that the trauma occurred, and they do so in a material context contiguous with the original context of the death.

For even if we do not know the narrative details, shrines on the side of the road insure that we remember that people die on the highways doing the exact thing we are doing when we see them: driving, going about the business of living everyday lives, believing in reaching a projected destination— believing, in short, that the future exists. After all, we can see the future up ahead, through the windshield, and we are driving into it, performing freedom and autonomy. But then again, the shrines are there to remind us that other drivers were doing the same thing when they died as well.

NOTES

1. Sylvère Lotringer and Paul Virilio, *The Accident of Art*, trans. Michael Taormina (New York: Semiotexte, 2005). For a more extensive engagement of Virilio, acceleration and car accidents, see Arnar Árnason, Sigurjón Baldur Hafsteinsson, and Tinna Grétarsdóttir, "Acceleration Nation: An Investigation Into the Violence of Speed and the Uses of Accidents in Iceland," *Culture, Theory & Critique* 48 (2007): 199–217.
2. Lotringer and Virilio, *The Accident of Art*, 103.
3. Ibid., 98.
4. Ibid., 102; italics in original.

5. Ibid., 96.
6. Raymond Williams, *Towards 2000* (London: Hogarth Press, 1983), 187–89.
7. See National Highway Traffic Safety Administration, "Traffic Safety Facts: 2008 Traffic Safety Annual Assessment—Highlights." Retrieved June 16, 2009 from http://www.nrd.nhtsa.dot.gov/Pubs/811172.pdf.
8. While car crashes may be "hard to see" within spaces of automobility, they are continually rehearsed—even fetishized—in cinema and television. See Mikita Brottman, ed. *Car Crash Culture* (New York: Palgrave, 2001); and Paul Newland, "Look Past the Violence: Automotive Destruction in American Movies," *European Journal of American Culture* 28 (2009): 5–20.
9. In the U.S., several states offer individual survivors the option of purchasing an official state-produced sign that memorializes crash victims. For example, where I live, in Texas, the Texas Department of Transportation (TxDOT) has a Memorial Sign Program that allows survivors of victims of "impaired driving" fatalities to pay to have official "Please Don't Drink and Drive" signs installed at the site of a fatal crash. The survivors must apply to be considered for such a sign, and program guidelines also explicitly stipulate that "An impaired driver is not eligible for a Memorial Sign." Accessed July 10, 2009, http://www.txdot.gov/public_involvement/memorial_program.htm. This is clear example of the necropolitics of road death memorialization, where states use their control over the roads to make some road deaths more abject than others. When the state determines that a car crash death is abject, the road death is institutionally forgotten. See Achille Mbembe, "Necropolitics," trans. Libby Meintjes, *Public Culture* 15 (2003): 11–40.
10. See Robert M. Bednar, "Touching Images: Towards a Visual/Material Cultural Study of Roadside Shrines," *Brown Working Papers in the Arts & Sciences*, Southwestern University, 7 (2007), http://www.southwestern.edu/academic/bwp/vol7/bednar-vol7.pdf, accessed June 29, 2009; Robert M. Bednar, "Making Space on the Side of the Road: Towards a Cultural Study of Roadside Car Crash Memorials," in *The World is a Text: Writing, Reading and Thinking About Culture and its Contexts*, vol. 3, eds. Jonathan Silverman and Dean Rader (Upper Saddle River, NJ: Pearson, 2009), 497–508, available online; http://www.southwestern.edu/~bednarb/roadsidememorials, accessed June 29, 2009; and Robert M. Bednar, *Road Scars: Trauma, Memory, and Automobility* (forthcoming).
11. See Rudolfo Anaya, Denise Chavez, and Juan Estevan Arellano, *Descansos: An Interrupted Journey* (Albuquerque: El Norte Publications, 1995); Alberto Barrera, "Mexican-American Roadside Crosses in Starr County," in *Hecho en Tejas: Texas-Mexican Folk Arts and Crafts*, ed. Joe S. Graham (Denton, TX: University of North Texas Press, 1997), 278–92; Bednar, "Making Space on the Side of the Road"; Jennifer Clark, "Challenging Motoring Functionalism: Roadside Memorials, Heritage and History in Australia and New Zealand," *The Journal of Transport History* 29 (2008): 23–43; Jennifer Clark and Ashley Cheshire, "R.I.P.: A Comparative Study of Roadside Memorials in New South Wales, Australia and Texas, USA," *Omega: The Journal of Death and Dying* 35 (2003–2004): 229–48; Jennifer Clark and Majella Franzmann, "'A Father, a Son, My Only Daughter': Memorializing Road Trauma," *RoadWise* 13 (2002): 4–10; Jennifer Clark and Majella Franzmann, "Authority From Grief: Presence and Place in the Making of Roadside Memorials," *Death Studies* 30 (2006): 579–99; Charles Collins and Charles Rhine, "Roadside Memorials," *Omega: The Journal of Death and Dying* 47 (2003): 221–44; Holly Everett, *Roadside Crosses in Contemporary Memorial Culture* (Denton, TX: University of North Texas

Press, 2002); Sylvia Grider, "Roadside Crosses: Vestiges of Colonial Spain in Contemporary New Mexico," in *Descansos: The Sacred Landscape of New Mexico*, ed. Joan E. Alessi (Santa Fe: Fresco Fine Art Publications, 2006), 11–28; Kate V. Hartig and Kevin M. Dunn, "Roadside Memorials: Interpreting New Deathscapes in Newcastle, New South Wales," *Australian Geographical Studies* 36 (1998): 5–21; Rebecca Kennerly, "Getting Messy: In the Field and at the Crossroads With Roadside Shrines," *Text/Performance Quarterly* 22 (2002): 229–60; Mirjam Klaassens, Peter Groote, and Paulus P. P. Huigen, "Roadside Memorials From a Geographical Perspective," *Mortality* 14 (2009): 187–20; Anna Petersson, "Swedish *Offercast* and Recent Roadside Memorials," *Folklore* 120 (2009): 75–91; Jon K. Reid and Cynthia L. Reid, "A Cross Marks the Spot: A Study of Roadside Death memorials in Texas and Oklahoma," *Death Studies* 25 (2001): 341–56.

12. My work on automobility is situated in a larger body of work on the "discourse of automobility." For an introduction to the field of automobility studies, see Mike Featherstone, "Automobilities: An Introduction," *Theory, Culture & Society* 21 (2004): 1–24. See also Mimi Sheller and John Urry, "The City and the Car," *International Journal of Urban and Regional Research* 24 (2000): 737–57; Sheller and Urry, eds., *Mobile Technologies of the City* (London: Routledge, 2006); John Urry, *Sociology Beyond Societies: Mobilities For the Twenty-First Century* (London: Routledge, 2000); John Urry, *Mobilities* (London: Polity Press, 2007); Tim Cresswell, *On the Move: Mobility in the Modern Western World* (London: Routledge, 2006). For work specifically on automobility as a discourse and apparatus of neoliberal governmentality, see Jeremy Packer, "Disciplining Mobility: Governing and Safety," in *Foucault, Cultural Studies, and Governmentality*, eds. Jack Z. Bratich, Jeremy Packer, and Cameron McCarty (Albany: SUNY Press, 2003), 135–61; Sudhir Chella Rajan, "Automobility, Liberalism, and the Ethics of Driving," *Environmental Ethics* 29 (2007): 77–90; Jeremy Packer, *Mobility Without Mayhem: Safety, Cars, and Citizenship* (Durham: Duke University Press, 2008); Cotten Seiler, *Republic of Drivers: A Cultural History of Automobility in America* (Chicago: University of Chicago Press, 2008).

13. Cathy Caruth, "Trauma and Experience: Introduction," in *Trauma: Explorations in Memory*, ed. Cathy Caruth (Baltimore: Johns Hopkins University Press, 1995), 3–12; Cathy Caruth, "Recapturing the Past: Introduction," in *Trauma: Explorations in Memory*, ed. Cathy Caruth (Baltimore: Johns Hopkins University Press, 1995), 151–57; Cathy Caruth, *Unclaimed Experience: Trauma, Narrative, and History* (Baltimore: Johns Hopkins University Press, 1996); Bessel A. Van Der Kolk and Onno Van Der Hart, "The Intrusive Past: The Flexibility of Memory and the Engraving of Trauma," in *Trauma: Explorations in Memory*, ed. Cathy Caruth (Baltimore: Johns Hopkins University Press, 1995), 158–82. See also Judith Herman, *Trauma and Recovery: The Aftermath of Violence—From Domestic Abuse to Political Terror*, 2nd edition (New York: Basic Books, 1997).

14. Roger Luckhurst, "Traumaculture," *New Formations* 50 (2003): 28.

15. E. Ann Kaplan, *Trauma Culture: The Politics of Terror and Loss in Media and Literature* (New Brunswick, NJ: Rutgers University Press, 2005), 34.

16. See especially Caruth, *Unclaimed Experience*, and *Trauma: Explorations in Memory*; Dominick LaCapra, *Writing History, Writing Trauma* (Baltimore: Johns Hopkins Press, 2001).

17. Alison Landsberg, *Prosthetic Memory: The Transformation of American Remembrance in the Age of Mass Culture* (New York: Columbia University Press, 2004).

18. See Kaplan, *Trauma Culture*; see also Susan Sontag, *Regarding the Pain of Others* (New York: Picador, 2003).

19. Roger Luckhurst, "Traumaculture," 38.

20. Marianne Hirsch, *Family Frames: Photography, Narrative, and Postmemory* (Cambridge: Harvard University Press, 1997).

21. Kaplan, *Trauma Culture*, 106.

22. Divya Tolia-Kelly, "Locating Processes of Identification: Studying the Precipitates of Re-Memory in the British Asian Home," *Transactions of the Institute of British Geographers* 29 (2004): 314–29 (316).

23. Ibid.

24. Ann Cvetkovich, *An Archive of Feelings: Trauma, Sexuality, and Lesbian Public Cultures* (Durham: Duke University Press, 2003), 3–4, 7.

25. Kathleen Stewart, *Ordinary Affects* (Durham: Duke University Press, 2007), 39; See also Lauren Berlant, *The Queen of America Goes to Washington City* (Durham: Duke University Press, 1997); Lauren Berlant, ed., *Compassion: The Culture and Politics of an Emotion* (London: Routledge, 2004); Eve Kosofsky Sedgwick, *Touching Feeling: Affect, Pedagogy, Performativity* (Durham: Duke University Press, 2003); Mark Seltzer, "Wound Culture: Trauma in the Pathological Public Sphere," *October* 80 (1997): 24; and Mark Seltzer, *Serial Killers: Death and Life in America's Wound Culture* (New York: Routledge, 1998).

26. Stewart, *Ordinary Affects*, 39.

27. Elizabeth Hallam and Jenny Hockey, *Death, Memory & Material Culture* (Oxford: Berg, 2001), 125–6.

28. Jack Santino, "Performative Commemoratives: Spontaneous Shrines and the Public Memorialization of Death," in *Spontaneous Shrines and the Public Memorialization of Death*, ed. Jack Santino (New York: Palgrave, 2006), 5–16. See also Erika Doss, "Death, Art, and Memory in the Public Sphere: The Visual and Material Culture of Grief in Contemporary America," *Mortality* 7 (2002): 63–82; Erika Doss, "Spontaneous Memorials and Contemporary Modes of Mourning in America," *Material Religion* 2 (2006): 294–319; Erika Doss, *The Emotional Life of Public Memorials: Towards a Theory of Temporary Memorials* (Amsterdam: Amsterdam University Press, 2008); Sylvia Grider, "Public Grief and the Politics of Memorial: Contesting the Memory of 'The Shooters' at Columbine High School," *Anthropology Today* 23 (2007): 3–7; C. Allen Haney, Christina Leimer, and Juliann Lowery, "Spontaneous Memorialization: Violent Death and Emerging Mourning Ritual," *Omega: The Journal of Death and Dying* 35 (1997): 159–71; Jack Santino, ed. *Spontaneous Shrines and the Public Memorialization of Death* (New York: Palgrave, 2006); Marita Sturken, *Tourists of History: Memory, Kitsch, and Consumerism from Oklahoma City to Ground Zero* (Durham: Duke University Press, 2007).

29. Diane E. Goldstein and Diane Tye, "'The Call of the Ice': Tragedy and Vernacular Responses of Resistance, Heroic Reconstruction, and Reclamation," in *Spontaneous Shrines and the Public Memorialization of Death*, ed. Jack Santino (New York: Palgrave, 2006), 233–54 (243); Haney, Leimer, and Lowry, "Spontaneous Memorialization," 160.

30. Ibid., 161. Spontaneous shrines speak to and from "highly conflicted" contemporary attitudes towards death, and thus reflect and are structured within larger trends in death, dying and bereavement practices. See Doss, *The Emotional Life of Public Memorials*, 27. Modernist practices of medicine, death, and burial that institutionalized living, dying, and burial made death more predictably ritualistic, but also much less present in everyday life. Cultural codes against showing grief in public have also shifted, emphasizing

if anything that people are now expected to actively grieve. Contemporary practices are both more visible and more improvised, giving over to (or leaving it up to, depending on your perspective) private individuals to decide the most appropriate ways of memorializing individual deaths. See Cas Wouters, "The Quest for New Rituals in Dying and Mourning: Changes in the We-I Balance," *Body & Society* 8 (2002): 1–27. This seems to be a foundational impulse towards what may best be called the "public-izing" of death and memory in contemporary culture. More important, the private-in-public nature of spontaneous shrines is also related to a growing emphasis on the continuity between life and death in the culture. See Doss, *The Emotional Life of Public Memorials*, 20.

31. Santino, "Performative Commemoratives," 13, 5.

32. Ibid., 10.

33. See Marita Sturken, *Tourists of History: Memory, Kitsch, and Consumerism from Oklahoma City to Ground Zero* (Durham: Duke University Press, 2007).

34. Jill Bennett, "The Aesthetics of Sense-Memory: Theorising Trauma Through the Visual Arts," in *Regimes of Memory*, ed. Susannah Radstone and Katherine Hodgkin (London: Routledge, 2003), 28, 32–33. See also Jill Bennett, *Empathic Vision: Affect, Trauma, and Contemporary Art* (Palo Alto: Stanford University Press, 2005).

35. Ibid., 37.

36. Doss, *The Emotional Life of Public Memorials*, 7. Doss extends this work further in *Memorial Mania: Public Feeling in America* (Chicago: University of Chicago Press, 2010). For related work on the "contemporary culture of public commemoration," see Carole Blair and Neil Michel, "The AIDS Memorial Quilt and the Contemporary Culture of Public Commemoration," *Rhetoric & Public Affairs* 10 (2007): 595–626; Kristin Hass, *Carried to the Wall: American Memory and the Vietnam Veterans Memorial* (Berkeley: University of California Press, 1998); Marita Sturken, *Tangled Memories: The Vietnam War, The AIDS Epidemic, and the Politics of Remembering* (Berkeley: University of California Press, 1997).

37. Marita Sturken, *Tourists of History*.

38. Gregory Ulmer, "Traffic of the Spheres: Prototype for a MEmorial," in *Car Crash Culture*, ed. Mikita Brottman (New York: Palgrave, 2001), 336.

39. Ibid.

40. For instance, in *Roadside Crosses in Contemporary Memorial Culture*, Everett quotes a mother of a teen car crash victim who maintains a shrine on the roadside more than the cemetery site because "the last place that Nathan was" before going "straight to heaven" was the accident site (95). She says she visits the site frequently not only to maintain the memory of her son but to talk to her son; she says the shrine serves this purpose well because "that's kind of where I felt his spirit was last" (96). Similarly, Charles Collins and Charles Rhine noticed that many who leave written messages to people who have died address victims as if they are "departed" instead of "dead" or "deceased"—as dis-placed, disembodied, or transformed, but not "ceasing to exist." Collins and Rhine, "Roadside Memorials," 234.

41. Clark and Franzmann, "'A Father, a Son, My Only Daughter,'" 8.

42. Clark, "Challenging Motoring Functionalism," 23, 33; see also Kurt Möser, "The Dark Side of 'Automobilism,' 1900–1930: Violence, War and the Motor Car," *Journal of Transport History* 24:2 (2003): 238–58.

43. See Hastings Donnan, "Material Identities: Fixing Ethnicity in the Irish Borderlands," *Identities: Global Studies in Culture and Power* 12 (2005): 69–105 (96–99).

44. Kenneth Foote, *Shadowed Ground: America's Landscapes of Violence and Tragedy*, 2nd edition (Austin: University of Texas Press, 2003).
45. Pierre Nora, "Between Memory and History: *Les Lieux de Mémoire*," *Representations* 26 (1989): 7.
46. Beckmann, "Mobility and Safety," *Theory, Culture & Society* 21 (2004), 81–100 (94).
47. Ibid., 94–95.
48. Ibid., 97.
49. Divya Tolia-Kelly, "Locating Processes of Identification: Studying the Precipitates of Re-Memory in the British Asian Home," 316.

8 Dark Elegy

The Embodiment of Terrorism in the American Memorial Landscape

Dee Britton

The American memorial landscape reflects an ongoing contestation between public and private visualization of memory. Prior to the Civil War, commemorations of the dead were primarily limited to private burial sites. After the Civil War, a national memorial landscape was created by the construction of national cemeteries, town square memorials, and numerous Federal and Confederate memorials in public space. The wave of Civil War commemoration in public space continued through the 1920s. The national memorial landscape then remained essentially unchanged for the next fifty years as commemorative activity was decentralized to local communities. Another wave of nationalized commemoration was triggered in the 1970s by demands for public commemoration of members of the military who were lost in the Vietnam and Korean military conflicts. There was however an evolving disconnection between contemporary global conflict and the nationalized commemorative representation. During the last half of the twentieth century in Western civilization, international and intra-national conflict began to be focused upon civilian targets instead of the military and/or political entities of declared (or undeclared) wars. The first U.S. aircraft was hijacked in 1961. Munich became the site of two terrorist attacks in the early 1970s: the bombing of its airport in 1970 and the attack on Israeli athletes during the 1972 Munich Olympic Games. Airports and airplanes continued to be primary terrorist targets: the Rome airport was bombed in 1973; an Air France airplane was hijacked by members of the Popular Front for the Liberation of Palestine in 1976. Although U.S. military and diplomatic personnel continued to be primary targets in the global arena, American civilians were rarely a focus of terrorist attacks in the 1970s and the first half of the 1980s. When civilians were involved, there were rarely fatalities. For example, a Trans-World Airline aircraft was hijacked in 1985 with 153 people on board; all but one (a U.S. Navy sailor) survived. Over time the attacks became more lethal throughout the West. Bombings of airports in Rome, Vienna, and Greece in 1985 and 1986 killed twenty civilians and injured 105 people. On December 21, 1988, Pan American Flight 103 exploded over Lockerbie, Scotland, killing the 259 passengers on board and eleven people in the village. After

Figure 8.1 Suse Ellen Lowenstein, *Dark Elegy*, Montauk, New York. Photo by author.

extensive examination of debris collected from sites throughout the Scottish countryside, Scottish and American authorities determined that the explosion was caused by the detonation of explosives that had been in the plane's luggage compartment. The World Trade Center was bombed in 1993, killing six and injuring more than 1,000. The Federal Building in Oklahoma City was bombed in 1995, killing 166 and injuring hundreds. The September 11, 2001 attacks resulted in the deaths of nearly 3,000 people. Clearly, the era of American civilians' exceptionalism from terrorist violence had ended. In 2001, the U.S. declared its first war of the twenty-first century, a "War on Terror."

There have been many local memorials constructed to the victims of terrorism. But it is not surprising, with the exception of the Oklahoma City bombing, that a national memorial to victims of terrorism is absent from the memorial landscape. The Oklahoma City bombing could be memorialized because its perpetrators were American and it was not widely perceived as an attack on American identity or lifestyle. Newspaper columnist George Will stated that "paranoiacs have always been with us but have never defined us."[1] Indeed, other interpretations of McVey's and Nichols' actions identified them as "quintessentially American, securely located in the nation's tradition of populist violence."[2] Although the Oklahoma City bombing is an important violent event in American memory studies, it differed from the bombings of Pan Am 103, the World Trade Center in 1993, and the attacks of September 11, 2001. The latter were attacks on American civilians by foreign nationalists or groups adhering to an anti-American ideology that was formed outside of the U.S.

I suggest that a national memorial to victimization contradicts the American metanarrative of strength and power. Maurice Halbwachs [3] believed that all memory is constructed and deconstructed within social groups. My research suggests that "memorial worlds" [4] are composed of nine categories of people: the Lost, the Invisible, the Bereaved, the Survivors, The Creators, the Interpreters, the Agents, the Gatekeepers, and the Perpetrators. National public memorials are typically contested between the Public Agents (government officials), their Gatekeepers, the Bereaved, and the Interpreters. The collective memory or amnesia that gains dominance in the social narrative depends upon the group that gains control of the "memorial world." Therefore, collective memories may be constructed, maintained, or altered by either instrumental or cultural forces. Instrumental memories, constructed by power elites, are used to manipulate memory for current or future nationalistic purposes. Instrumental memories may significantly differ from the cultural persistence or transformation of memory which are created from social interactions of the masses.[5] Therefore, any construction of a national collective commemoration of victims of terrorism involves contestation between both the instrumental and cultural interpretations of terrorist attacks on U.S.' citizens.

There have been two Congressional proposals for the installation of a memorial in Washington D.C to commemorate civilians killed in terrorist attacks. The first bill, H.R. 2982, was introduced by Congressman Jim Turner (D-TX), co-sponsored by 121 Representatives, and passed by the House of Representatives by a vote of 418–0 on September 25, 2002.[6] This bill authorized "the establishment of a memorial to victims who died as a result of terrorist acts against the United States or its people, at home or abroad." [7] Barely a year after the attacks of September 11th, eloquent supporting testimony reflected a national mood that was very supportive of the construction of memorials to terrorism. The House bill was introduced in the Senate the following day; it was referred to the Committee on Energy and Natural Resources, where it then expired due to lack of Congressional action. Five years later, on October 1, 2007, H.R. 3707, the "Memorial Dedicated to All Victims of Terrorism Act of 2007," was introduced by Congressman Timothy Bishop (D-NY). The legislation noted that:

> This memorial serves to remind the world community of the devastation that terrorism leaves in its wake, serves as a lasting testament to the victims of terrorism worldwide in the unending struggle to eradicate this menace from the globe, and stands as a beacon for all peace-loving people throughout the world to unite.[8]

The bill was then referred to the National Capital Memorial Commission, which is a primary gatekeeper of public space in Washington. After a hearing in February 2008, the NCMC unanimously refused to support the bill. Why were these bills allowed to die in committee? The U.S. was actively nationalistic during the time that both of these bills were introduced to Congress. The country had committed substantial troops and its national budget to the "War on Terror." U.S. civilians were subjected to significant privacy invasions by numerous government agents. What explains the void in the commemorative process during a time of renewed nationalistic identity? *Dark Elegy*, the memorial designated by H.R. 3707, demonstrates the contestation between the instrumental and cultural interpretations of civilian victimization due to terrorism.

THE CONSTRUCTION OF *DARK ELEGY*

Dark Elegy was created by Suse Lowenstein, an artist born and raised in Hamburg, Germany. One of Lowenstein's sons, a Syracuse University student, was returning home from a fall semester in London on Pan Am Flight 103 when it exploded over the skies of Lockerbie, Scotland. Lowenstein described the origin of *Dark Elegy*:

> I started sculpting . . . because it is normal for me to do that . . . to create and sculpt things that are relevant in my life. Clearly Alexander's murder was the most relevant event to ever occur in my life. There is nothing more painful for a mother to have loved and nurtured a child and to have the child murdered . . . and never be heard of or thought of again. I started a sculpture of my body at the way that it felt at the very moment of learning of his death. [When that sculpture was completed] I actually created another me, symbolically . . . [one] that is helping the 'other' me that is doubled over, [one that would] stay up and stay alive . . . because your first instinct is to die. You do not want to go on. [9]

After Lowenstein completed the first two sculptures, she turned to a woman who also attended meetings of a group of family members of those killed on board Pan Am Flight 103:

> I observed one woman in particular who carried her grief with such depth and dignity that in itself it created such a physical beauty . . . I asked her if she would be interested in participating in my project, explaining to her what I was doing. And she was excited about the idea and agreed to do it and while I was speaking to her, another woman overheard what I was talking about and she approached me and asked if she could also participate . . . she really liked the idea of memorializing our loved ones. And it was at that moment that it

occurred to me how incredible it would be if the actual people came to me and allowed me to sculpt them at the very moment that they heard their loved ones had died.

The work *Dark Elegy* was born. Each person visited Lowenstein's studio and spoke about the moment when they heard that their loved one would never come home. This experience provided important support for those who participated in the *Dark Elegy* project. In modern and post-modern Western society, the bereaved are expected to quickly conclude their mourning and immediately reintegrate into society. Many of the Pan Am 103 bereaved noted the isolation that resulted from their grief and mourning. In 1988, it was unimaginable to many Americans that they could die as a result of an act of terrorism. A mother of a Pan Am Flight 103 victim stated:

> [W]e are truly in a denial. No one wants to lose children . . . nobody wants to go there in thought. I remember soon after it first happened that I would run into people in the supermarket and they would turn on their heel just so that they didn't have to deal with me . . . and I remember being furious and angry at the time. Not only was I stuck with this horrible, horrible loss . . . but I also had to deal with all these people who couldn't deal with me and that was more than I could bear. I needed friends . . . and to see them turn around and shy away . . . and now after some time has passed, I view it . . . as that they don't know any better. They don't know how to deal with it because our entire society doesn't know how to deal with it. Death is something that you get over: 'are you over it yet?'; 'is it better yet?'; 'time heals all wounds'. It doesn't happen like that.[10]

Shared trauma and bereavement rituals often provide a sense of communality to those who are bereaved. Lowenstein commented on the unique understanding that they shared:

> Thinking back to that part of the process, what comes to mind is how incredibly privileged I felt about the fact that these women could open up to the bottom of their core to what happened that particular night and also what happened before then . . . their relationship with their loved one . . . some had a huge fight the last time they spoke to their loved one. I would guide them back to that very moment . . . I wanted to be intimately familiar with where they were, who called, how did they hear and boy, would their body change . . . the sound [of their voice] would change . . . they would either weep or be dead quiet or scream, bang their fists on the ground, pull their hair.

Lowenstein photographed family members as they relived their experience, and she then helped them return to their present reality:

Often times, I would have to hug them and kind of bring them back to the here and now . . . there would be crying and hugging . . . and the sharing was really overwhelming. And again, it could have only happened because I am one of them. And I feel so good that I am one of them . . . that I could do this . . . not only for my Alex, but for all of them. Because I have the gift to have them remembered.

Lowenstein first created maquettes[11] from the photographs and then seventy-six sculptures of mothers, wives, and grandmothers of those lost on board Pan Am 103. A single figure, if standing, would be approximately seven to eight feet tall; the weight of each sculpture varies from 250 to 450 pounds. The figures are composed of a synthetic stone and fiber glass modeled over a steel armature. Lowenstein's choice of color reflected her perception of the model's emotional strength:

[Some] of the women were a lot more fragile than others . . . so the ones that I felt were more fragile in their emotional strength were paler in color than those who were more robust in their emotional make-up. Also, if you stand away and look at the whole sculpture together, it is much more interesting to have dark and light and reddish and yellowish [hues].

All of *Dark Elegy's* bereaved are women. Lowenstein believes that gendered roles are the reason that men did not volunteer to model for *Dark Elegy*:

Most of the men in that group were of a generation where the boys don't cry and they are not soft . . . what I was describing and portraying in *Dark Elegy* was (a person) at their most helpless and softest and most desperate. And I think that deep down, men of that generation did not want to be portrayed that way. Another explanation is that by the time that they could have participated, it was already all women and so it would have been extraordinarily courageous for the first man to come forward and say that 'I would like to be a part of this too'. And that never happened. And I think that many of the men were somewhat inhibited by the fact that so many women had posed and been sculpted that they didn't want to be the first.

Her choice to represent the bereaved in the nude was also deliberate:

[T]he bodies are undressed . . . because at the moment when we learned that our loved ones were dead, we were stripped of everything that we ever had. Our skin color didn't matter, our wealth or poverty didn't matter . . . all that mattered was that our loved ones were killed. It stripped us to the same level . . . and how better to portray that than to physically strip us of our clothes? It was a beautiful symbolism of that very moment that we were stripped to the very core. How else can I portray those who were stripped to the core except for the most obvious?

It is interesting to note that the subjects of *Dark Elegy* are the bereaved family members. *Dark Elegy* does not represent those lost to terrorism but instead commemorates the enduring pain of those left behind. Although memorials of the bereaved are rare, *Dark Elegy* is similar to Käthe Kollwitz's sculptures, *Mother with Dead Son* and *Grieving Parents* that are installed in Germany and Belgium.[12] *Dark Elegy* is commemoratively unique; it was created by the bereaved, modeled by the bereaved, and memorializes those who were still alive after the traumatic event.

THE EXHIBITION OF *DARK ELEGY*

Although Lowenstein initially created *Dark Elegy* as a commemoration to those lost as a result of the Pan Am 103 bombing, the project's scope rapidly expanded to include a remembrance of all victims of terrorism:

> [This] sculpture has no borders. A woman, from Asia, from Africa, from Greece, from anywhere, will understand . . . [what is] left behind in the wake of hate between people and countries . . . because it is so universal . . . it never changes . . . it is always the same. The people left behind from 9/11 look exactly like that. The Klinghoffer family[13] look exactly like that . . . the Rome airport bombing look just like that. Pan Am 103 relatives look just like that. It is so universal which is why I always stress the fact that even though *Dark Elegy* was spawned from the tragedy of Pan Am 103, it is truly and always has been dedicated to the victims of terrorism.[14]

Dark Elegy was first described as a memorial dedicated to all victims of terrorism in a Pan Am 103 family group's newsletter that was ironically dated September 11, 1991, exactly ten years prior to the attacks on the U.S.

Dark Elegy has been exhibited in numerous locations including art galleries, town centers, and numerous high school and college campuses. Throughout many years of installations in a variety of public space, there was only one incident of deliberate damage to *Dark Elegy*:

> [I]n one place (there) were two figures were literally taken out of the group and dragged several blocks away and smashed in the street. That was the worst of the damage. And the community at large felt absolutely horrific about it, really. And then in other locations it would be maintenance people who wouldn't be careful and maybe drive over a leg or arm with a tractor and the arm or leg would break but in

general, there was very little damage and that indicated a respect . . . of the people of that town for what the sculpture portrayed.

Unprotected public art installations frequently are damaged by graffiti and vandalism. Public art projects that are either created by community members or represent community sentiment are projects that are the least likely to be damaged. Projects that represent "outsider" status invariably invite the greatest destruction. It is notable that this work was not subject to numerous issues of vandalism. Many of *Dark Elegy's* traveling installations were scheduled as a result of a communication between the artist and a local bereaved person. The majority of people in those communities did not hold a personal identification with the Pan Am 103 disaster. I strongly believe that the lack of destruction during *Dark Elegy's* public exhibitions directly relates to the emotional power of the work. Lowenstein described the reaction of others who have experience *Dark Elegy* for the first time:

> I see people come around the corner and be faced with the sculpture and it's almost like a physical blow. I have seen grown men slow down and look as if they are totally out of control. It's remarkable. I don't usually go . . . there when people are there because that piece speaks louder than anything that I can say so I don't usually talk about it . . . but I observe their reaction of it . . . And it's really that reaction that I have been observing for a number of years now that has me convinced that the sculpture needs to be out there. It needs to be out there in the public to be viewed by all.

As the number of figures in the work increased, it became impractical to continually move the work from place to place. The complete work is approximately sixty-five feet in diameter. The artist temporarily placed *Dark Elegy* at her home in Montauk, New York and opened her property to the public for two hours each day. Lowenstein hoped that her work would one day be in a primary public space that provided access to large numbers of people. Initially, she had hoped that the work would be located at the United Nations:

> [P]eople always [try to] make me aware that it is an organization of many faults. But I don't like to look at that, but rather concentrate on the . . . symbolism of it . . . where all nations come together with the hopes of being able to work together . . . and live in peace next to one another. Because of that symbolism, I think that Dark Elegy would be ideal at the United Nations. This sculpture needs no language, it is understood by all. It is not political in any partisan sense. It knows no borders. Today, people all over the world are affected by terrorism.

The United Nations' gatekeepers posed challenges that were virtually insurmountable obstacles. The United Nations does not accept gifts from individuals; all gifts, including works of public art, must be offered by a member nation. Once a gift has been offered, there is an extensive review process to determine if this transnational agency will accept the gift. Lowenstein faced several essential obstacles in her wish to gift *Dark Elegy* to the United Nations. The first was the refusal of the George W. Bush administration to schedule a meeting to discuss her offer to give the work to the U.S. government. The George W. Bush administration did not welcome interaction with the Pan Am 103 family members. Although there was an initial reluctance by the George H.W. Bush administration to publicly discuss the bombing of Pan Am 103, it did designate Bush's Chief of Staff, John Sununu, as an administrative contact person for the organization representing family members.[15] The first Bush administration also created a presidential commission to investigate the bombing of Pan Am 103. The bereaved continued to have access to the executive branch throughout the Clinton administration. This access however became substantially limited during the George W. Bush administration. During the first four years of the administration, Secretary of State Colin Powell briefly met with the organization that represented the Pan Am 103 family interests. During the first two years of George W. Bush's second term, the group did not receive a written response from Secretary of State Condoleezza Rice. The first step of gifting *Dark Elegy* to the United Nations could not be met as the Lowensteins were not given a forum to discuss the gifting of *Dark Elegy* to the U.S.

There was another substantial obstacle for *Dark Elegy's* installation at the United Nations. Assuming that a member nation would both accept and re-gift the work to the United Nations, the United Nations must follow protocol in the acceptance of a gift from its national member. *Dark Elegy* provided significant commemorative challenges to the United Nations. There is no international consensus in defining the term "terrorism." The first attempt to operationalize terrorism in an international context occurred when the League of Nations proposed a 1937 convention that defined terrorist acts as "All criminal acts directed against a State and intended or calculated to create a state of terror in the minds of particular persons or a group of persons or the general public."[16] This convention was never adopted. The United Nations attempted to resolve this ongoing quandary with a 1999 resolution that stated that the United Nations:

1. Strongly condemns all acts, methods and practices of terrorism as criminal and unjustifiable, wherever and by whomsoever committed;
2. Reiterates that criminal acts intended or calculated to provoke a state of terror in the general public, a group of persons or particular persons for political purposes are in any circumstance unjustifiable, whatever the considerations of a political, philosophical,

ideological, racial, ethnic, religious or other nature that may be invoked to justify them.[17]

This resolution failed as well. Herein lies an essential reason that *Dark Elegy* will not be installed on the grounds of the United Nations; it is impossible for an organization to commemorate victims of an act that it is unable to officially define.

Lowenstein also had another dream: that *Dark Elegy* would be located in Washington, D.C. When Congressman Timothy Bishop introduced H.R. 3707 in October 2007, he recommended that *Dark Elegy* be designated as the national memorial honoring all victims of terrorism. Securing congressional sponsorship for a memorial designation is the first step of a complicated process. Gatekeepers have immense control of the public space in Washington. The Commemorative Works Act of 1986 delineates very specific regulations for the construction and placement of monuments, memorials, and plaques for virtually all of the public spaces in the metropolitan capital area. The act requires that no event or person may be commemorated in the District of Columbia proper for a period of twenty-five years from either the designated event or the death of the last member of the commemorated cohort. H.R. 3707 states that *Dark Elegy* shall be dedicated to all victims of terrorism. Certainly, terrorism's initial victims have more than met the twenty-five year criteria. Given the current globalization of activity that may be defined as "terrorist," there is ongoing victimization. If the twenty-five year rule is applied to the last victims rather than initial victims, it is then impossible for a terrorism victimization memorial to meet this requirement. There have been exceptions to CWA's twenty-five year rule. For example, President George W. Bush dedicated the Memorial to the Victims of Communism on June 13, 2007. This memorial, located within view of the U.S.' Capital, certainly faces the same challenges as a memorial to victims of terrorism. However, the Victims of Communism memorial represents an important instrumental visualization of the American metanarrative while a Victims of Terrorism memorial is a contradiction of American exceptionalism.

Dark Elegy also did not fit several other requirements of the Commemorative Works Act. The act requires the establishment of a not-for-profit organization to raise funds and coordinate the construction and maintenance of approved memorials. The Lowensteins offered to sponsor the work as individual citizens. If *Dark Elegy* was approved for placement in the District of Columbia, the artist planned to use the funds that she and her husband received from the Libyan government [18] to move, bronze, and maintain the sculptures. The CWA design process also ensures that memorials will be future works of art. The regulatory design process does not consider that a completed work of art may be presented as "the commemorative work. . .of preeminent historical and lasting significance to the United States."[19] There have been precedents of memorials having accepted designs without competitions (e.g. the *Three Soldiers* addition to the Vietnam Veterans' Memorial), but *Dark Elegy* would have been the first completed work to have been designated a national memorial. Although there have been CWA exemptions granted for other memorials (the WWII memorial on the National Mall is the most significant example), *Dark Elegy* faced numerous challenges in the Washington commemorative arena.

THE *DARK ELEGY* HEARING

On February 26, 2008, the National Capital Memorial Commission conducted a public hearing for H.R. 3707, the bill dedicating *Dark Elegy* to all victims of terrorism. The NCMC is the primary gatekeeper that is charged with the planning, design, and construction of federal buildings and public space in Washington D.C. and surrounding counties in Virginia and Maryland. NCMC commissioners are appointed by federal and local officials. During the H.R. 3707 testimony, Suse Lowenstein and her husband Peter reaffirmed that *Dark Elegy* was not exclusively a commemoration of the victims of Pan Am 103, but was dedicated to all victims of terrorism. A number of Pan Am 103 bereaved testified about the importance of the work. Academics testified to the aesthetic value of the work and the precedence of exceptions to the Commemorative Works Act.[20] After public testimonies were completed, the commissioners commented upon the bill. Several noted that the twenty-five year rule would be violated by this bill. The commissioners' comments then veered from discussion of legal and policy issues. One commissioner noted that the National Park Service had several concerns about *Dark Elegy*. John G. Parsons, an associate regional director for the National Park Service, expressed reservations because *Dark Elegy's* figures were all female. He noted that men had also been victims of terrorism and would not be represented in this gender-specific work. There is precedent for this concern. When Frederick Hart's *Three Soldiers* was installed at the Vietnam Veterans' Memorial, female veterans complained that they were excluded from representation. This led to the installation of the *Women's Vietnam Veterans Memorial*. It is ironic that *Dark Elegy's* gendered representation would be problematic in a national commemorative space that is dominated by male representation.

Parsons also noted that there would be substantial objection to nude sculpture on public land. In addition, he stated that "because some of the poses of the various figures create an opportunity for irreverent behavior by visitors, there is serious concern about activities that would be disrespectful of your purpose."[21] Peter Lowenstein, the artist's husband, responded to this concern by asking the commission "Do you really feel objections like that are valid, and not a fantasy of someone's mind? Because my first instinct was to keep Mr. Parsons away from them [the sculptures]."[22] Michael McGill, a commission member, then defended Parsons, "He

(Parsons) has for the past 30 years been a major figure in this city . . . He has learned by experience about problems that can arise. He was not being voyeuristic. He was not being odd."[23]

After deliberations, the National Capital Memorial Commission voted unanimously against H.R. 3707. The nudity of the sculptures was a continued theme during the commission's hearing, and perhaps citizens of the U.S. would not accept nudity in a public memorial. Although the controversy regarding the sexualized reception of the work was both riveting and unusual in the negotiation of public commemorative works, I suggest that there are two other reasons that *Dark Elegy* will never be situated in the District of Columbia or surrounding environs.

The first challenge is that the work is dedicated to all victims of terrorism. Since there is no internationally accepted definition of the term terrorism, it is difficult to commemorate an undefined act. Mark Juergensmeyer notes that the term terrorist

> depends on whether one thinks that the acts are warranted. To a large extent, the use of the term depends on one's world view: if the world is perceived as peaceful, violent acts appear as terrorism. If the world is thought to be at war, violent acts may be regarded as legitimate.[24]

Given the lack of consensus in the definition of the term terrorism, some interpreters of *Dark Elegy* might include victims killed by acts of the U.S. government. The gatekeepers of the national public space are very unlikely to place any commemoration that may possibly include the government as perpetrators of terrorism.

The second challenge to *Dark Elegy's* designation as a memorial to victims of terrorism is its vivid representation of loss. A NCMC commissioner specifically questioned whether such a "violent" memorial should be located in public space. He suggested that a more "benign" work would be more appropriate and proposed that the government place a plaque commemorating those lost to terrorism somewhere within the District of Columbia commemorative space. This recommendation is reminiscent of the official reception of George Segal's commemoration of the Kent State University shootings in the U.S. In May 1970, National Guard soldiers fired upon a group of students who were protesting the Vietnam War. Four students were killed and nine were injured. This defining moment of the Vietnam era remained officially unmarked on the state university campus for over seven years. In March 1978, the Mildred Andrews Foundation, a private foundation, commissioned a memorial for the Kent State campus and selected George Segal, an internationally known artist. Segal visited the campus and mentioned to the executive assistant to the president that he was "exploring the Abraham and Isaac story." McCoy said, "I don't know how that would work. We'd better be careful." [25] Segal commented that "There is a strong connection in my mind between the image of

Abraham and Isaac and the killings at Kent State. It's an attempt to introduce difficult moral and ethical questions as to how older people should behave toward their children." Segal also viewed the May 4 shootings as "a genuine tragedy in that both sides were well meaning, each convinced of its own point of view and unable to see the other's."[26] Several days later, the college administration wrote a letter to the foundation, accepting the commission. Upon the work's completion in July 1978, the university administration unanimously rejected *Abraham and Isaac* and asked Segal to create another sculpture. Robert McCoy, executive assistant to President Golding said, "Most people, when they erected statues of commemorative things chose subjects that appeared not to incite violence."[27] McCoy also suggested that the new sculpture "would be more appropriate to show a guardsman fully dressed, and a girl casting roses into a gun. She could maybe be nude, or if you drape something over her . . . I have a feeling we could sell that metaphor."[28] Unlike Washington D.C., nudity apparently was not a commemorative issue in Ohio in the late 1970s. Segal refused to change the memorial and *Abraham and Isaac* was ultimately installed at Princeton University.

CONCLUSION

In the "memorial worlds" context, public art memorials are installed through negotiations with gatekeepers who literally provide the ground for permitted commemorations. There is an important instrumental concern about constructing a visualization of terrorist victims. It is essential to remember that victims of terrorist are often randomly or symbolically selected to serve as message generators for the perpetrators.[29] Although the construction of memorials, monuments, and commemorations to victims of terrorism may enable gatekeepers an opportunity to establish an instrumental interpretation of terrorism, these visual representations also risk the amplification and perpetuation of that violent message.

Since the National Capital Memorial Commission's rejection of *Dark Elegy* as a national memorial to all victims of terrorism, there has been some discussion about locating the work in the town of Montauk, New York. Several town elders believe that it could become a "part of the Montauk picture" and fill a perceived cultural gap in the community. [30] There is some support for *Dark Elegy* to remain in the community. The artist and her husband are residents; their son Alexander spent summers surfing off of its shores. There are also community members who want to maintain Montauk's fishing, surfing, and tourism identity and oppose locating the work in the town's public space. Lowenstein stated that she has scaled back her view of *Dark Elegy*:

> When I first started working on Dark Elegy, I never intended for it to be public. It was something that I could do for Alexander . . . and then

for all victims of terrorism. Others wanted me to make it public. What really bothers me is the process. Powers that be determine what people should feel and think . . . and that is not what America is all about.[31]

The term "War on Terror" has not been used since the inauguration of the Obama administration yet American troops continue to be sent to Iraq and Afghanistan. Certainly, a memorial honoring the military members killed in the first wars of the twenty-first century will be constructed on the National Mall. It is also likely that the civilian victims will remain invisible in the national memorial landscape as the "naked" women of *Dark Elegy* search for a permanent home.

NOTES

1. Edward T. Linenthal, *The Unfinished Bombing: Oklahoma City in American Memory* (New York: Oxford University Press, 2001), 19–20.
2. Ibid., 21.
3. Maurice Halbwachs, *On Collective Memory*, ed. and trans. Lewis Coser (Chicago: University of Chicago Press, 1992 [1952]).
4. Dee Britton, "Arlington's Cairn: Constructing the Commemorative Foundation For United States' Terrorist Victims," *Journal of Political and Military Sociology*, 35:1 (Summer 2007): 19–27.
5. Jeffrey Olick and Joyce Robbins, "Social Memory Studies: From 'Collective Memory' to the Historical Sociology of Mnemonic Practices," *Annual Review of Sociology* 24 (1998): 129–30.
6. US Congress 2002. H.R. 2982, 107th Congress, 2nd session.
7. Ibid.
8. US Congress 2007, H.R. 3707, 110th Congress, 1st session.
9. Suse Lowenstein, interview by Dee Britton, Montauk, NY, March 26, 2006.
10. Mother, Pan Am 103 victim, interview by Dee Britton, March 2006.
11. A maquette is a small, preliminary model of a sculpture.
12. Kenneth Foote, personal correspondence with Dee Britton, February 24, 2008.
13. Leon Klinghoffer, a sixty-nine-year-old American who was confined to a wheelchair, was murdered on the Italian cruise ship, the Achille Lauro, in 1985.
14. Suse Lowenstein, interview by Dee Britton, Montauk, NY, March 26, 2006.
15. Allan Gerson and Jerry Adler, *The Price of Terror* (New York: Harper Collins, 2001), 63.
16. United Nations Office on Drugs and Crime, "Definition of Terrorism," 1999, GA Res. 51/210, Measures to eliminate international terrorism. Retrieved June 19, 2007 from http://www.unodc.org/unodc/terrorism_definitions.html.
17. Ibid.
18. In 2003, Libya agreed to pay ten million dollars for each Pan Am 103 victim.
19. National Park Service, Subcommittee on National Parks, Recreation and Public Lands of the House Committee on Resources concerning H.R. 452, 2001. Retrieved November 13, 2005 from http://www.nps.gov/legal/testimony/107th/rrmemdc3.html.

20. During this hearing, I testified to the NCMC regarding Commemorative Works Acts exceptions granted for other memorials in the metropolitan D.C. area.
21. Mark Weiner, "Terror victim memorial soundly rejected: Flight 103 theme and nudity are given as reasons," *Newhouse News Service*, February 26, 2008. Retrieved March 7, 2008 http://www.chron.com/disp/story.mpl/nation/5573157.html.
22. Ibid.
23. Ibid.
24. Mark Juergensmeyer, *Terror in the Mind of God: The Global Rise of Religious Violence* (Berkeley: University of California Press, 2003).
25. Laura Putre, "In Memory Of. . .: The Twenty Year Search for a Quiet May 4 Monument," *Kent State University Burr*, May 4, 2000. Retrieved March 8, 2008 from http://burr.kent.edu/archives/1990/memory/memory2.html.
26. George Segal, "Abraham and Isaac: In Memory of May 4, 1970 Kent State University," n.d. Retrieved March 8, 2008 from http://speccoll.library.kent.edu/4may70/exhibit/memorials/segal.html.
27. Laura Putre, "In Memory Of. . .:."
28. Ibid.
29. United Nations Office on Drugs and Crime, "Definition of Terrorism."
30. Suse Lowenstein, telephone interview by Dee Britton, July 2, 2009.
31. Ibid.

Part III
Media and Mediums

9 Memory through the Perpetrator's Lens

Witnessing via Images Taken by *Wehrmacht* Soldiers and Officers on the Eastern Front

Frances Guerin

As the number of images taken by perpetrators, bystanders, and accomplices of the Holocaust continues to grow, privilege is, nevertheless, still given to images taken by victims and survivors in the ongoing and urgent search to remember and memorialize World War II and the Holocaust. Even as we rapidly approach a time when those who suffered and survived at the brutal hands of Nazi Germany will no longer be alive to tell their stories, an insistence on theirs as the only authentic perspective on the violent crimes continues. Furthermore, the denigration of perpetrator and bystander images as "biased" and "unreliable" comes in spite of repeated instances of unself-conscious dependence on visual representations taken by Germans—civilians, officers, soldiers, Nazis and non-Nazis—in discussions and historical exhibitions focused on the Holocaust and World War II.[1] Lastly, there is a persistence of critical and historical discourses that malign the effectiveness of the image—no matter who has taken it—in favor of the use of written and oral texts for processes of witnessing. Such prejudices persist in spite of the proliferation of images that can contribute new and unusual perspectives to the work of memory, not only of World War II, but also, of other historical traumas in the late twentieth and early twenty-first centuries.

Even though it is often submerged within these discussions, the privilege given to images made by survivors and victims is based on the belief that those taken by German soldiers and officers, their accomplices, and even resistance workers, are violent in and of themselves. They are always dismissed on the basis of their saturation with Nazi ideology. As critics such as Bernd Hüppauf have argued, this interpretation is predicated on two blind assumptions: first, that the image can be equated with the political allegiance of the one who looks through the viewfinder.[2] And second, that the soldier behind the camera shares the "positionality," the perspective, even the identity of those high-level Nazis who authored and disseminated the racist concepts of "Jews," "Slavs," and other "types" to be destroyed.[3] While neither of these assumptions stands up to scrutiny, the "misleading over-simplifications," as Hüppauf would have them, do manage to keep the past in the distance and alleviate the potential threat it poses to an extension into the present.

Today, sixty-five years after the end of World War II and the Holocaust, there is an urgency to find new ways of remembering its crimes and traumas. We have no choice but to go beyond the testimony of survivors as they become fewer and fewer in number. In addition, the nature of their incarceration was such that access to photographic equipment was extremely rare, and mostly non-existent. Thus, many of the images that survive were taken by others. In this chapter, I am interested in how amateur photographs can be used in processes of witnessing the atrocities of the Holocaust and World War II. In particular, I discuss photographs taken by *Wehrmacht* soldiers and officers on the Eastern Front between 1939 and 1941. I put forward a way of seeing the images that speaks to their usefulness, and that of amateur images more generally, in the ongoing work of remembering, and ultimately, witnessing such events, albeit at an emotional, physical, and historical remove. Thus, within my discourse, these images are placed as a "material site of memory" that enable a preservation of new memories, our memories, for the twenty-first century.

I choose these amateur images as sites of memory for a number of reasons. Perhaps the most important being that the amateur image is typically ambiguous, indefinite, fluid, and, for want of a better word, flawed. In turn, the inconsistencies and "flaws" in the photograph create "distance," or open up spaces that allow us to assume a contemporary responsibility for the memory of the depicted events. We are required to notice the image, to imagine its completion, to narrativize it in a way that the amateur image does not and cannot do for itself. As I shall demonstrate, this indefiniteness of amateur images offers them as agents in our memory work today. And to reiterate, as agents, they also create memories, a process that is mobilized by a series of structural, visible, and metaphorical distances that are endemic to the amateur image, to these amateur images. The various levels of distance and, in turn, the various ways that perceptual, emotional, and intellectual spaces are created encourage us to take up the images in our own narratives of memorializing the events that they see, and we, by extension, witness from a distance. As I say, distance is critical here—distance invites reflection, frustration, provocation, and judgment. Distance, as I conceive of it, thus enables and even encourages us to insert ourselves, what we know and don't know, what we believe and what we doubt, what we feel and don't feel, into the communicative relations created by the image. And so a conversation, an argument, comes alive and the memory of the heinous Holocaust events is re-vivified in the mind of the viewer. Thus, the distance of the amateur reanimates the events from another perspective, our perspective.

The distances that I identify in the chosen photographs are typical of the amateur image. For example, amateur images commonly forge a distance between the events depicted and the camera. We see this distance in the physical remove of the events from the photograph: amateur photographs typically show events in long shot, in the distance, to the point where we sometimes have difficulty discerning what is taking place. Other "imperfections" of the amateur photograph create a self-conscious image that draws attention to its status as representation: mistakes, repetitions, out-of-focus blurs, underexposure, and overexposure. In such examples, we are reminded of the presence of the camera as an instrument of mediation, thereby forging a disconnect with the events it photographs. Similarly, there is a distance between the meaning of the image in the late 1930s/early 1940s and its meaning today. We recognize this through the age of the photograph: the fading of the color dye, stains on the image, tears and creases that tell the story of the photograph's being folded up and placed in a wallet or a pocket for safe keeping. Similar to this, there is a historical distance between the events depicted and the images themselves, a distance that has often been collapsed in the interests of indicting the image for its violence. This distance might alternatively be conceived of as the distance between what the officer or soldier sees through his viewfinder and the events as we see them represented all these years later.

All viewers may not perceive the events in the same way: thus, there is an inscription of distance between various levels of possible viewing, possible interpretations among different viewers (maybe even for the same viewer). All of these "distances" create still more tensions within the photographs. These various distances foreground the openness of the image, a lack of clarity to what it represents and how. In turn, the openness leads to literal and metaphorical spaces for the contemporary viewer to reflect on both the events and the photograph as an event performed in the past. To put it another way, within these spaces we are called upon to take responsibility in the contemporary moment, to take up the process of witnessing the traumatic events of the past. Thus, the amateur photograph lends itself as an agent in our memory work today. This process not only demonstrates how a collective memory is transformed through temporal and geographical distances, where old memories are dissolved and new ones born, but it shows how the changing status of images as sites of memory more generally can be exploited for memory work that accords with the contemporary political and historical responsibility to the past.

A theoretical justification for the generative spaces created through the various distances is not so imperative, particularly, because its conception is born of the photographs themselves. However, I will clarify that my thinking here leans on a tradition of looking at the realist image from a perspective that begins with the work of André Bazin and the French documentary film movement.[4] My approach to the realism of the amateur image in particular draws on statements made by Péter Forgács, a filmmaker who works extensively with amateur film, re-editing and re-fashioning it into documentaries that re-vision World War II and the Holocaust through the eyes of the private, everyday worlds in the footage.[5] According to Forgács, the so-called flaws and imperfections of the amateur image are its most exciting traits because they give it its claim to truth. While the so-called truth of these images is not static or one-dimensional, Forgács is concerned to validate the amateur image as an aesthetic object. I mention this because, while the idea of the image's imperfections as the site of possibility is useful to an interpretation of the amateur photographs taken by soldiers and officers on the Eastern Front, they are not, and must not be understood as aesthetic—the images produce a meaning that does not depend on seeing them as art. To be sure, I engage the photographs through certain assumptions about modern art, but I must be clear to reinforce that this does not mean they can be seen as art works.

Before looking at the photographs, I also clarify what, within my discourse, it means to "witness" the Holocaust. In our anthology, *The Image and the Witness*,[6] Roger Hallas and I extend the groundbreaking work of Dori Laub and Shoshana Felman to conceive of the potential for images to be used in processes of bearing witness to traumatic historical events. We argue that the image can be conceived to mediate between intersubjective relations that are commonly accepted to animate the process of witnessing itself.[7] For Laub and Felman, the inter-subjective relationship that gives rise to witnessing is established between the survivor as speaker/analyst and the listener/analyst. Through this relationship, the survivor's trauma is brought back to consciousness and she is able to narrativize and to externalize events that are otherwise too profound to be realized. The ethical weight of this process demands that the psychoanalyst-listener also be witness to his or her self, and thus, to the process of witnessing. The one who bears witness is not the passive facilitator of knowledge, but rather, must also listen to herself, her responses, her experiences, in order to keep the testimony alive. And lastly, the psychoanalyst-interviewer must bear witness to the "flow" of "trauma fragments" and respond to them to ensure their continued flow.[8] As we argue in *The Image and the Witness*, the presence of an image has a capacity to generate an inter-subjectivity: the image opens up a site at which a witness (in this case us) who did not directly observe or participate in the traumatic historical event, now has the ability to witness, at a distance, to the ordeal of those photographed. When we see the photographs, it is our responsibility to bear witness to ourselves, as we revivify and prolong the historical memory of the traumatic events.[9]

Of critical significance to my concept of witnessing here, and to my consequent interpretation of the photographs, is that the author or photographer of the image is not present to the documentary image. The soldier-photographer is necessarily absent, unidentifiable, in effect, he is anonymous. To emphasize: it is not that the documentary image offers a window onto the reality of the events it sees, but rather, that we believe in the power of the image's phenomenological capacity to give the event a visual presence. And our engagement with that presence is only made possible through the absence of the photographer as mediator. Consequently, we have the opportunity to become openly receptive to the experiences of those who were present at the event. Thus, knowledge or identification of the national and political allegiance of the photographer is not necessary to a revivification of the photograph, to our process of witnessing. Indeed, as I shall illustrate through reference to specific photographs below, his removal gives us the freedom to look from different perspectives, through different eyes, our eyes.

THE DISTANCE OF THE SOLDIER-PHOTOGRAPHER AS AUTHOR

The distance incurred through my specific conception of the amateur image as anonymous is a conceptual, not a literal definition. Thus, within my argument, an image can be anonymous even when the photographer can be identified. Anonymity is better defined as an inability to infer the meaning of the photograph based on the identity and presence of the maker. Even when the photographer can be named, his photographs are generic, often identical to thousands of others. Similarly, the photographs were freely reproduced and distributed, passed on from party to party throughout the war. Again and again, the same image resurfaces in the archives with conflicting attributions, contentious ownership, and inconsistent contextual information. In addition, the *mise-en-scène* is frequently abstracted, the historical context is vague and the post-war provenance can be sketchy at best. From the outset, these images remain unable to be pinned down: an evasion that I refer to as a type of anonymity. The absence of the photographer from how the image makes its meaning, thus the role of the image in processes of witnessing is perhaps best illustrated through looking at the photographs taken by an officer, who is identified as the author of the images he takes.

A 1984 interview with Gerhard Gronefeld in which he discusses his photographs illustrates the distance of the soldier-photographer from the image he produces. These images are neither anonymous nor amateur in the traditional sense of these terms. Gronefeld was officially employed by the illustrated journal *Signal* and in 1941 was sent to what is now Serbia to report on the fighting. He was, thus, a professional photographer assigned to the *Wehrmacht*. Thus he is neither an amateur and nor is there ambiguity around him as the photographer. Nevertheless, even though Gronefeld the photographer is identified in the image, the soldier-photographer we locate can be different from the one he believes himself to be.[10] Such multi-perspectival possibilities of the images, together with their multiple layers of distance, are at the basis of the specific form of anonymity I identify. The interview reproduced in *Fotogeschichte* focuses on a series of photographs of executions in Pančevo, a city just north of Belgrade. The images represent "hostages" being led to the gallows by guards (German army) to be hung in revenge for the killing of SS officers by Serbian partisans. We see the hanging of seven well-dressed men in suits, complete with neckties, and their hair slicked back. In another of the photographs we see not so well-dressed victims on the gallows, from different angles, in long shot, but their facial characteristics are still identifiable. And we see the brutal shooting of prisoners, taken at right angles to the cemetery wall against which some are already slumped, the arm of the lone executioner in uniform is still out-stretched with a gun in his hand. His superior stands next to him clearly watching the soldier "at work." In a number of photographs a shoulder, a head or some other unidentifiable object intrudes into the frame, but never obscures the focus of the image.

Gronefeld is nowhere to be found in his photographs. He is emotion-ally, physically, and intellectually absent from these images of a series of executions of hostages in Yugoslavia taken in 1941. We could argue that Gronefeld's camera is distant from the events because such a photograph is known to be prohibited, therefore he must stand well back from these brutal actions.[11] Alternatively, we may want to infer that the long shot of Gronefeld's vision of these executions Pančevo is the result of technol-ogy that at this time would not have permitted close-ups. Gronefeld offers another interpretation in his retrospective account. He argues that he is repulsed by what he sees, so horrified at the gruesome murders that he vomits when he comes to photograph the executions.[12] He claims to stand at a distance, to photograph the lynchings from afar as a way of separat-ing himself from the perpetrators of these crimes, as a way of asserting his aversion to the crimes taking place before his camera. They, "the Germans" referred to by Gronefeld, are placed in the background to the murders as a sign of his condemnation of their acts.[13] Simultaneously, as Gronefeld relates his disgust at the murders, he expresses no remorse or shame for his presence at, or role in, the Nazi crimes in Eastern Europe.

If we are to accept his narrative, we are immediately faced with a contra-diction. On the one hand, the long shot of the lynchings and shootings of partisans lined up along a wall strongly suggests a cold, detached bird's-eye view of these highly-charged events, and, on the other hand, the photogra-pher claims to have been so deeply moved by their extremity that he reacts with physical disgust. Nowhere can we find these conflicted emotions in the images of brutality. Gronefeld's presence at the event, his vision of it through photography, would have to be taken into account when consider-ing the author-effect or construction thereof. Gronefeld as photographer of these particular images points to the complications with an approach that privileges him as the author. One might argue that it is not necessary to take Gronefeld's testimony into account when interpreting the photo-graphs as expressions of an identified author. However, there is nothing to distinguish Gronefeld's photographs from those taken by countless other soldiers at countless other executions. There is nothing in the image that would identify him as the author. Therefore, if Gronefeld's memories are not the springboard to an authorial reading, then what is? Thus, even when the author is known, this information does not guarantee a straightforward interpretation of the photographs.

Instead, I propose that the same distance which confuses an author approach to photographs like Gronefeld's be foregrounded to facilitate alternative interpretations that privilege a heterogeneity of viewer responses. Not only the emotional distance, but also the distance between camera and event, between perpetrator and victim, between viewer and photograph, between then and now, can be mobilized as the basis for our recognition and remembrance of these past events. It creates a space into which we are invited to reflect on the events depicted in the image. Thus, these same photographs have a power to reignite historical memory and perpetuate processes of witnessing the past. To place these images of brutality on the historical stage of witnessing is a controversial move. If, for no other reason than that I turn to photographs most often taken by perpetrators for the purposes of historical witnessing. The other criticism that can be levelled at my approach is that it potentially places the images in a light that sees them, and my discourse, in a way that fails to do justice to the human magnitude of the events they witness. That is, it is a strategy that does not focus primarily on the suffering of those victims of the historical trauma as they are seen by the camera.[14] And yet, as documents involved in processes of witnessing, these images are among all we have left for the continued memory of, most importantly, World War II and the Holocaust.[15]

At the most immediate level, the image testifies to the brutal, if not absolute, reality of the events depicted. The specific details of the images may be indeterminate—the precise time and place of the image production, who appears in the image and so on—but on this most immediate level, many of them see, and thus testify to brutal slaughters, the parades of hangmen, the violence of the perpetrator, bodies left to rot, prisoners obeying orders for fear of their lives, and other atrocities. The photographs may be cropped and some events consciously included in the image, while others fall outside of the frame. Nevertheless, there is every reason to believe in the correspondence between the representation and the event depicted.[16] Unlike official propaganda images that were taken in abundance by Nazi photographers such as Gronefeld, given the sheer number of amateur images produced, together with the costs involved in manipulation, and that they were not at least initially intended for any commercial or public use, we can assume that the amateur photos were spared retouching and fabrication in the processes of production. Due to their status as amateur and private photographs, they were taken and processed with abandon, with little attention paid to technical mistakes, unwanted details or uncensored inclusions. Thus, the events they depict can be seen as real. There may be other realities, particularly those which do not appear in any of the photographic images which are only ever fragments of the time and place of which they are traces. Nevertheless, the photos in existence are documents of the events at which the camera was once present.

THE DISTANCE OF PROHIBITIONS

Although somewhat remote from the process of witnessing the Holocaust, like the role of the theological witness, these photographs are evidence of the existence of events and happenings that were typically prohibited, denied, or repressed by official (German) histories. The prohibitions on representation of German crimes are key to an understanding of the importance of these images in processes of witnessing what took place on the Eastern Front. Again and again, these and other photographs (such as Gronefeld's) see what they are not supposed or allowed to see.

The many photographs available do not obey the censorship laws that were in place during the war in the East. The list of prohibited material was not long, but it was definitive. All locks, bridges, and harbors, close-ups of weapons and machinery, anything that would give away attack and defense strategies, or in any way endanger the authority of the German army. While it was acceptable to photograph the "enemy" who was already dead, it was strictly forbidden to capture the execution in motion. In short, any image that slurred the name of the *Wehrmacht* was also prohibited and censored.[17] Similarly, any image that might compromise the Germany army by leading to potential imprisonment was prohibited.

The soldiers photographed the censored subject matter anyway. Images of violence, brutality, and slaughter are everywhere in the archives. Moreover, the transgressions displayed in these images are critical to their role in processes of witnessing. Most obviously, the photographic image is evidence of what is not officially documented. In addition, the photographs have an unacknowledged power to disturb the authority of official history by representing what is denied and suppressed. This potential challenge to authority, to expose the existence of events that must be denied to maintain power, is familiar territory for the amateur image. Because the amateur sees and remembers events that otherwise fall through the cracks of official history, it opens a window onto an alternative view of history. In turn, these otherwise unexplored visions prompt us to reconsider this historical moment anew. Thus, while on the one hand, the photographs taken on the Eastern Front are suspect because they are the battlefield seen through German eyes—even when they are taken by bystanders or other participants, it is a German perspective—they also evidence the plurality of alternative histories seen by the perpetrator.

It must be acknowledged that in spite of the uniqueness and potential transgression of the often forbidden perspective of the amateur photographs, they also offer an unethical perspective of the crimes in the East. Images that depict anything from a dozen local Jews lined up before a firing squad through lynchings in process and lynched corpses hanging like decorations from light posts in the streets of small Polish towns, to piles of slaughtered corpses being bulldozed into self-dug pits are, according to some discourses, categorically unacceptable as testimonies to the heinous crimes of the German soldiers. They are unacceptable because to witness the survival of the Holocaust goes hand-in-hand with a moral and ethical imperative to be responsible to the events in some way. Accordingly, these photographs are so ideologically saturated: they objectify the victims, ignore their suffering, and foreclose the possibility of the victims' "speaking" their own stories.

The many photographs that see rows of dead bodies, groups of emaciated, cowering figures holding tightly to each other, or hands to their sides, lined up for execution, or corpses hanging from balconies like Christmas decorations for all to marvel at, register a brutal distance rather than a necessary intimacy and "total presence of the [soldier and his photograph] as other."[18] As Hüppauf convincingly argues, these images are drained of human content, and often verge into the terrain of abstract, formal compositions.[19] The trauma and experience of the victim is certainly not seen or experienced from the inside—the human figure is often so far removed from the lens of the camera that it is impossible to respect the individuality of his or her internal experiences, the singularity of his or her trauma. As a result of this distance, there is no relationship established between victim and perpetrator's image (as mediator). Seen from this vantage point, the camera and resultant images take no responsibility for the traumatic experience of the victim. Not a thought is spared for their suffering, but rather, the victims appear like points of interest on a sightseeing tour, or they become merged with the landscape.[20] If we are to follow the framework for witnessing as I outline it above, witnessing does not take place as an experience between a subject and an intimate other because these photographs are too intent on calling attention to the authority and distance of the one who sees. Lastly, the discourses into which I place these photographs depart significantly from the accepted notion of witnessing because they do not narrate the story of survival. Rather, the victims of the photographs have already been killed, and to witness their trauma would be akin to psychoanalyzing a dead man. They are far removed from the profound processes of self- and historical-realization as we have come to associate them with the processes of witnessing.

While I want to hold on to this possible interpretation as it is seen through the lens of Laub and Felman's witnessing, it is not the only perspective from which to see. As Barbie Zelizer and others have claimed, often in passing rather than through sustained argument, the images taken by the amateur German soldier-cameramen can bear witness to the Holocaust.[21] But these same critics also stop short of explaining how the said images witness. It is not enough to claim the photographs as evidence of what lies before them:

how precisely can they be taken up in our efforts to witness World War II and the Holocaust responsibly?

In his renowned collection of amateur and official photographs and documents that tell the history of the Jewish Holocaust, Gerhard Schönberner argues in *Der Gelbe Stern* that the images of the perpetrator reveal a curiosity that speaks their very troubling "tactlessness."[22] The images collected in his book are of the same genre as those taken by Gronefeld and other soldiers: long shot documentations of violent crimes. According to Schönberner, the images are almost a lie because they are superficial visual representations that do not even approximate the brutality and incomprehensibile experiences of the other senses.[23] The same images of slaughter and inconceivable human destruction may tell other realities: they show the thinking of the Nazis, their self-identity as heroes and their victims as subhuman, what they deemed worthy of photographing, and the anti-Semitic ideology that motivated them.[24] We will note that, for Schönberner, the images exist only at the level of the optical, that is, their only reliable truth is in their presentation of what they "see": the events that take place before the camera. Thus, the perspective of the perpetrator, and in particular, the impact of Nazi ideology on this perspective, renders the photograph superficial, useless in any attempt to "witness" the inhumanity of ghettoization, deportation, torture, execution, and mass expulsion. This impotence in the process of witnessing that is the logical extension of the identified opticality is in keeping with the thoughts of Laub and Felman. Following their logic, to witness is to experience the sensuous richness of the events, not simply as visual occurrences. Thus, to witness entails the experience of other senses; the stench of bloodied, decomposing bodies, the taste of death, the sound of bullets ringing out and orders being yelled, the feel of those emotions experienced by the participants. Certainly, none of these experiences are had at the most immediate optical level of the atrocity photographs. Thus we must go further. As Zimmerman says *vis-à-vis* amateur and home movie images, we must "mine" the photographs for their buried truths.[25] And one way to go further and deeper is to look at our reception of and interactions with the photographs.

Whether we are German, Russian, American, Jewish, Christian, or of any other identity, when we see the photographs seventy years later, the eyes of the German perpetrator behind the camera only directs what we see for so long. That is, we do not see in the image what the cameraman once did. We see with the advantage of seventy years of history, and we see from different cultural and political perspectives. First and foremost when we look at images such as a group of Russians or Poles or Gypsies, huddled together, heads bowed, their only protection at the point of a gun being their choice to look away, we recognize a confrontation between the soldier-cameraman and his victims. We imagine the trauma of the mass, unidentifiable subject, the perceived injustice, the underlying fear, and promise of death. In others we note the camaraderie, curiosity, and obligation of those grouped by the threat of execution before the camera. In fact we are likely to notice a whole spectrum of responses, emotions and meanings, a whole range of circumstances and dispositions.

The disquiet stirred in us when we see the photographs places them as catalysts in the process of witnessing the events of World War II, both as past historical events to be remembered in the present and as visual objects that testify to their one time presence at these events. Nevertheless, in addition to the reasons outlined above, for Laub and Felman, these images could not be witnesses because representation is always a medium and never a conduit to bearing witness. While neither discusses the image, we can extrapolate and speculate that, following their logic, the image could only ever mediate the intersubjective relationship between survivor-witness and the listener/viewer-witness.[26] However, I argue that via the spectator's engagement with the manifest visual details of an image, an intersubjective relationship is created, and this relationship can facilitate a process of bearing witness to historical trauma.[27] The photographic images are always in relationship with a viewer or viewers, and they become agents of historical memory and historical witnessing as we view them from the distance of seventy years. This relationship between viewer-viewed-subject matter, or I-photograph-unfathomable crimes, gives the photographs a power of involvement in the picturing, and today, the revivification of history. In the temporal, geographical, and emotional spaces between the viewer and the events taking place, in the inter-subjective process of reception, history becomes re-energized, it is witnessed with these images as instigators of the process. It is true that these particular photographs will open up different memories from those enabled by survivor images. However, this difference does not invalidate, it actually fuels, the memories and histories spawned by the perpetrator photographs.

Cathy Caruth points us toward one potential interpretation of the images as vehicles for the articulation and re-articulation of history, that is, as agents in the process of witnessing. Caruth argues for the "double telling" of the narrative of trauma in a model which is very close to that of Felman. Nevertheless, for Caruth, the double telling is in the image itself. Following Freud, for Caruth, witnessing makes available to consciousness a traumatic experience that was not assimilated when it occurred through telling a story. Thus confrontation with or witnessing the trauma comes in the reiteration of the same trauma. According to Caruth, the listener as witness to the trauma of an other (the pictured) faces an encounter between life and death in oneself.[28] Accordingly, when faced with the contentious perpetrator photographs taken on the Eastern Front, we are forced into a devastating awareness of the death of the victims as human beings, and we are repeatedly struck by the soldier's survival before and behind the camera. Before we judge the victims' death and the soldiers' survival, the reawakening of these historical events to consciousness is in itself a process of witnessing.

To extend the interpretation along the lines opened by Caruth, Kathrin Hoffmann-Curtius argues that the death of the victim as other reinforces the exposure of the *Wehrmacht* soldiers' own vulnerability. Thus, the photograph as agent is understood to invite the viewer—no matter her historical period—to see the soldiers (both those in and out of the frame) wrestling with or negotiating their own potential death through the creative act of photographing the victim.[29] Accordingly, the photographs enable a vision and re-vision of the co-dependent relations between victim and aggressor on the battlefield in the depicted historical moment. Of course, this is only one interpretation.

Another interpretation might see photographs such as one in which a soldier aiming his rifle at resistance fighters lined up along a nondescript wall in Russia—an image in distant long shot framed by two soldiers—as a narrative of self-surveillance. The same photograph brings to light the rebellion within the ranks of the German army as the photographer takes a photograph that is strictly forbidden. Such an image can become an agent in the witnessing of the complex relations and self-positioning of soldiers within the army, especially as they relate to the orders handed down to them, the beliefs being instilled in them. Another interpretation might be that offered by Hüppauf in his insightful theorization of the same genre of photographs in "Emptying the Gaze." Accordingly, such photographs depict a de-corporealized "gaze" that, in turn, effectively creates a timeless and "objective," "space of destruction" that has different meanings for different viewers of the image.[30]

Whatever the interpretation, the ability to position ourselves at a distance from the eye behind the camera due to the distance of the pro-photographic event, to see the photograph as evidence of the presence of a traumatic event in the past that took place between an aggressor and his victims, between various ranks within the army, enables the events to come back to memory as a complex historical experience. The most important recognition is that only when the image is detached from the one behind the camera, and the specific identity of the subject, is it possible to see it as an agent in the process of witnessing the atrocious events of World War II. The image must be anonymous for this process to be effective.

Most significantly, as viewers, we do not automatically assume the position of the soldier: for example, we do not look with glee and pride at a photograph of Jewish elders being mocked and tormented, all the time trying to assert our power and hide from our own fears of death and guilt of persecuting others.[31] Such a reading could not be further from the reality of our experience of the photographs. The images belong in a process in which our responses can vary significantly: we are horrified by the violence, we are outraged by the suffering, perplexed by the soldier's dependence on the corpses for his identity as a loyal servant of his country, repulsed by his sadistic violence, disturbed by the care taken in image composition as though it were of a picturesque landscape. Our complex responses to the photographic evidence of atrocities on the Eastern Front as testimony to the trauma bring the events into our present. In turn, this is the process by which they can be validated for their role as agents in the process of witnessing this war.

It is true that our responses are, to a certain extent, determined by the photographs as evidence that, in turn, are not naïve or unbiased. And it is true that any interpretation is clouded by cultural and historical persuasions, just as the image is soaked in the ideology of life in Nazi Germany. Thus, there is no objective or authentic interpretation of the photographs. Nevertheless, the minute they engage a viewer, they are vehicles in a vivification and re-vivification of history. They have a potential for involvement in the process of witnessing the pogroms in the East from a position removed in time and place. And this animated process is enabled through the complex web of distances that are woven into the photographs: the distance of the subject from the camera, the psychological and emotional distances between the perpetrator and his victim, the distance between subject and viewer created through focal-length. In addition, the process is generated by the flaws of the image such as blurring, scratching, and writing, all of which further distance us from the events represented. All of these distances are, to reiterate, the result of the photographs' status as amateur. Professional photographs tend to depict their subjects with greater clarity, at a short focal-length, and with a sharper focus, and are usually intent on clarity of context, narrative, and intended significance. Contrarily, the figurative and metaphorical distances identified by examining the visual details of amateur photographs are at the heart of their openness, and the resultant multiplicity of possible interpretations. Moreover, these same distances are what invite us to insert ourselves into the worlds they visualize, and thus, to remember with new insight the acts of violence they depict. Similarly, the potential of the photographs to act as agents in new histories and memories is enabled by the distance of seventy years. As Hüppauf points out the time that has elapsed means that these photographs "no longer produce the urge to look away."[32]

I want to hold open the possibility of differing experiences, differing sensory and emotional responses to the photographs taken by Germans on the Eastern Front. Indeed, this variety is expected given the changing historical, political, ideological, and cultural contexts of reception. While readers may want to challenge the emotions experienced by the contemporary viewer as inauthentic, non-empathic, or removed from the victims', even the survivors', traumatic experience, we do well to remember that this is the nature of memory or "post-memory," and second generation witnessing as Marianne Hirsch has formulated it.[33] For all of the doubts cast over the authenticity of the witnessing in which the photographs taken on the Eastern Front play a part, it does not make the histories they represent any less valuable, the memory they create less profound than those produced by photographs taken by Jews or Allies. In fact, Hirsch points out what is now an evident fact, but was once—in the 1980s—a radical idea: it is impossible for any photograph to reproduce the perspective of the victim, or to narrate history in the voice of the dead because it is necessarily silent.[34] Furthermore, if a representation attempted to reproduce the original trauma on behalf of the one to whom it belonged, this would be considered tasteless itself. Thus, the only perspective from which these images might represent is, in fact, that of distance. Finally, it is imperative to preserve the ethical rights of the victim while also questioning the moral privilege of the same victim's perspective on these events. It is true that while the perpetrator deems the events important enough to capture on film, the resulting images are more than mere documents. There is always a violence in and to the images. We cannot and do not ignore the pride and sense of achievement expressed by the soldiers in some of the photographs. And yet, we do not imitate these responses. If we understand them to represent a complex relationship between the perpetrator and his victim, between the photograph and its subject, between the viewer and the photograph, then we can mobilize the images in the process of witnessing these traumatic events. Moreover, we can exclude the soldier in our witness to the slaughters on the Eastern Front enabled by the images. There is no obligation to invite him to explore, act as a guide or a companion on our journey. As a result, therefore, the status of the image as agent is not dependent on the photographer's respect or disrespect of the silence of the dead. Most significantly, the German perpetrator-photographer is not the conduit for testimony, the testimony of the victim. On the contrary, as viewers, it is our responsibility to assume the unique opportunity offered by these amateur images to witness, to have our memories of events to which we have previously not had access ignited and reignited again and again. Of critical importance to the understanding of the photographs in discourses of witnessing is their conception as amateur, and anonymous images. Seeing the photographs taken on the Eastern Front by an array of photographers as tools of destruction that mirror or contribute to the abhorrent happenings before the camera not only limits the understanding of the images. But it also stymies the possibility of our continued witnessing of World War II and the Holocaust from different perspectives. When we see these photographs through the multiple optics opened up by their status as amateur images in the twentieth century, we gain insight into their discursive coincidence with the phenomena and structures of looking that give them meaning. Seen from varied perspectives, these otherwise reviled photographs as sites of twenty-first century memory processes are, despite their infusion with the conflicts of Nazi ideology, more complex than a designated focus on this same ideological content would allow for. Moreover, this complexity is what lends them as agents in processes of witnessing, as the place where a historical memory of twentieth century crimes can be preserved in the twenty-first century.

NOTES

1. For more on the reuse without adequate attribution of perpetrator images, see my book: *Through Amateur Eyes: Film and Photography in Nazi Germany* (Minneapolis: University of Minnesota Press, 2011).
2. Bernd Hüppauf, "Emptying the Gaze," in *War of Extermination: The German Military in WWII 1941–44*, ed. Hannes Heer and Klaus Naumann (New York and Oxford: Berghahn Books, 2000), 347. See also, Georges Didi-Huberman, *Images In Spite of All: Four Photographs from Auschwitz*, trans. Shane B. Lillis (Chicago: University of Chicago Press, 2008).
3. Hüppauf "Emptying the Gaze," 351. A good example of how the photographer of the crimes on the Eastern Front is always guilty comes in the work of Hanno Loewy, ". . .'without masks' Jews through the lens of 'German photography' 1933–1945," in *German Photography 1870–1970*, ed. Klaus Honnef, Rolf Sachsse, and Karin Thomas (Köln: Dumont, 1997), 106.
4. André Bazin, "The Ontology of the Photographic Image," trans. Hugh Gray, *Film Quarterly* 13:4 (Summer, 1960): 4–9.
5. Péter Forgács, "Wittgenstein Tractatus: Personal Reflections on Home Movies," in *Mining the Home Movie: Excavations in Histories and Memories*, ed. Karen L. Ishizuka and Patricia R Zimmermann (Berkeley: University of California Press, 2008), 47–56. Here he claims: "Mistakes are never part of a film's intentions, yet they are always present. In fact, mistakes make the genre of home movies powerful and real. Even the best, most sensational feature film or journalistic newsreel cannot compete with the latent authority of the home movie. I call that the 'perfection of imperfection.'" (51). In his films such as *The Maelstrom* (1997) and *A Danube Exodus* (1998), he often reuses footage from private home movies to trace the plight of European Jews between 1939 and 1942.
6. Frances Guerin and Roger Hallas, eds., *The Image and the Witness: Trauma, Memory and Visual Culture* (London: Wallflower Press, 2008).
7. Shoshana Felman and Dori Laub, *Testimony: Crises of Witnessing in Literature, Psychoanalysis, and History* (New York: Routledge, 1992).
8. Ibid., 71.
9. For a more thorough explication of this use of the image as an agent in our contemporary process of bearing witness, see Frances Guerin, "Witnessing from a Distance, Remembering from Afar: Historical and Theoretical Grounds" in Guerin, *Through Amateur Eyes*, chapter one.
10. Diethart Kerbs, "Da kommen Menschen zu Tode," *Fotogeschichte* 13 (1984): 51–64.
11. See below for details of prohibitions.
12. Kerbs, "Da kommen Menschen zu Tode," 55–56.
13. Ibid., 54.
14. Marianne Hirsch, "I Took Pictures: September 2001 and Beyond," in *Trauma at Home: After 9/11*, ed. Judith Greenberg, (Lincoln: University of Nebraska Press, 2003), 69–86. On this notion of the documentary image's engagement with the issue of the magnitude of the historical trauma, see Bill Nichols, *Representing Reality: Issues and Concepts in Documentary* (Bloomington: Indiana University Press, 1991), 232. For Nichols, magnitude involves our ethical relationship to the victims of historical trauma, thus it requires that the traumatica historical experience is the basis of the image and its understanding.
15. My concept of witnessing here builds on and should be read in conjunction with the theoretical discussion of the use of the image as witness to traumatic historical events in *The Image and the Witness*. See Guerin and Hallas, *The Image and the Witness*, 1–20.

16. The most well-known here is that of Roland Barthes' discussion of the photograph as an authentication of the occurrence of the past, albeit now lost. Indeed, for Barthes the photograph even takes on the life of what it represents in the mind of the viewer. See Roland Barthes, *Camera Lucida: Reflections on Photography*, trans. Richard Howard (New York: Hill and Wang, 1981), 88–89.

17. Ulrike Schmiegelt, "Macht euch um mich keine sorgen . . ." in *Foto Feldpost: Geknipste Kriegserlevnisse 1939–1945*, ed. Peter Jahn and Ulrike Schmiegelt (Berlin: Elephanten Press Verlag, 2000), 26. Bernd Boll traces the history of prohibition on photographing executions. He also comments that soldiers were not permitted to photograph dead or injured German soldiers. These injunctions were in keeping with the Nazi policy to propagate a very specific image of Germany's success in the war. See Bernd Boll, "Das Adlerauge des Soldaten. Zur Fotopraxis deutscher Amateure in Zweiten Weltkrieg," *Fotogeschichte* 22:85–86 (2002): 75–87. This prohibition is reiterated by most scholars who examine the material. See also, for example, Honnef, Sachsse, and Thomas, *German Photography 1870–1970*.

18. Dori Laub, "Bearing Witness or the Vicissitudes of Listening," in *Testimony: Crises of Witnessing in Literature, Psychoanalysis, and History*, ed. Shoshana Felman and Dori Laub (New York and London: Routledge, 1992), 64.

19. Hüppauf "Emptying the Gaze," 356–57.

20. This is where the concept of soldier as witness is most significantly undermined. Because the photographs violate the humanity of the victims, they automatically preclude any hint of the responsibility of the soldier as witness, let alone a recognition of his own responsibility either for the murder of his enemy or the testimony of his trauma.

21. Barbie Zelizer, *Remembering to Forget: Holocaust Memory through the Camera's Eye* (Chicago: University of Chicago Press, 2000), 10.

22. Gerhard Schönberner, *Der gelbe Stern: Die Judenverfolgung in Europa 1933–1944* (Munich: Bertelsmann Verlag, 1978), 6. The introduction to which I refer was written in 1960.

23. Ibid., 5–8.

24. Ibid., 7. This insight of Schönberner is in itself striking because he is using the photograph as historical document in which the biases form the basis of the discursive value of the images. It is striking because he wrote this in 1960 at a time when there was a blanket of silence over these events in the German cultural and historical imaginary. And it would be another forty years before the same value will be ascribed to the perpetrator's photographs. However, it is also noticeable that, despite his argument, the book includes images taken by a variety of photographers for a variety of purposes, including resistance fighters. He is not interested so much in the images as he is in the making public of the Jewish Holocaust.

25. Ishizuka and Zimmermann, *Mining the Home Movie*.

26. For the argumentation on the translation of Felman's theory for the study of images, see the Guerin and Hallas, "Introduction," in *The Image and the Witness*, 1–20.

27. Guerin, "The Grey Space Between: Gerhard Richter's *18. Oktober 1977*," in *The Image and the Witness*, ed. Guerin and Hallas, 111–26.

28. Cathy Caruth, *Unclaimed Experience: Trauma, Narrative, and History* (Baltimore and London: Johns Hopkins University Press, 1996), especially chapter 3, 57–72.

29. Kathrin Hoffmann-Curtius, "Trophäen und Amulette. Die Fotografien von Wehrmachts- und SS-Verbrechen in den Brieftaschen der Soldaten," *Fotogeschichte* 20:78 (2000): 71.

30. Hüppauf, "Emptying the Gaze," 345–77.

31. Schönberner, *Der gelbe Stern*, 36–37.
32. Hüppauf, "Emptying the Gaze," 349.
33. Hirsch also supports the argument that the photographs are witnessing. See for example, her essay "Nazi Photographs in Post-Holocauast Art. Gender as an Idiom of Memorialization," in *Crimes of War: Guilt and Denial in the Twentieth Century*, ed. Omar Bartov, Atina Grossman, and Mary Nolan (New York: The New Press, 2002), 100–20.
34. This notion was first articulated by Jean-François Lyotard in *La Différend* in his discussions of existential and metaphysical shifts. He talks about the impossibility of proving death in the gas chamber. The only way to prove the existence of the killings is to have the witness testify, and all witnesses are dead. See Jean-François Lyotard, *La Différend: Phrases in Dispute*, trans. Georges Van Den Abbeele (Minneapolis: University of Minnesota Press, 1989), 3–5.

10 Inherited and New Memories*

Ernesto Pujol

INTRODUCTION: FOUR KINDS . . .

Susan Sontag writes that victims are always interested in the representation of their suffering. Therefore, undocumented memories are the intangible journals of the disempowered, and sighted memories their haunting rare monuments. I am neither a victim nor a hero. But, as an artist, I seek to manifest the unspoken.

VISIBLE MEMORIES

During the late 1950s, my parents supported the Cuban Revolution. But they were not communists. They were Christian socialists pursuing human rights, free education, and health care for all citizens regardless of class, gender, and race. Thus, my mother endured the last month of her pregnancy during the harshest days of the battle for power in Cuba, bravely going to work no matter what, to keep the economy going and her dependents fed. Mom always tells the story of one particularly violent morning, when her office work was interrupted, everyone was sent home, and because public transportation had broken down, she had to run heavy with a nine-month belly through Havana's empty streets, seeking shelter under doorways, while sniper bullets flew by and open trucks carried the smoking corpses of fighting men burned beyond recognition. I have heard the story so many times that *I can see it*, not so much like a film, but as if I were there, across the street, watching a pregnant young woman bravely struggling to get home.

Nevertheless, when the new Cuban government aligned itself with the former Soviet Union, tragically transforming the island into yet another Soviet Republic, a chess piece of Cold War players, and shortly after the Bay of Pigs Invasion, which seemed to mark the beginning of increasing armed conflict between the US and Cuba, my parents, who were conscientious objectors, applied to emigrate in 1961. At that time, it was possible but socially shameful to apply for emigration. You were publicly subjected to various forms of official humiliation. Among them was the notorious *home inventory of personal belongings*. Thus, my mother had to spend days going through all the contents of her home, listing all its items, counting and describing them, de facto creating an *intimate inventory of embodied memories*; a *personal inventory of visible memories*.

That is one of my first major inherited memories, that stressful inventorying, that painful detailed *taxonomy of memory*. Moreover, once you completed and handed this immoral document over to a government official, it meant that none of those objects belonged to you anymore. Possessions that had been in your family for generations, items like silver spoons, embroidered cloth napkins, porcelain dishes, fine glasses, a mahogany rocking chair, a first-born's crib, a grandmother's quilt; cheap and expensive, old and new things that you were still living with and using, they all now belonged to the government. So, nothing had changed in your immediate surroundings, and everything had changed: your *relationship* to visible memories had changed.

It was as if you had suddenly been given *the task of detaching memory from object*, so that you could take yourself with you, so that your heart did not remain behind, making it impossible to have a new life beyond that moment, those things, that place. You suddenly had to *learn not to depend on visible memories in order to take your past, your identity with you,* in secret, invisibly.

Looking back, this new overnight relationship to visible or embodied memories definitely triggered a life-long process of almost monastic, Zen Buddhist-like detachment; a brutal process which reached its tragic peak at the dramatic moment of exit. My mother had to walk away forever from those treasured things and that sacred space only with the clothing that she was wearing and her son tight in her arms. From that fateful moment she would have to forget the objects but not the memories, because to go on remembering those things and their loss forever would be devastating, paralyzing, death-like, yet she had a life to live and children to take care of. But she simply could no longer take care of *the visible past*.

And so, although the old photographs that she smuggled out of the country increasingly became sacred family relics, during the rest of her life my mother had no desire to own anything, to hold on to anything, because she had learned in one instant that *visible memories are very fragile*. We make the mistake of thinking that they are weighty, more enduring than fragile human bodies of vulnerable flesh and brittle bone. But monuments of all sizes lose their meaning over time, tumble, or are stolen from us, so that we have no access to them, intellectually nor materially.

However, not every woman in my family walked on into the future so clearly.

Figure 10.1   Ernesto Pujol, *Mother of All Souls*, 2010, from the *111 Days in Deseret* series.

BORROWED MEMORIES

My grandmother and her sister, my great aunt, were great *memory machines*. They sat all day long in rocking chairs and remembered the past, hardly using their bodies except to rock, hardly living below their necks. They left their native land as seniors, so they were too old to learn a new language and get jobs. But, more significantly, the weight of the things they left behind, *the weight of their visible memories*, as embodied in objects, houses, streets, neighborhoods, landscape, people, and the graves of people, were all impossibly heavy anchors that did not let their tired ships sail on.

Thus, they were still alive but their lives were over. They spent the next twenty-five years remembering intensely, teaching/telling me incredibly vivid stories of their childhood, adolescence, and adulthood, repeatedly going over their autobiographies until I learned/knew their stories as well or better than they did. This was fortunate, because at one point they began to lose their minds, and they could not remember anymore. So, I would tell them their own stories, even correcting them when they were wrong about their own facts.

Of course, when you are a child, no matter how precocious you are, you have few memories, because you are mostly a new vessel. Therefore, if you are constantly handed over other people's memories, there is an effect, a *formative memory-shaping effect*. It was amazing to grow up at the feet of these old women because, at one point, I had m-e-m-o-r-i-z-e-d their memories, and I did not know where their memories ended and where my memories began. We were one collective mind. It was as if I had been there at the turn of the century, with these late Victorians, living in the manor house of a palm plantation in the Caribbean, with all its colors, textures, and smells. I was an urban child of the late twentieth century, but I walked around feeling the hot rain of a nineteenth century monsoon, going out to fields of memory to watch sugar cane grow, ride horses, listen to a piano we did not have, travel daily through a world long gone of which I had absolutely not a single object to anchor me to, but a spider web of inherited memories. Brain cell by brain cell, they constructed a way of remembering by embedding memories so intense that they felt more real than reality, ultimately forming my creative way of relating to lived and appropriated experience as a man and an artist.

Many years later, after they died, I finally traveled to Cuba to work with the Ministry of Culture and the National Union of Artists and Writers in the creation of four site-specific non-profit art projects. I traveled to the island source of all this mythical remembering, like the grandchild of fallen aristocrats who returns to the former czarist Russia, mysterious Atlantis, or the ruins of Troy for a reality check of its former riches against the epic *Iliad*. I tested family memories as best as I could, one by one, and, to my surprise, I found them lacking. Everything had been altered, idealized; with some extreme exceptions, mostly the best had been remembered. Because memory, wondrous magical memory, is so subjective, selective, fragmented. *Memory is so incomplete a method of harvest, so cracked a vessel for storage.* It was a sad moment, like losing the key to the door of an invisible world. But it was also a freeing, liberating moment, because I got the opportunity to generate my own set of memories about late twentieth century neo-Revolutionary Cuba; ironically, a set of memories probably just as haunting as the ones I carried before. And it was reality, and there is no fantasy greater than the complexity of reality.

So I am now both like my mother and my grandmother: on one hand, like my mom, I personally continue to chose not to own very much; and, on the other hand, like my grandma, I professionally stop the river of time in my durational performances, to pause and make others pause. Cannot envision life without reflection.

MUSCLE MEMORIES

Other than the opposing poles of attachment and detachment, the third variation that has informed my experience of memory has been that of muscle memories. Muscle memory has definitely taken a very long time to surface in me as a dynamic for remembering. I think that it is the mid-

Figure 10.2   Ernesto Pujol, *Lamb 1*, 2010, from the *Baptism* series.

life result of having spent time in a cloistered monastery, combined with Bikram yoga, Five Rhythms dance, and performance art practice.

Several years ago, I began to hear my Bikram yoga teachers speak about muscle memory. And I thought, *how can there be memory outside the brain, outside the mind?* Then, two things happened that began to alter my understanding of memory, as I knew it: first, my body decided to perform in public. And please note that I say my body, not my mind; *my body decided to perform.* I had been performing for photos and video for years, but never live. So I began to do live performances through some sort of below the neck, separate, non-intellectual drive, definitely through a non-mental force that had to do with torso, hips, and appendages needing and seeking to move. It was, literally, as if my body was driving a car while my brain took a back seat. In fact, most of the time my mind was a terrible passenger, nervous, anxious, suffering motion sickness, stomach cramps, wanting to cry and throw up, like some unwilling brat acting out that one wishes we could just leave at the curb. More often than not, my mind was terrified but my body kidnapped it and dragged it along across spaces and places, landscapes it did not want to move through for fear of embarrassment and hurt.

My body had a secret set of memories that it wanted to revisit and exorcise in my pilgrimage toward an integrated consciousness, and it also harbored other people's memories, lending itself to them as a public vessel and triggering tool. For years, as a contemporary installation artist, I created site-specific, ephemeral, full-immersion environments of memory through borrowed furniture and objects, into which people would come to experience their individual and collective memories.

After all those years, *the mind and its products were not enough for remembering,* so my body put itself forward, and also recruited the bodies of others. In a 2003 project titled *Becoming the Land* at the Salina Art Center in Kansas, I intuitively asked the grandchildren and great-grandchildren of farmers to loan me their bodies, to come out with me to the short grass prairie and revisit their horizon while I photographed them. They did not know it, but I was photographing their muscle memories, their secret embedded imprints. In fact, my mind did not fully know what my body was doing. However, my body seemed to know what it was doing managing those people's bodies; there was a memory dialogue between our bodies.

The second thing that began to happen was an increasing awareness of *the subtleties of remembering.* I began to notice when I was *remembering with the mind* and when I was *remembering through the body.* I began to tell the difference, which I had never noticed before. For example, I returned to an acupuncturist that I had not visited for several years. And before I moved, as I thought about my upcoming appointment, my mind remembered the neighborhood, the building, the office, and the old Chinese lady who barely spoke any English. Therefore, I got there just fine. But then, I suddenly needed to go to the men's room, and my nervous body (about to get pin pricked) got up without thinking about directions, went to the office door, picked up a big set of keys hanging from a hook to the left, went out and turned left into the hallway, walked its length, turned a sharp right, and walked into the men's room. The whole map of bodily need was imprinted in my body and it followed it like wiring. But if you had asked me hours before, the strictly mental I would not have remembered where the men's room was.

That was a rudimentary example, literally. But a more poetic example happened after my 2007 *Memorial Gestures* performance at the Chicago Cultural Center. I choreographed fifteen performers dressed in white for a durational performance mourning the violence of the armed conflict in the Middle East. I used a Civil War *memorial* as the setting if not the excuse to make it politically safe for audiences to challenge our war without being unpatriotic.

The Chicago Cultural Center has a mosaic floor with a checkerboard grid pattern. And without any mental directive, my secular body spontaneously found itself formally walking its memorializing architecture, like many years before when I was a contemplative monk doing walking meditation within a cloister. And my mind embraced it. I intuitively trusted and accepted *the body's non-verbal directive* and I taught the group to imitate my monastic walk. In the end, we performed from 10:00 AM to 10:00 PM. After it was over, after we walked, paused, knelt, stood, walked some

Figure 10.3   Ernesto Pujol, *Memorial Gestures*, 2008, Chicago Cultural Center. Stock photo.

more, sat, got up, and moved on, repeating this for twelve hours, a day into night, embodying both the Civil War memories of a long-gone Victorian generation, and the memories of a new generation of Iraq War widows and orphans, my mind did not know that my body was now *imprinted* with that site-specific choreography.

The day after, when I revisited the site to say goodbye and my body walked unto its checkerboard floor, it began to perform! It refused to walk normally but moved very carefully, walking in slow motion from square to square. So my brain had to order my body stop. *What are you doing? You cannot go back there. It's over. You must resume normalcy.* But my body did not want to obey. And it was only very slowly, with great effort, during minutes that seemed to last for hours in psychic time, that my body finally grudgingly responded, began to walk normally, and was able to say goodbye.

FUTURE MEMORY

I attend a weekly class of Five Rhythms where I try to flow through a dance studio with an empty mind, moving in and out of chaos. But as a Zen Buddhist, the hardest teaching about death is the notion of the total loss of memory, the fact that in the great recycling and reunification of energies in the Great Ocean of Being, most, if not all, of the memories of an entire lifetime are lost. As a humanist, it does not make sense because it would make for a better humanity if we remembered our mistakes and carried on wisdom gained. But then, perhaps human evolution is not the result of a refinement of memory, but a refinement of actions that refine an intangible animating energy. Of course, I do not know, I only try to make peace with my current not-knowing and this future not-knowing. But I stubbornly keep hoping that I remember something next time around, because it took a lifetime to heal the memories of a violent revolution, communism, and stressed and devastated individuals during childhood. It took a lifetime to heal the memories of the AIDS epidemic, and all the illness, dying, death, and mourning I experienced as a young adult. And, more recently, it is taking another lifetime to get over the recent loss of men I love to the depressions and addictions that prey people with *unhealed memories.*

America is undergoing a crisis of memory. Our increasingly sick American economy, which has not hit the bottom yet, is the result of collective Alzheimer's. The American Dream is anti-memory. Its dangerous ignorance of the distant and even recent past, its embarrassment before old age, its denial of death and worship of eternal youth, its cult of entertainment, its addiction to fun, to endless distractions, only makes use of memory as a marketing or political strategy. *American memory has been reduced to slogans*, backdrops, or superficial sentimental points of reference for marketing product and ideology. It is pure copy. I do not know what is going to force us to remember, to return to being a people who remember where we come from, beyond all Hollywood myth. And yet, this true self-critical remembering is the only way by which we will reach the humbling meditation of what we should become, at home and abroad. I do hope that it does not take a nation in ruins for us to awaken to consciousness.

*This chapter was the opening artist lecture during the 2008 Visible Memories Conference at Syracuse University, written in what Peggy Phelan describes as performative writing.

11 The Diffusion of an Atomic Icon
Nuclear Hegemony and Cultural Memory Loss

Ned O'Gorman and Kevin Hamilton

In America, visual imagery related to the "Atomic Age" stands ready for recall as a style, easily appropriated into retro-fashion and nostalgia. But Americans with access to the Atomic Age as style don't necessarily stand ready to recall the era's inaugural event—that of the bombings of Hiroshima and Nagasaki. Thus, within Atomic Age aesthetics, understood as the performance of collective memory, there exists a gap. This chapter considers how that gap might not be so much the product of a collective mental block, but the extension of the structure of the Atomic Age archive as it was built in the Cold War. For the horrible imagery of nuclear destruction was not so much forgotten as it was *lost*, and it was lost as it was managed, even displaced, by competing iconography.

To tell this story we begin where any critical visit to a museum or archive typically begins, with a look at taxonomy. Buried within the U.S. Psychological Strategy Board's 1952 archive sits a two-page catalog of "Photo Branch material for psychological [propagandistic] use," which begins:

> 52–1818P—USN's [Navy's] new F9F-6 "Cougar" jet plane that flys [*sic*] more than 600 mph.
>
> 52–1827P—USAAF's C-124 "Globe Master" cargo airplane takes in AF H-19 helicopter into its belly.
>
> 52–1399P—USN displays its newest carrier-based bomber, the XA2J-1.
>
> 52–1459P—One man helicopter, developed by USN.
>
> 51–17498P—Three French agriculturists study plant disease & insect control in U.S.
>
> 51–17479P—Four French agricultural economists studying in U.S.
>
> 52–1458P—Two technicians at U.S. Atomic Energy Commissions plant in Oak Ridge, Tennessee.[1]

We stop here and make two notes: first, the photo of nuclear technicians was filed alongside those of U.S. air power and agricultural technology, swords and plowshares. Second, the nuclear technicians here are pictured *at Oak Ridge*, squarely allying them with the regime of swords *over* plowshares.

From 1945–1962 some 220,000 personnel were involved in atmospheric nuclear weapons testing alone, and many more contributed to the engineering, construction, storage, protection, and readiness efforts of America's nuclear arsenal.[2] The majority of these personnel were nuclear technicians: engineers, mechanics, pilots, and other kinds of operators of machines. Together, they formed the backbone of American nuclear production, linking science to engineering, theory to application, and design to practice, as well as civilian life to the defense establishment, private enterprise to public service, civil society to the state, and peace to war. For much of the early Cold War, as the Psychological Strategy Board's files suggest, nuclear technicians were canonical icons of American nuclear hegemony, integral to the complex process by which American nuclear power was symbolically sustained and regularly recreated. In as much as American power rested firmly on a claim to technological superiority over the Soviet world, America's nuclear elite rested the claim to both nuclear legitimacy and hegemony on technical mastery. The icon of the expert technical operator visibly reinforced, and indeed performed, this claim. It is thus no coincidence that parallel to America's rise to nuclear power, images of technical experts proliferated throughout mass culture.

Despite the ubiquity of the image of the expert operator in even contemporary iconography, its origins and significance in nuclear production have faded from public memory. It exists as a sign without a referent. Visible yet vacant, contemporary representations of the technical expert at his console, which so dominated early nuclear iconography, now tend toward camp or anachronism. Like monuments to a forgotten war, these mute representations obscure a highly effective program of myth construction. The *origins* of nuclear hegemony have faded from view, hence granting it a quality of permanence, intransigence, even timelessness. We thus truly *suffer* from cultural memory loss.

Those who benefit from American nuclear hegemony might feel understandably ambivalent about the historic violence that produced such a power. If forgetting keeps us subject to the Bomb, it also protects us from its implications. The very iconography that enabled this process of forgetting can also serve in the recovery of collective memory and shared ethical responsibility.

In this essay we give a critical-historical account of a process of cultural memory loss. We trace the course of the icon of the nuclear technician into mass culture's practices and artifacts, arguing that the symbolic power of the nuclear technician in the early Cold War lead to a diffusion, in the sense of widespread use, and thus to a defusing, in the sense of symbolic integration into the mundane. Like the archive of its cataloging, the icon of the nuclear technician came to be buried, so to speak, within the artifacts and practices of mass culture, effectively rendering the nuclear technician as such invisible, and thus largely forgotten—remembered only as it pops up as an anachronism within popular culture, or, as we will discuss in our conclusion, as a suddenly scarce national resource within the nation's defense apparatus.

This history of the diffusion of an icon, we argue, allows us to follow the complex course of the creation, re-creation, and transformation of nuclear hegemony in the U.S. We argue that the diffusion of the icon of the nuclear technician—condensed into the image of an *operator*—eventually encompassed Americans *en masse*, rendering everyone an operator, and the (nuclear) operator a kind of ideal American citizen. This, in turn, eventually transformed the nature of nuclear hegemony in the U.S. from the province of the sublime to that of the mundane.

The first section of our essay, therefore, recounts the state-sponsored visual practice of foregrounding the nuclear technician, with emphasis on the rhetorical functions of this state-created icon with respect to nuclear hegemony. The second section, in turn, looks at the diffusion of the operator in American mass culture, arguing (1) that it is a relic of the nuclear technician, and (2) that it represents the defusing of nuclear hegemony in America from the sublime into the mundane.

Our study would thus make both historical and theoretical contributions to the study of visual practices and practices of memory. Here, we are interested in the *history of an icon* over several decades in the second half of the twentieth century, with special emphasis on the pivotal decade of the 1950s. Like histories of ideas and concepts, our history is guided by particular interests, in our case the relationship of the icon of the nuclear operator to the creation, recreation, and eventual transformation of nuclear hegemony in the U.S. We hope that the particular history we offer here might contribute to other nuclear histories, as well as function for visual studies as one significant example of a history of an icon. Theoretically, we explore the link among aesthetics, memory, and the processes of political hegemony, for the history we offer here gives us insight into one means by which political hegemony, in the words of Raymond Williams, "has continually to be renewed, recreated, defended, and modified."[3] Hegemony has to be formed, reformed, and transformed, and thus includes an aesthetic aspect concerned with what, how, and when a people see an object, idea, and/or concept. We suggest that the transformation of nuclear hegemony in America in the second half of the twentieth century entailed a process of forgetting that was also a process of converting the sublime into the mundane. Thus, we explore the political implications of the aesthetics of memory.

NUCLEAR HEGEMONY AND THE NUCLEAR OPERATOR

Since Hiroshima and Nagasaki, the most spectacular of the nuclear icons has been the image of the mushroom cloud, "the godhead of Annihilation and Ruin."[4] There have been, to be sure, other nuclear icons: bomber airplanes,

ICBMs, and chubby bombs. And then there have been iconic personalities: nuclear scientists, military brass, and presidents. But the mushroom cloud completed each of these signs, and has perdured as the central nuclear icon. At once apocalyptic and admonitory, the image of debris billowing up into a giant white "T" has gained in the modern world the significance of both an augury, forewarning a future fate, and the injunction "Never again."

In fact, this is but one of several dualisms endemic to the iconicity of the mushroom cloud, making it a powerfully polyvalent sign. It is at once an object of "experiment," a product of the development of modern natural sciences, and "experience," a product of the collective imaginary, an object of fantasy, fetish, and futuristic narratives. And within the former, it is at once the apogee of the scientific project, the unlocking of a key to the universe, and the ultimate undoing of that project, unleashing the universe's power in an uncontrollable manner. Similarly, within the world of experience (or "aesthetics"), the image of the mushroom cloud is the consummate sublime object—invoking fear and awe, tropes of magnitude and terror, and doing a kind of violence to the imagination—and, as David Nye has argued, "A technology so terrifying [that it] ceased to seem sublime," and became simply horrifying.[5]

These dualisms have presented serious obstacles to nuclear hegemony. By "nuclear hegemony" we mean the ongoing processes by which political, social, and cultural forces combine to establish and enforce the dominant power of the nuclear-industrial complex, which since the Manhattan Project in the 1940s has had power to command resources, protect secrets, control publicity, and establish professional and political classes and hierarchies of personal and institutional authority. What Raymond Williams writes of "lived hegemony" more broadly we appeal to in conceiving of nuclear hegemony:

> A lived hegemony is always a process. It is not, except analytically, a system or a structure. It is a realized complex of experiences, relationships, and activities, with specific and changing pressures and limits. In practice, that is, hegemony can never be singular. Its internal structures are highly complex, as can readily be seen in any concrete analysis. Moreover (and this is crucial, reminding us of the necessary thrust of the concept), it does not just passively exist as a form of dominance. It has continually to be renewed, recreated, defended, and modified. It is also continually resisted.[6]

Thus hegemony rests on a dynamic "claim to," rather than being the "possession of" the ruling class. Hegemony can never be the "possession of" because it is not total or undivided. It must regularly work to control counter- and alternate-hegemonic forces.[7]

In the case of nuclear hegemony, the "claim to"—as Andrew Feenberg has argued more generally regarding the elites of modern industrial civilization—has been a claim to "technical mastery."[8] Indeed, precisely because the mushroom cloud, the central icon of nuclear power (both in the natural and political sense of "power"), is so volatile, unstable, and polyvalent, *mastery* has been a particularly vital claim to establish and re-establish within the processes of nuclear hegemony. Yet, within its actual evolution, readily available representatives of mastery in American culture have been notably ineffective in sustaining this claim. Theoretical scientists, whose mastery of the "natural" world would seem to solidify a claim to technical mastery, have in fact been repeatedly rendered in public and popular culture alike as potentially "mad," either because they are maniacally obsessed with the power they posses, or because they posses a form of intelligence "out of touch" with "society" (e.g. Jerry Lewis's *Nutty Professor*). Similarly, military men (indeed, they've been *men*), have been portrayed as consumed with destructive power of their nuclear arsenals, ready to sacrifice all life, including their own, in their martial quest (e.g. Air Force General Jack Ripper in *Dr. Strangelove,* or Colonel Cascio in *Fail-Safe*). Even presidents have been rendered weak-kneed, reckless, ill-informed, or as tools of a manipulative conspiracy (again, most notably in *Dr. Strangelove*).

On the other hand, nuclear technicians—at least until the accident at Three Mile Island, and we would argue still after—have been remarkably reliable icons of technical mastery within the hegemonic discourses of nuclear power. By "technicians," we mean those positioned as immediately responsible for the instrumental operation of nuclear power. They include what typically falls under the category "technician" (persons charged with the care and operation of instruments in industrial and/or experimental settings) but also may include engineers, pilots, mechanics, programmers, electricians, etc. All are, in essence, *operators*, charged with the disciplined performance of instrumental feats. Therefore, unlike theoretical scientists, military brass, or politicians, the nuclear technician has enjoyed a unique claim to "technical mastery," one evinced in a myriad of ways in the represented and actual performance of instrumental control over nuclear technologies. In the next section, we explore in some detail the iconicity of the nuclear technician by looking at a number of instances of visual media concerned with the claim to technical mastery vis-à-vis nuclear power: the U.S. government's *Operation Ivy* (1953), Columbia Picture's *Fail-Safe* (1964), Looney Tunes' *Crockett Doodle-Doo* (1960), the U.S. government's atomic energy exhibit in Geneva (August 8–20, 1955), and Frederick Wiseman's *Missile* (1987). Our argument is that the iconic reliability of the nuclear technician resides in the convergence, within his (and even *her*) figure, of three fundamental associations within twentieth century American industrial society: the association of "rationality" with instrumental control, the association of the "model American" with a science-and-technology savvy middle class, and the association of mass military enlistment with mass consumer technologies.

"Men are responsible"

In the fall of 1952 the U.S. tested two nuclear devices in the so-called Pacific Proving Grounds in the Marshall Islands. Detonated from Eniwetok Atoll, the tests were designed to gauge the operability of a hydrogen bomb, and marked the rapid acceleration of the nuclear arms race. Indeed, atomic tests had by 1952 become critical elements in America's "psychological war" with the Soviet Union, intended as much to prove America's nuclear superiority over its adversary as to scientifically test new atomic technologies.

However, Operation Ivy—the codename given to the tests—presented immediate publicity problems for the U.S. government. While the events and images of the operation were tightly guarded, some letters from observers were apparently leaked to the news media, which in turn prompted official statements from the Atomic Energy Commission. To the chagrin of the government, news media relayed the contents of the AEC statements with visuals from Hiroshima and Nagasaki, as well as stock photos from the Pacific Proving Grounds. As Colonel Byron Enyart of the Air Force wrote Truman's Psychological Strategy Board but two days after the completion of the tests, "Along with every statement, the commentators or the television newscasters showed pictures of Hiroshima and Nagasaki, as well as atomic artillery being displayed in our proving grounds, with speeches by Pace and General Officers, showing what great potential war capabilities we have." Such a repertoire of words and images, he warned, "affects the war nerves of Western Europe, and for that matter, the entire world, which in turn makes possible the continued effective use of peace as a leading theme in Soviet psychological operations." To its own detriment, the U.S., Enyart suggested, had not yet dissociated its nuclear testing from warmongering.

Enyart consequently urged the PSB to heed the advice of Dr. Stefan T. Possony, who in an October 1952 government study concluded, "In the field of psychological warfare, too, the atomic bomb is being used effectively against the U.S. Our enemies contend that reliance on this 'weapon of mass destruction' reveals the 'barbarous' character of American 'imperialism.'" Possony thus recommended that, in order to gain the mantel of "peace" in the world, the U.S. government begin to aggressively pursue a non-military "international atomic program" that could in promise if not in deed achieve the "acceleration of industrialization in countries with small investment capacity," "the provision of electric power on a quid-pro-quo basis to countries exporting vital raw materials and fearing depletion and exploitation," "the acquisition of a capability to cultivate large areas of the jungle and steep slopes through cheap power," "the irrigation of large desert areas," the "enlargement of the transportation potential of the world," the "political integration or federation of national states," and the "restructuring of industrial societies."[9]

In this way, Possony's report linked the effective application and operation of atomic energy to technical revolution in industrial society, and indeed to a restructuring of the world order. At the heart of Possony's proposal was the material and "psychological" power of instrumental rationality, which could harness, he asserted, the seemingly infinite potential of atomic energy. Indeed, later—this time advising the Eisenhower administration in the winter of 1954—Possony would stress the iconicity of instrumental control in the Cold War psychological battle for the mantel of peace. Having looked at secret footage of the 1953 Operation Castle tests only to determine there was "no way to produce a movie of the operation in which the hydrogen weapon can be minimized or ignored," he advised

> that the film (about Operation Castle, which would be released on a limited basis later that year) highlight the scientific, systematic and typically American way by which we have been going about developing nuclear energy. We should show the effort involved, our regard for human lives, and the various construction, logistical and technological activities, in order to drive home the idea that American technology can accomplish many gigantic undertakings efficiently. In this particular case, the audience should be convinced that such a problem is "right up our alley" and can be handled without strain.[10]

Operation Castle, in other words, could be presented as an effortless operation, the epitome not of technology spiraling out of control, but of the "rationality" of instrumental control.

To be sure, even in framing atomic tests as "operations"—borrowed from military parlance—elites embedded what were in fact highly experimental and unpredictable scientific and technological ventures within the values of instrumental rationality: success would be tied to technical mastery, and technical mastery could be asserted and reasserted as long as it could be shown that technical instruments did their job monitoring and measuring the tests.

It was precisely such an approach that the U.S. government's *Operation Ivy* took in the 1950s. Importantly, the film—produced by the Air Force's Lookout Mountain Studios in Hollywood to cover the detonation of the "Mike" device—was created *both* for government officials and for the general public (with different cuts of the film for the different audiences), and the discourse of technical mastery vis-à-vis instrumental rationality pervaded both versions. Therefore, the emphasis on technical mastery was not strictly a matter of "audience adaptation" or "pulling one over." Rather, it represented the articulation of an ideology that helped sustain—in the face of both the escalation of the arms race and the mounting challenges of containing the circulation and fallout (literal and metaphorical) of weaponized nuclear energy—the illusions of instrumental rationality with regard to the competent control of machines.

After a short introduction from a government official, *Operation Ivy* (in both versions) begins with a guided tour of the testing complex at and around Eniwetok Atoll, lead by Reed Hadley, a Hollywood movie actor, primarily known in the early 1950s for Westerns. Hadley stands on the *U.S.S.*

Estes, the vessel carrying the lead scientists and engineers overseeing the test. Walking into the ship's control room, he introduces viewers to Stan Burress, Commander of the Scientific Task Group. Burress, in turn, turns to panels of instrumentation and begins to explain their role: "If you'll look close you'll see that it is now 59 minutes before HR. As time clicks off, more and more lights come into operation. This kind of display panel is new to atomic test work because of the large number of remote control and metering problems encountered in this operation." The panels of instrumentation repeatedly return to view in the film: viewers see numerous shots of timing and metering devices, as well as cameras, antennas, receivers, and monitors. Such technologies, viewers are told, ensure the thorough monitoring of the tests. Cameras in particular are foregrounded as reliable instruments of measurement and monitoring. As Burress explains, "The lens of a television camera rather than human eyes is watching events." Nothing, it appears, can escape the "eye" of this network of monitoring and measuring devices—not even, as the film puts it, "one the most momentous events in the history of science. . . . [T]he most powerful explosion ever witnessed by human eyes." Instrumentation thus assures the rational appraisal of the sublime.

Yet, it is not the instruments per se which assert the power of instrumental rationality over this world-historical explosion. It is the bodies before the instruments, the engineers and technicians who establish and assure their proper functioning, who manipulate their controls, who interpret their signals, and who display, in their operational agility, technical mastery.

Figure 11.1   The operator at his console in *Operation Ivy*. http://archive.org.

In fact, instruments without operators, control panels without pilots, or gauges without interpreters would only heighten the anxieties of technology run amok. Within a world of nuclear hegemony, it is thus the iconic figure of the nuclear technician that assuages these anxieties, and assures audiences. Indeed, *Operation Ivy* squarely addresses the "gamble" of nuclear testing by pointing, literally, to the personage of the nuclear technician. Upon the deck of the *U.S.S. Estes* Los Alamos's Robert Graves tells Hadley that the U.S. "must take risks" if it is to achieve "great gains." Hadley responds, "but then the uneasy state of the world puts everything on a gambling basis I guess." "Yes," Graves responds, "but not as much as a gamble as you might think." He then points to an engineer standing upon the deck: "Take that man over there, he and his company have put a great deal of thought into the engineering and design of 'Mike.'" The ideology of technical mastery is in this way concentrated on the *human*, not the machine. Indeed, at the conclusion of the public version of *Operation Ivy*, Val Peterson, Chairman of the AEC, exhorts viewers of the film, "In light of the picture [of the mushroom cloud] which you have just seen I ask to ponder these concerns in your heart and in your conscience as *a responsible American citizen*" (emphasis added). Humans, not machines per se, appear both aboard the *U.S.S. Estes* and in America as a whole as the locus of nuclear control.

Or, as Henry Fonda's presidential character in *Fail-Safe* (1964), another film about nuclear risk (this time a fictional film about losing big), says in a moment of crisis, "All I know is that men are responsible!" This responsibility, however, is fraught with tensions inherent within the association of "rationality" with instrumental control. Fonda's character most directly means "culpable," but his cry and the Peterson's identification of the "responsible American citizen" carry with them other senses of "responsible," particularly, "having control over" and "trustworthy." Implicit within *Fail-Safe*'s narratives about the catastrophic breakdown of machines and humans in the atomic age is a strong argument that, as the film's screenwriter Walter Bernstein has said, "Humans made it, humans can do something about it."[11] While *Fail-Safe* is a powerful protest of the atomic age—and thus a kind of counter-hegemonic narrative—this pivotal claim is but a re-articulation of that made by Peterson in explaining "responsibility" at the conclusion of *Operation Ivy*:

> Two course of action must be followed in the long and difficult road to peace: first, unceasing efforts to reach international agreement upon such a sound proposal as President Eisenhower made to the United Nations for the constructive use of atomic energy in the service of all mankind. This requires better and deeper understanding of the problems it faces upon the part of the American public. Second, prudence dictates steadfast preparation by us at home to back up our president as he goes into the counsels of the world in order that he may lead from

strength, strength based upon an assurance that the American people are prepared to withstand any assault. This is no simple thing to do.

Indeed, the complexities of "better and deeper understanding" and "steadfast preparation . . . to withstand any assault" mirror the ideology of technical mastery: national survival, in Peterson's view, hinges on the American people themselves becoming rational instruments of the arms race. Both Bernstein and Peterson agree that humans—that is, a certain class of humans—can "fix" through instrumental action the crises of the nuclear age. They differ only on the nature of the crisis.

"Men are responsible" in part because nuclear hegemony depends on a particular vision of the human, a vision embodied in and performed by the technician: competent; rational but not "mad" with science or power; capable of "great feats" but only as a member of a dependable work force. The nuclear technician represents a *class*, a decidedly "middle" class. He is expert but not genius, hard-nosed yet humane, a master of machines with no evident wish to be an overlord of people. He is, in short, thoroughly socialized to middle-class values within American industrial society: dutiful, responsible, patriotic, even cowboyish. In the 1960s it was the space program more than any other cultural text that asserted this view of the technician. NASA's "Houston" stood as a visible "pacific" model of the cloaked Strategic Air Command, reassuring Americans and the world that, as Columbia Picture's disclaimer read at the end of *Fail-Safe*, "a rigidly enforced system of safeguards and controls insure that occurrences such as those depicted in this story cannot happen." If American astronauts had the "right stuff" to make them national heroes, Houston's flight controllers, engineers, and managers represented the middle-class basis of the American technological exploit that assures the "responsible" pursuit of complex tasks.

A caricature of this vision is evident in the Looney Tunes' 1960 *Crockett Doodle-Doo*. The plot is cartoonishly simple: Foghorn Leghorn, an overgrown rooster with a strong Southern accent, meets the little Egghead Jr. on the edge of the woods, just past the farm. Egghead is seated on a barrel, reading a book, *Basic Research in the Physical Sciences* by "Prof. Newt Ronn." Foghorn declares to the audience, "Now that, I say that, is no way for a kid to be wasting his time, reading that long-haired gobbledygook." "Boy, I say boy," he shouts, turning toward Egghead, "I say I'm gonna take you out to the woods, and learn ya 'bout scoutin, woodcraft, real Davy Crockett stuff!" Egghead, who does not speak, shakes his head to express his lack of interest. Nevertheless, Egghead joins Foghorn in the woods for a series of challenges: who can make a fire, who can call ducks, and who can produce smoke signals. In every case, Egghead puts down his book and betters his rival with "up to date" technologies: matches, a manufactured duck call, and a projection device. Then Foghorn, now wearing an Indian headdress, admits, "Pretty sneaky. But I got, I say I gotta, show the

Egghead I still got a couple of Indian tricks up my sleeve." Using a hidden watering can, he prances about "Indian style" and pretends to make it rain. Egghead in turn, makes a simple paper airplane that he loads with a small container bearing a chemical compound. The compound, in turn, produces a thundercloud that ends up not only soaking Foghorn, but frying him. The cartoon then culminates with battle over who can build the better trap, with Foghorn, of course, ending up hung upside down from a tree in Egghorn's contraption. "Hey boy," he says, "got anymore of those long-haired books?"

The class and regional markers in *Crockett Doodle-Doo* are evident. Foghorn is backwoods, primitive, poor, white, and Southern. Egghead is a would-be Yankee, studiously aspiring to "get off the farm" and enter a civilized technological order. The class hierarchy of the piece is even clearer: Foghorn is "schooled" by Egghead, and left "lynched" from his feet, begging for some "long-haired books." (Foghorn is a caricature of the Southern white supremacist—intolerant, assertive, and brutal.) White middle-class Yankee society thus decisively triumphs over Dixie barbarity. Circa 1960, the tale no doubt evoked, among other things, the recent memory of Little Rock. However, this class-based story is catalyzed not by a conflict over inclusion, but by Professor Newt Ronn's *Basic Research in the Physical Sciences*, which Egghead so studiously reads. Indeed, "basic science" was a major concern of the Eisenhower administration: it was a concept critical to the nation's military defense enterprise, to civil defense, and to internal security.

With regard to military technologies, "basic science" was seen as the foundation of American technological superiority over their Soviet rivals. On March 15, 1956, Eisenhower's National Security Council requested a presentation "on the problem of technological superiority be made by the Department of Defense, the Office of Defense Mobilization, and the National Science Foundation." The White House had grown increasingly concerned that the Soviets were "making rapid strides" in basic scientific research and was on the cusp of overtaking the U.S. "in the education and training of scientific and technical personnel."[12] On May 31, the representatives of the DOD, ODM, and NSF made their presentation to the NSC. Alan Waterman of NSF argued that "basic research" was the key ingredient to maintaining America's technological superiority, and thus edge in defense. "The most decisive factor for us in the struggle to maintain scientific and technological leadership is manpower, and above all its quality and competence," he argued. The broad promotion of "basic research" could be the bedrock of a large corps of scientists, engineers, and technicians.[13] Consequently, shortly after the presentation Eisenhower directed that DOD, NSF, and the Department of Health, Education, and Welfare develop programs "to meet the problem of maintaining free world technological superiority over the Soviet bloc," of which *Crockett Doodle-Doo* was a reverberation.[14]

With respect to civil defense, "basic science" represented a dispositional ideal. Scientists, engineers, and technicians embodied a model of calmness, rationality, and deliberation—a kind of "democratic" deliberateness before great challenges, where problems are "internalized," solutions objectively debated, and action-plans followed with discipline. Indeed, the 1956 "Report to the President and the National Security Council by the Panel on the Human Effects of Nuclear Weapons Development" advised the president to embrace the scientific study group as a model for educating the public on the risks of nuclear war. It discouraged a "mass communications media approach," urging instead locally-run discussion groups which would, like a scientific study group, abide by norms of calm and collected rational consideration: "We believe that such issues can be discussed in an atmosphere of calm deliberation with less emphasis on the symbols and images of disaster that so often characterize the emergency approach to attention getting, but which carries the danger of provoking apathy and hysteria."[15] In this way, the studious Egghead, calmly reading Prof. Newt Ronn's book and applying its basic principles to his tango with the barbarous Foghorn, represented a *dispositional* model integral to the processes of nuclear hegemony. Neither apathetic nor hysteric before Foghorn's "feats," Egghead simply takes his book knowledge and outdoes his rival.

Finally, "basic science" was a concept implicated in matters of internal security against espionage, treason, and other forms of disloyalty to the nation. According to a 1955 FBI pilot study, *laborers* posed a significantly greater risk to internal security than engineers and technicians among government contractors. Technicians, draftsmen, and mechanics, on the other hand, had the fewest incidents of subversion (with engineers having more incidents than the latter, but far less than laborers). In fact, labor, especially labor strikes, presented serious challenges to both the Truman and Eisenhower administrations in the 1950s. The 1950 Defense Production Act was aimed at ensuring government command over defense production, granting the executive branch power to requisition plants and property, raw materials, and to institute wage and price controls. On April 9, 1952, Truman notoriously nationalized the steel industry as the steel workers prepared to strike amidst the war in Korea, only to be rebuffed by the Supreme Court in *Youngstown Steel & Tube Co. v. Sawyer*. And in 1954, labor strikes at the nuclear production facilities in Oak Ridge, Tennessee and Paducah, Kentucky caused the Eisenhower administration a great deal of trouble. Eisenhower's AEC warned that they "will have a serious effect on programs of the Commission which are directly related to the national safety," a conclusion with which the president's specially appointed Board of Inquire concurred. Thus, on August 11, 1954 Eisenhower requested, and was granted, an injunction against the strike.[16] In this way, the FBI's "findings" were not surprising: the "disloyalty" of laborers was part and parcel of a governmental structure of differentiation, in which laborers were pitted against other working-class groups like technicians and engineers who were seen as not only more competent, but more loyal, than laborers by virtue of their grasp of the unique challenges of the nuclear age.

With the centrality of "basic science" to government visions of national defense and security in mind, Egghead retains all of his Yankee middle-class identity, but gains even more definition. Studiously reading Prof. Newt Ronn's book, he is a nascent nuclear technician, and, as such, a model American citizen. His ability to apply the basics of science seemingly effortlessly to the operation of tools, instruments, and technologies signifies that he is capable of contributing to the national defense via the upkeep of America's "technological superiority," that he will be calm, collected, and rational in the face of nuclear risks, and that he will be loyal to the nation, attune to the challenges of a nuclear age. Egghead is a "post-industrial" *operator*, a loyal and contributing member of a nuclear nation. Foghorn, on the contrary, is Southern laborer who, like the laborers in Tennessee and Kentucky, still operates within the politics of an older "industrial" order, and thus undermines the nation's nuclear defense measures.

EVERYONE AN OPERATOR, EVERYONE A SOLDIER

If Egghead was a model American because he studiously masters basic science and thus achieves technical mastery, then technical mastery was no longer being protected as the exclusive possession of an elite class, as it had been well into twentieth-century industrial society. Technical mastery had been popularized, making its way even into the backwoods of the South (at least among the young). Publications like *Popular Mechanics,* which were widely popular among boys in the 1950s and which were dominated by pieces on atomic science, testify to an expanding technical class, one that became virtually identical with a white middle-class and thus with "main-stream America."

The evolution of American technical expositions overseas shows this expansion. While such expositions had a relatively long history—most notably, the 1893 Columbian Exposition in Chicago—in the 1950s, amidst the battle for "technological superiority" between the Americans and the Soviets, they took on special importance in state-sponsored propaganda efforts. The first such U.S. sponsored exhibit focused exclusively on atomic energy was the International Conference on Peaceful Utilization of Atomic Energy in Geneva in August, 1955, a key component of Eisenhower's expansive "Atoms for Peace" propaganda program. The exhibition—facilitated with the cooperation of American corporations—featured atomic technologies for medicine and industry. For example, a machine for calibrating "thyroid uptake" (likely using radioactive iodine) was shown, featuring a young, white, and nude female mannequin as its subject (the thyroid affects metabolism, protein levels, and sensitivity to various hormones). Diagrams of chemical plants related to atomic energy were also featured.

A principle attraction was an atomic reactor built at the Oak Ridge facility and shipped to Geneva. Throughout the exposition, in both American and Soviet exhibits, lab-coat donning scientists and technicians displayed massive control panels, worked instruments, and explained dials and gauges.[17] Thus, *le personnel technique* (masc.) and their atomic machines dominated the Geneva conference.[18]

The U.S. and the U.S.S.R. engaged in a series of such expositions on the "peaceful uses" of atomic energy in the latter years of the 1950s, each government trying to claim for itself the mantel of peace. In the judgment of the U.S. government, the U.S. efforts were "highly successful." "The United States," a joint AEC and Department of State report on a 1958 exhibition stated, "held a dominant role generally through the quality and number of its technical papers and impressive technical exhibits. The latter was regarded as the finest scientific exhibition ever assembled."[19] Atomic science and technology, therefore, came to stand in for science and technology more broadly.

However, the well-known 1959 American National Exhibit in Moscow was different. Housed under a giant "sunburst pattern" aluminum dome in Sokolniki Park, thus architecturally establishing atomic science as the overarching American technological achievement, the Moscow exhibit was a far more expansive elaboration of the wonders of atomic energy than the prior conferences on the "peaceful uses" of atomic energy had been. The U.S. exhibit featured the themes of "Land and People," "America Lives," "America Works," "America Produces," "America Consumes," "America Learns," "America Explores Man and the Universe," "America Creates," "America Travels," "America Plays," and "American Community Life." The idea behind the plethora of themes, formulated by the U.S. Information Agency, was "getting our message to the Soviet people" in kaleidoscopic fashion, focusing on the benefits of American technological superiority for a consuming middle class.[20]

Thus, perhaps surprisingly, the *kitchen*—the site of the infamous "kitchen debate" between Soviet Premiere Khrushchev and Vice President Nixon— proved to be one of the most highly charged "messages." Thematized as "America Consumes," the display featured such things as a demonstration of a "DeLuxe kitchen," plastic, rubber and aluminum kitchen equipment, electrical appliances, a food demonstration (including packaging, preservation, cooking, ready mixes, frozen foods, canned foods), and snack bars and automatic food and drink vending machines. In the so-called Kitchen Debates, Khrushchev dismissed these consumer items as "silly," provoking Nixon's poking finger and an apparent *non sequitur*: the Vice President's demand, in response, that the Soviets not make any unilateral demands at the upcoming Four Powers Conference.

A *non sequitur*, however, it was not, at least not from the perspective of an expanding nuclear hegemony. The kitchen in the 1959 Moscow exhibit represented the diffusion of the American nuclear technician into the domestic, everyday, and feminine. No longer the subject of atomic technology—vulnerably positioned before the machine—the white, middle-class American woman gained at the Moscow exhibit the status of an "operator," seamlessly manipulating a myriad of devices in running her efficient, technologically sophisticated home. Indeed, the American exhibit subtly collapsed a series of distinct spaces by focusing on the technological possibilities of "small" spaces (e.g. the kitchen, the micro-apartment, and the modest prefab home). The exhibit testified to the possibilities technology had created for the airship, the space station, the fallout shelter, the bunker, and the underground atomic control room. "America," it asserted, can "work," "produce," "consume," "play," "explore," "create," "learn," and even "travel" within small, technologically sophisticated spaces.

Thus the point of the Moscow exhibit, albeit implicit rather than manifest, was that *all* Americans were coming into the atomic age, *all* Americans were becoming technical masters, capable of thriving within the new, smaller confines of atomic architecture. Even as Radio Free Europe and Radio National Liberation tried to convince peoples behind the Iron Curtain that Soviet technological success—most spectacularly in *Sputnik*—came at the expense of the people's general standard of living, America's supremacy in consumer goods and maneuvering in small spaces suggested the presence of a citizenry prepared, en masse, to manage a technological war. Thus, what was conspicuously missing from the themes at the Moscow exhibit was in fact its overarching implication: America *fights*, and fights as technical masters. Even the *women* of America, as the kitchen exhibit stressed, can manipulate the machine.

The development of this sort of American universal conscription was provocatively explored in Frederick Wiseman's *Missile* (1987), a documentary film about the 4315th Training Squadron of the Strategic Air Command at Vandenberg Air Force Base in California. The film follows, among others, several women being trained to work as Minute Man II (a land-based nuclear ICBM) operators at Whiteman Air Force Base in Missouri. Whiteman had distinguished itself in the 1980s as the home of the first Strategic Missile Wing to accept women operators, and *Missile* hinges on the image of a two-woman team operating a nuclear control panel as efficiently as the women of America's "kitchen" in the Moscow exhibit.

Indeed, *Missile* explores *Fail-Safe*'s claim "Men are responsible!" by complicating it. A daylong session on ethics and "deterrence" makes up, by far, the longest scene in the documentary, and is a window into SAC's conception of "responsibility." At the beginning of the session, students are told that at the end of the day they will be asked to sign a statement expressing that they have "no reservations" about inserting launch keys if given the order from the president. The purpose the day's session, the senior officer explains, is to help the trainees prepare for signing the statement. "We want you to fully comprehend the awesomeness of this responsibility," he explains. "We don't want you to be robots." Nevertheless, they are told that their signature means that they will, without question, follow the orders given, trusting, as the senior officer says, that "the president of the United States is not going to ask you to insert those launch keys until there's just no other option. It's the final solution." The moral responsibility of the trainees therefore is condensed into a signature of assent. On the other side of the signature, the only responsibility of the SAC operator is instrumental efficacy: transcribing code, reading gauges, rotating dials, flipping switches, and turning keys. In this way, the focus in *Missile* on the daylong ethics instruction plays on the evident disproportionality of SAC training: one day of a fourteen-week program is devoted to the question of the moral responsibility of the nuclear operator, and that responsibility is reduced to what is an essentially legal procedural act. The remaining ninety-seven days are devoted to strictly instrumental concerns. Nuclear hegemony, *Missile* suggests, is contingent on a more fundamental instrumental hegemony.

This instrumental hegemony is most subtly explored as the film probes the inclusion of women within the training of nuclear operators. On the one hand, *Missile* shows the trainers speaking and acting before the training squadron as if there were no sex-and-gender differences among the group; everyone is neutered into an operator-soldier. On the other hand, in featuring a meeting exclusively among the all male trainers, where the men are exhorted to avoid "fraternization" with students, especially now that women are among the group, *Missile* shows that the "egalitarian" approach of SAC is consciously created, even enforced. Women trainees have in fact disrupted the norms of behavior at SAC, but the operational life of the program must not show it. In this way the assertion of instrumental neutrality that underlies the claim "Men are responsible!" is extended to personnel. To retain "feminine" and "masculine" within the program would be undermine the fundamental logic of instrumental neutrality precisely because, as *Missile* shows, *operators are instruments*, having signed off their moral selves to an operational command-and-control structure.

Still, sex-and-gender differences are manifest in the film's portrayal of the training program. In an introductory session on instrumental operation, several of the women trainees tell the squadron that Whiteman's unique initiative to bring women into the ICMB corps drew them to the program. And we see SAC forming their two-person commander and deputy teams along sex lines, evidently to avoid any problems feared from coupling male and female in small underground control rooms for extended periods of time. Indeed, the film's denouement comes when a two-woman team moves through a launch practice run without any errors, earning an "outstanding performance" mark. "Your crew coordination throughout the evaluation was outstanding," a senior male officer tells them during a debriefing. "Checklist discipline especially . . . You can tell that you trained very hard to get to this level readiness." Relative to the typical modes of expression among the subjects of the film, the women become effusive upon hearing the news, emotionally embracing one another. *Missile* thus does for issues of sex and gender what it did for issues of morality, highlighting the contradictions of the training program through disproportionate attention to the tensions of SAC's participation within an instrumental hegemony.

Within this hegemony, the nuclear technician is an ideal American citizen because its (*nuet.*) technical mastery can be thoroughly neutralized, militarized, and operationalized. If, as Susan Zaeske has argued, the "signature" has played a crucial role in the assertion of political agency in U.S. history, especially for women, SAC's signature is an emblem of a counterforce in modern democracy: the universal subscription of all citizens into the instrumental war aims of the modern democratic state (first seen in Napoleon's *Grande Armée*).[21] The passage of women in the 1950s from subjects of atomic technology, seen in the 1955 thyroid calibrating machine at the Geneva exposition, to the operators of technologies housed under an atomic canopy, seen in the 1959 Moscow exhibit, to atomic operators, seen in *Missile*, represents a significant advance for nuclear hegemony, "democratizing," as it did, the nuclear operator, diffusing "it" into the whole of American mass culture. Just as a giant sunburst pattern aluminum dome covered the American exhibit in Moscow in 1959, so the diffusion of instrumental, interface-based technologies into American mass culture in the 1950s, 60s, and beyond brought the entire nation under the cover of nuclear power.

CONCLUSION

Ignition keys, "touch and go" microwaves, GPS, push button toasters, easy control blenders, equalizers on stereos, digital gas pumps, television remote controls, dial-up pizza delivery, programmable thermostats, synthesizers, text messaging, CB radios, voting levers, toy ray guns, parking meters, dialysis machines, surveillance devices, drones, robotic manufacturing, programmable waffle makers, keypad entry systems, combine cabs, video games, digital dashboards, personal computers, Lite-Brite, kiosks in subway stations, computer notebooks, jet airplane cockpits, droids, credit card machines, technical support menus, markable pdf files, shoe phones, cell phones, iPhones, and the vast interface mediated realm we call the internet. "We are all operators," or so it would be.

To be sure, post-war American consumer technologies had a complex life, one that can be looked at apart from the development of nuclear technologies. Yet, our argument is that nuclear hegemony, understood as a dynamic "claim to" nuclear-centric political power by a ruling elite, came to cover in the 1950s the whole of American consumer culture. The nuclear operator, once standing heroically as an icon of technical mastery, was transformed into the technologically savvy housewife, the tricked-out farmer, the increasingly digitized office worker, the disco drummer, the videogame junkie, and the countless iterations of technicians operating everything from air-conditioning units to stadium public address systems.

This transformation, we suggest, was at once aesthetic and mnemonic. Aesthetically, nuclear hegemony claimed the American consumer-citizen as a kind of mundane metonym. Just as in the mid-1950s the nuclear technician stood as an iconic figure of rational control and technical mastery within official government rhetoric, so the Moscow Exhibit bore witness to the transference of this iconic logic to the middle-class American. The mundane absorbed the sublime, turning "every" American into a metonym for the rationality of nuclear technologies.

This aesthetic movement, of course, follows the logic of "hegemony" as explicated by Antonio Gramsci, Raymond Williams, and others, wherein the dominated class comes to "consent" to its own domination by a ruling class. It also, to be sure, makes nuclear hegemony vulnerable to counter-hegemonic resistance as operators "seize the controls" to put into question the nuclear state (e.g. as in *War Games* (1983), which like *Fail-Safe* challenges the reliability of our machines, but this time through the mundane figure of a computer-happy "whiz kid"). Yet, in acceding through consumer culture to the claim of technical mastery and instrumental rationality, we invariably perform in our most mundane operational actions the logics that created nuclear hegemony.

Curiously, contemporary reappropriations of the Atomic Age forget the crucial role operators played in rationalizing nuclear technologies. The memory practices of modernity are inextricably tied to the sublime. To be remembered, to be registered as significant within collective memory, is to be marked with some aspect of fear, wonder, or awe. That within the memory of nuclear iconography, still remarkably active in the discourses of nuclear energy and nuclear terrorism, the operator has been forgotten, buried both within mass culture and in the archives the nuclear complex, means only that our modern memory culture is oblivious to the mundane, and thus to the myriad of ways subjection is realized, indeed operationalized.

This is an important function of the visual in memory practices. Through their participation in the sublime, traditional monuments resist being operationalized—we return to them the way we return to a park, a liminal space that does not fit in everyday flows. For ambivalent memories, this is not a desirable rhythm, we wish to forget these events altogether. There are few better ways to collectively forget than to hide such unpleasant memories in plain sight, and there's no better place to hide them than in the mundane visual flow of media images.

At the same time, what has been forgotten, the operator, was crucial to the public record of the specific, historical origin of the Atomic Age in the destruction of Hiroshima and Nagasaki being *lost*. A myth of origins has acceded to a myth of timelessness—indeed a boon to nuclear hegemony. For even if the archive of nuclear power and production is around us, as a kind of living repository of memories of how "we" achieved the right to nuclear dominance, our internalizing it to the point that we do not recognize it as having originated—as *historical*—means that with respect to nuclear power we live in a memory culture without referents. One function of monuments without referents is to establish the state as timeless. Where there is no myth of origins, there is nothing transitory, contingent, or precarious. And this can only serve nuclear hegemony.

Yet, it can undermine it too, for in forgetting the special status of the nuclear technician we may see its increasing scarcity within the means of nuclear production. Indeed, the 2008 Report of the U.S. Commission on the Prevention of Weapons of Mass Destruction Proliferation and Terrorism, *World at Risk*, suggested as much, admonishing the U.S. government to "protect," as a "national resource," the nuclear technician:

> With regard to nuclear weapons, the number of technical experts available to the intelligence community is declining because of retirements and the reduction in innovative nuclear weapons-related work at the U.S. national laboratories. Nuclear expertise remains in high demand by the intelligence community because it serves as a hedge against breakout capability and other technological surprises by state and non-state adversaries. Accordingly, such expertise should be protected as a national resource.[22]

Thus, as the icon of the nuclear technician has been forgotten, so the survival of the nuclear technician itself has been endangered. Indeed, nuclear power in America has been folded into the mundane infrastructures of the energy industry and national defense. Once lionized as a singular source of American security, prestige, and prosperity, it has become but one option among several sites of energy and defense exploitation, creating for the state a crisis in available resources.

NOTES

1. Harry S. Truman Library, Papers of Harry S. Truman, SMOF: Psychological Strategy Board Files, Box 3.
2. F. R. Gladeck, et al., *Operation Ivy: 1952* (Springfield, VA: National Technical Information Service, 1982), 5.
3. Raymond Williams, *Marxism and Literature* (New York: Oxford University Press, 1977), 112.
4. Don DeLillo, *Underworld* (New York: Scribern, 1998), 563.
5. David E. Nye, *The American Technological Sublime* (Cambridge: MIT Press, 1994), 254.
6. Williams, *Marxism and Literature*, 112.
7. Ibid., 113.
8. Andrew Feenberg, *A Critical Theory of Technology* (New York: Oxford University Press, 1991), v.
9. Byron Enyart, Memo for the Record, November 18, 1952; Stefan T. Possony, "An Outline of American Atomic Strategy in the Non-military Fields," October 6, 1952. Both documents can be found at the Harry S.

Truman Library, Papers of Harry S. Truman SMOF: Psychological Strategy Board Files, Box 37.

10. Martin Medhurst, "Atoms for Peace and Nuclear Hegemony: The Rhetorical Structure of a Cold War Campaign," *Armed Forces and Society* (1997): 23.4, 576–77.

11. Jeffery Scwarz, director, *Revisiting Fail-Safe*, DVD (packaged with *Fail-Safe* Special Edition, 2000) (Los Angeles: Automat Pictures, 2000).

12. Memo from the National Security Council, March 15, 1956, "Basic National Security Policy"; Robert H. Johnson introductory remarks on "Technological Superiority" prior to NSC presentation; see folder "NSC 5602 (1)" in Dwight D. Eisenhower Library, White House Office, National Security Council Staff: Papers, 1948–61, Disaster File, Box 14.

13. "Maintenance of Technological Superiority," Presentation before the National Security Council, May 31, 1956, folder "NSC 5602 (1)" Disaster File, Box 14.

14. NSC Memo, June 5, 1956, "Technological Superiority"; folder "NSC 5602 (1)" Disaster File, Box 14.

15. See "Report to the President and the National Security Council by the Panel on the Human Effects of Nuclear Weapons Development," (November 1956), 13, 21, Eisenhower Library, Ann Whitman Files, Administrative Series, Box 4.

16. See "Statement of the Atomic Energy Commission as to the Strike by Locals 288 and 550 United Gas, Coke and Chemical Workers, CIO" and "Report to the President by the Board of Inquiry Created by Executive Order No. 10542" in folder labeled "Atomic Energy Commission 1953–54 (3)" in Eisenhower Library, Ann Whitman Files, Administrative Series, Box 4. For Eisenhower's request for an injunction see "Letter Directing the Attorney General To Petition for an Injunction in Labor Dispute at the Atomic Energy Commission Facilities at Oak Ridge and Paducah," August 11, 1954, at John T. Woolley and Gerhard Peters, The American Presidency Project [online]. Santa Barbara, CA: University of California (hosted), Gerhard Peters (database). Retrieved October 31, 2010 from http://www.presidency.ucsb.edu/ws/?pid=9978.

17. Over seventy countries were said to have participated in the exhibit, but it was clearly dominated by the U.S. and U.S.S.R.

18. The French is drawn from a Union Carbide press release. See folder "Atomic Energy Commission—1955, Photographs," in Eisenhower Library, Ann Whitman Files, Administrative Series, Box 4.

19. See folder "Atomic Energy (9)," Eisenhower Library, White House Office, Nat Security Council Staff: Papers, 1948–61, Disaster File, Box 6.

20. Minutes of Cabinet Meeting, January 23, 1959, Eisenhower Library, Ann Whitman File, Cabinet Series, Box 12.

21. Susan Zaeske, "Signatures of Citizenship: The Rhetoric of Women's Anti-Slavery Petitions," *Quarterly Journal of Speech* 88:2 (May 2002): 147–68. See also Zaeske's *Signatures of Citizenship: Petitioning, Antislavery, and Women's Political Identity*, (Chapel Hill: University of North Carolina Press, 2003).

22. *World at Risk*, The Report of the Commission on the Prevention of WMB Proliferation and Terrorism (New York: Vintage Books, 2008), 97.

12 Silenced Memories

Forgetting War in Finnish Public Paintings

Johanna Ruohonen

War commemoration is an essential tool for nation-states to establish their official narratives. In Finland, a civil war in the early moments of independence in 1918 and a series of wars against the Soviet Union and Germany during the course of World War II not only had a great role in defining the Finnish nation-state, but have also been used in various ways to create a sense of national identity through commemorative art. Their public remembrance and commemoration has, however, been complicated. Following the civil war, the two sides had different histories to be commemorated. Following World War II, artists had to create monuments for a war effort that was not victorious, maintaining its glorifying nature while not offending the victors.[1]

Memorial monuments commonly glorify the military past of a country, show the justice of wars, and solidify official narratives.[2] As W. J. T. Mitchell has argued, much of the history of public art has served to monumentalize violence.[3] While monuments have also been employed in the official remembrance of the past wars in Finland, the focus of Finnish public paintings has more often been geared towards the future. Public painting bloomed especially in the context of the post-WWII reconstruction, an era strongly marked by the past wars, yet the subject of war is largely absent. Instead, the paintings depict a harmonious society, united in reconstruction. The ways in which Finnish wars have been addressed in public art, and also how the subject has been avoided, reveal a problematic relationship towards the remembrance of wars.

The traditional materials of monuments, bronze and stone, signal a lasting presence, which is essential for commemoration. Public paintings have more often been assigned didactic and propagandist, as well as decorative, functions, even though examples of systematic employment of commemorative public paintings are easy to find around the world.[4] Nevertheless, even without an explicitly commemorative function, officially produced public art bears direct relation to official memories. Choices over which locations are marked, who and what is depicted, and in what ways, offer a view into the institutional formation of official memories through public art. Public art may be used to foster both remembrance and forgetting in the society.

By official memory, I refer to an authoritative interpretation that guides, for example, history writing.[5] Public art production serves to create a coherent historical narrative, which has been considered necessary for justifying the existence of nation-states, especially in the moment of their forming. While striving for a coherent history, regimes often wish to control and delimit the individual memories of many citizens. Official memory is often accompanied by either subtle or powerful coercion on how things should be remembered.[6] In Finland, this tendency shaped history writing and memorialization for decades after the civil war. Commemorations of the losing side emerged slowly after World War II and issues relating to the civil war are still sensitive in Finnish society.

James E. Young has called monuments intersections between public art and political memory that create common spaces of memory. In this way, according to Young, "monuments propagate the illusion of common memory."[7] Jay Winter and Emmanuel Sivan describe the activity performed at a memorial as "collective remembrance," memories called upon collectively in public.[8] Indeed, remembrance at a memorial does not happen automatically but demands articulated acts of remembering by the spectators and enough background knowledge to recognize what is being commemorated. It also has been suggested that with monuments societies outsource the burden of remembering; while the monuments remember for us, we are allowed the luxury of forgetting.[9]

Just as wars are complex and controversial political nexuses, the situations that follow them are equally complicated: the peace that follows a war is not a "return" to a time before the conflict. Wars create a number of issues for the state to deal with, such as demobilization, solving economical problems, integrating the veterans, and minimizing the spiritual damages of the society.[10] According to Petri Karonen, the minimizing of the spiritual damages following a war is achieved by bettering the spiritual state of the nation, and remembering the war in all its forms but especially as honorable.[11] The last point is the most relevant in the context of art, and the one in which art can be most directly used.

In addition to the work of remembrance that shapes communal life after war, forgetting may also serve a number of functions in a post-war society. As Paul Connerton has demonstrated, forgetting does not necessarily equal a loss, but it may serve even a critical role for the creation of one's identity or a peaceful life in a society.[12] This chapter discusses the uses of officially produced art in the complex process of remembering and forgetting after war.

THE DIVIDED NATION

The Finnish civil war broke out soon after the declaration of independence, in January 1918, while much of Europe continued to battle in

World War I. Although labeled a civil war, the conflict was not merely internal, as the two opposing sides, the right-wing White and the leftist Red, were aided by Germany and Bolshevist Russia respectively. The division of the society generally followed class lines: the middle- and upper-class supported the Whites while the Reds consisted mainly of members of the working-class and peasantry. The Whites represented official Finland and fought under the command of the Senate, whereas the Reds were revolutionary and blamed for revolt after the war. The battles lasted only for a few months, from January until May 1918, but the losses were great on many levels. The total number of deceased has been estimated at 35,000 people, of which 30,000 were Red. As victors, the Whites incarcerated tens of thousands of people in prison camps, where up to 13,500 people were killed. Both sides committed terrorist acts, which deeply scarred Finnish society.[13]

After the war, the White side legitimized the event as a war of independence and commemorated their cause with monuments, often named "statues of liberty." As Paloma Aguilar has shown in regards to the Spanish Civil War, mourning is never a simple process, but for the victorious side of a civil war it is made significantly easier. In Spain, the members of the winning side enjoyed official support, and were able to express their grief in various ways. From the shared experience, they could achieve some form of moral and psychological relief.[14] Because the losing side in Finland was denied public mourning and shared manifestations of sorrow, its members were deprived of this relief. The Reds could not build monuments to commemorate their losses and their dead were buried without a Christian blessing, often in unmarked locations in the woods or swamps. The rare modest Red memorials, wooden crosses and stones, were frequently destroyed.[15] As Riitta Kormano has argued, the naming of the deceased Reds in memorials would have given the fallen a legitimate, individual value, which the Whites wanted to withhold. The Whites considered the Reds as having committed a crime, and, thus, they were treated as criminals.[16]

In the social hierarchy of early twentieth century Finland, artists belonged to the bourgeois class and, during and after the civil war, they largely remained passive or had White sympathies. After the war, Finnish sculptors and Suomen kuvanveistäjäliitto (The Association of Finnish Sculptors) eagerly took part in the production of White monuments. However, accepting commissions to create White monuments was not necessarily indicative of the artists' personal sympathies but can be seen as a matter of employment, as Eeva-Maija Viljo has pointed out.[17] The visibility of a sculptor or painter with monumental aspirations correlates to the desires of the commissioner.

During the first decade after the civil war, the White side erected 333 memorials around the country. At the same time, other public art commissions were rare and official support for art was scarce.[18] Public painting largely depended on private patronage throughout the first half of the twentieth century. Restaurants, banks, and other corporations commissioned large-scale works for their offices, and some patrons donated monumental paintings to public locations. The association Taidetta kouluihin (Art for Schools), established in Finland in 1906, commissioned ten public paintings for schools between 1906 and 1948; however, municipalities only started to allocate money for public paintings on a larger scale after World War II. The Valtion taideteostoimikunta (Arts Council of Finland) was established in 1956 with the mission of acquiring art for state locations.

AVOIDING INFLAMMATORY SUBJECTS

The monumental painting competition for the Parliament House in 1929–30 was an important milestone in the development of Finnish public painting. Designed by J. S. Sirén, and completed in 1931, the new Parliament House was intended to represent the greatness of the young independent nation. Parliament House historian Liisa-Maria Hakala-Zilliacus considers the building a representation of a national reconciliation after the civil war because the decoration of the building lacks symbols of the victors. The building does not celebrate the Whites, nor does it insult the Reds.[19] A mural painting was planned for the Chamber of Grand Committee, but none of the competition sketches was realized. The quality of the competition was considered so low that the first prize was not given out, and even though the jury justified its decisions largely on formal questions, the subject matters of the sketches are also revealing— they reflect a tension in the remembrance of the civil war. For example, as the Parliament House was the place of legislation, various artists proposed paintings with law themes.[20] However, because the legality of the war was contested (those sympathetic to a White perspective framed the war as an illegal uprising), such imagery was avoided in the decoration of the building.[21]

Ultimately, the jury for the painting competition could not reach an agreement.[22] Architects, who had the majority of votes on the jury, preferred the more decorative and allegorical suggestions that the artists on the jury disliked. *Navis Reipublicae* by Lennart Segerstråle (Figure 12.1), which won the second prize, the highest prize awarded, depicted a ship as an allegory of the state, led by a monumental, bare-breasted woman, identified by the artist as "Mother Finland," and accompanied by the allegorical figures of "Law" and "Defense." The classicist soldier standing in defense of Mother Finland, armed with a sword and shield, resembled the figure frequently used in the White monuments. The critique of the work, however, concentrated on formal aspects: the muscular woman was considered "tasteless" and the positions of the figures "pathetically artificial."[23]

Figure 12.1 Lennart Segerstråle, *Navis Reipublicae*, 1930, sketch for a mural. Photo by Simo Rista/Parliament of Finland. © 2011 Artists Rights Society (ARS), New York/KUVASTO, Helsinki.

Many of the awarded entries dealt with controversial subjects and narratives that resonated with White remembrance of the civil war. From the White perspective, they represented the organized, lawful society, while the Reds had participated in an illegal uprising. This dramatic ideological juxtaposition is presented, for example, in the awarded sketches *Yhteiskunta ja kaaos* (*Society and Chaos*) by Yrjö Ollila and *Elämänpuu* (*The Tree of Life*) by Uuno Alanko. In Ollila's painting, the organized society, lead by "Justice," proceeds firmly to the left, while the chaos has to back away toward the left edge of the frame. In *The Tree of Life,* a large tree divides the picture plane. On the "good" side, a happy family is running to greet a man accompanied by a white horse. On the "bad" side, a man is trying to tame a bolting brown horse, while another man is holding onto what could be an axe, bowing his head besides a man lying on the ground. This imagery easily reads as one man having killed the other, as "brother rising against brother."

The last prize was given to Henry Ericsson for his sketch *Kalvola*, which artists on the jury had rated the best. *Kalvola* refers to the site where the granite columns of the Parliament House had been mined. Work is among the central iconographical features in the decorative program of the Parliament House, but industrial workers are largely absent—likely due to the implications towards the workers movement and leftist ideologies. The situation in the Finnish building trade was very vulnerable in the late 1920s; labor disputes and strikes were frequent, and the conflicts were interpreted in the light of the juxtaposition between the working-class and the bourgeoisie. Also the miners working for the Parliament House had frequently been on strike. Thus, the artist's decision to foreground industrial labor over agrarian was likely seen inappropriate for the "monument of independence."[24]

None of the sketches were realized, and the suggested further competition was not arranged until 1961. Besides the poor quality of the sketches, the dominance of architects in the jury was seen as a main reason for the failing of the painting project.[25] Whether due to the unqualified jury or incompetent artists, the tricky political situation, unrealistic expectations or the limitations presented by the location, a widely accepted monumental painting for a nationally significant space proved impossible to be created a decade after the civil war.[26] All in all, Finnish public paintings were few in numbers during the first half of the century, despite the recurrent debate on the necessity of public art, also referred to as "art for the people."[27] Ultimately, national public painting was not produced on a larger scale until after World War II, when it was employed to foster the new narratives of national unity.

UNITING THE NATION

In November 1938, the newspaper *Uusi Suomi* published a petition, signed by the then president of Finland, Kyösti Kallio, alongside the Prime Minister and thirty-three other right-wing and Social Democratic politicians, as well as cultural and economic leaders of the country. In the petition, they pleaded with economic leaders to offer opportunities for artists when constructing new buildings. In this way, they hoped to guarantee the extensive decoration of the buildings and provide Finnish art the possibility of "fulfilling its greatest social function"—the moral uplifting of the people. According to the petition, Finnish art must "belong to the whole nation," and artists should be allowed to participate in "patriotic creation work."[28] The petition advertised that the government had submitted a proposal for the Parliament to establish a "Percent for Art" program in Finland.[29] The proposal was accepted in 1939 but it was never put to effect on a national level.

The Finnish discussion was by no means unique. It was openly inspired by European and especially Nordic developments; mural revivals took place all around Europe following both World Wars. Romy Golan has argued that the mural revival in Central Europe in the late 1920s was connected to the stabilization of the societies after the war. "The stability fostered a desire for a more permanent, monumental art form," Golan writes. Murals were seen to retrieve the communal role that art was believed to have had in past societies.[30] Interestingly, the particular political order was not centrally important: murals were produced in large numbers in Fascist Italy, in the Soviet Union, in the newly independent Norway, and outside Europe in Mexico in the 1920s and in the U.S. during the 1930s.

In Finland, the national character of monumental paintings was emphasized by multiple stakeholders also within the art establishment. In declaring a competition for the Finnish Normal School in Helsinki in 1932, the Art for Schools association established the subject as "otherwise free, except that it should be national and proper for youth in school age."[31] The artists, thus, needed to be conscious of—and able to represent—subject matters that would be understood as "national" and "proper for youth." The national character of Finnish public paintings, from the late nineteenth century to the post-WWII decades, was typically articulated through the depiction of Finnish landscape.[32] Accordingly, the realized sketches in the Normal School competition depicted a seaside fishing community and boys preparing their skis on a frozen lake or sea.

What in the end was needed for the creation of a new understanding of national unification was a war against a foreign aggressor. In 1939, when the Winter War against the Soviet Union broke out, only twenty years had passed since the civil war. The boys and men fighting on the front were sons of those who had fought in the civil war; some had even participated in it themselves. The Commander-in-Chief of the Finnish army was the commander of the Whites in the civil war, C. G. E. Mannerheim. Hence, memories of the civil war blended in many ways with new narratives of the war. From the Whites' perspective, the Winter War was considered the second war of independence. The earlier fight for freedom was now completed, since the aggressor was actually the country from which Finland had gained its independence. On the other hand, during the Winter

War, the Reds were fighting alongside the Whites; hence, they needed to be included in the society. From this perspective, the new victims were seen as redeemers of the previously divided nation.[33]

To signal the newly-found national unity after the end of Winter War, the annual celebration for the White victory ceased in 1940. Instead, the nation observed the first day of commemoration for all Finnish war victims. The moment also marked the first time that the Reds were allowed to commemorate their losses in the civil war with monuments.[34] The process of commemoration was, however, much more complicated for those commissioned to memorialize the Reds than it had been for creators of White monuments. The terminology and iconography used in White monuments could not be employed. Whereas the Whites claimed terms such as "fatherland" and "liberty" in their memorials, the phrase "fallen for their conviction" was introduced in reference to civil war victims from the Reds.[35] Furthermore, as most Finnish sculptors had participated in the production of White monuments, they could not be convincingly employed in designing monuments for the Reds. As a result of this, and also of economic issues, much of the Red memorial production was executed at commercial workshops. The common iconography included flags and a tree cut in two by lightning. In more complex memorials, mothers and children were depicted with men carrying torches and flags.[36] Allowing the erection of monuments was a gesture of giving the Reds back their legitimacy as citizens. In return, at this moment of external threat, they needed to put the past behind them. Riitta Kormano argues that during the Winter War, the coercion for speaking in the name of unanimity took the place of earlier right-wing pressure.[37]

"THE SPIRIT OF THE WINTER WAR"

In the Finnish national narratives, the Winter War (1939–40) against the Soviet Union is remembered as a heroic war, in which the small but perseverant nation defended itself gloriously against its great aggressor. The Continuation War (1941–44) creates more troubled narratives due to the German alliance and invasion of the Finnish army on Russian soil. It plays, therefore, a minor part in public remembrance, or is grouped together with the heroic narratives of the Winter War. Despite losing both wars against the Soviet Union, the end of the war has been formulated into a successful defense.[38] Finland was not occupied but the losses were great: the loss of life amounts to 84,000 people, in addition to which Finland lost large territories of land in the Eastern border, Karelia. Over one-tenth of the Finnish population had to leave their homes in Karelia and settle in what was left of Finland.[39] The conditions of the armistice in the Continuation War, dictated by the victor, led Finland into an armed conflict with Germany—known as the War of Lapland (1944–45)—as Finland was required to rapidly expel German troops from the Finnish soil. Also, the amount of war reparations was harsh, yet it boosted the Finnish industry, and thus fastened the urbanization and the rise of the standard of living in the post-war era.[40]

Since the Finnish fallen in World War II were transported to and buried in the graveyards of their own home parishes, memorials were needed even in the smallest municipalities. Classicism, which had been employed in the White memorials, was abandoned, and a more realist approach was used to fit the new democratic ideal. Riitta Kormano has suggested that the language developed for the Red memorials set an example for the commemoration of the lost war: the lack of uniforms and depiction of children, commonly used in this tradition, were first introduced in Red monuments.[41] The Finnish WWII monuments often feature heavily built common people on low pedestals; they are easily accessible both symbolically and literally. The pietá motif is frequently used. In addition, soldiers are often depicted in groups of two or three, emphasizing the common struggle, "brothers-in-arms," and creating a contrast to the sole allegorical soldier of the White monuments.[42]

Important representations of the "Spirit of the Winter War" in the painted format are the *Finlandia* frescoes by Lennart Segerstråle, executed for the Bank of Finland during the Continuation War (1943). The two large frescoes, *Suomi herää* (*Finland Awakens*, Fig. 12.2) and *Suomi rakentaa* (*Finland Builds*) depict wartime turmoil and anticipate reconstruction with a strong religious undertone, employing familiar imagery from both religious art and memorial monuments, such as the pietá motif. Painted in the middle of the war, they do not go as far as suggesting a victory in the war, but the justice of the Finnish cause is clearly shown in the heavenly light that is cast upon the Finnish people.

A central element in both frescoes is a mother and son, referring strongly to Christian iconography and commonly used in Finnish war memorials as well. In *Finland Awakens*, the pair is positioned as a pietá: a woman dangles a lifeless man from the armpits. Behind them, a group of Finnish soldiers in white winter uniforms are kneeling down, praying to heaven. In *Finland Builds*, the mother, dressed in white and holding a child on her shoulders, has turned her back to the viewer while a heavenly ray of light is cast upon them. Both of the women are haloed, underlining the religious interpretation. The other reading, articulated by the painter himself, is the woman as "Mother Finland," mother of the nation.[43]

In both of the frescoes, chaos and sorrow are depicted on the right side of the painting. In the upper right part of *Finland Builds*, a gloomy female figure in dark robes stands beside a tree stump—an element widely used in the Red monuments. The frescoes were originally commissioned in 1938, and the conflict from where their subject rose from was the civil war. However, it later transformed into and has been read as a depiction of the Winter War.[44] The building of new structures dominates the left side of the paintings: in *Finland Awakens* two men work side by side, and in *Finland Builds* the workers are a family. According to Segerstråle, the two men

Figure 12.2   Lennart Segerstråle, *Suomi herää* (*Finland Awakens*), 1943, Bank of Finland, Helsinki. Photo by author. © 2011 Artists Rights Society (ARS), New York/ KUVASTO, Helsinki.

symbolize "brothers-in-arms," "a mutual understanding between classes and language groups," that is, a unified nation after the division of the civil war.[45] The rebuilding family in *Finland Builds* refers to the reconstruction, a united nation working for a common future, and the family as the basic unit of the nation.

In these frescoes, Segerstråle could finally carry out the vision of "Mother Finland" he had outlined also for the Parliament House competition, but in a more realistic manner. Also, differing from the classicist soldier Segerstråle had depicted in *Navis Reipublicae*, the Finnish soldiers were now dressed in contemporary uniforms. Indeed, compared to *Navis Reipublicae* from 1930, the *Finlandia* series correlates with the changes in memorial art, insinuating the new democratic ideals instead of the White remembrance.

PUBLIC PAINTING IN THE RECONSTRUCTION

In the two decades following World War II, Finnish public painting production was at its peak. Vast municipal building construction, together with ideological discussions about the importance of public art, resulted in a dramatic increase in public painting commissions in the course of the 1950s. This boom coincided with the rapid changes in the Finnish society through not only the growth of cities, infrastructure, and public services, but also due to industrialization, the post-war baby boom, and the mass relocation of Finnish citizens from the ceded Karelia province. Finnish public paintings frequently touched on the theme of reconstruction, a changing society largely in consequence of the past wars.

Besides the reconstruction of buildings, the spiritual reconstruction of the nation was an essential context for the production of public paintings. The "patriotic creation work" that had been called for in 1938 and full blossoming of national public art finally became possible at a moment when national narratives proclaimed unity instead of division.

The most frequently used location for municipal public painting commissions in post-war Finland were schools, which were built in large numbers as the "large generations," those born between 1945–49, reached school age from 1952 onwards.[46] The placing of public paintings in schools continued the earlier established art educational ideologies that had been promoted in Finland, especially by the Art for Schools association, and emphasized the importance of mural painting as an educational tool. Furthermore, it symbolized the importance of investing in future generations. Schools were a prime location where the official narratives and values could be passed on for future generations.

As they were painted in large numbers, the themes of post-war public paintings expectedly show variation. Yet, a number of typical elements can be pointed out: the paintings commonly depict children playing, often in the Finnish countryside; they present an ideal family unit of father, mother, and children, and gender division within it; they emphasize construction work and the importance of work in general; and they present united people, often solemn and modest folk, working for a common goal. They avoid mythological or historical subjects; nudes and exotic landscapes; depictions of "difference" or "otherness," for example in gender roles, sexual orientation, or physical appearance; as well as depictions of war, conflict, or terror.

Kaupunki nousee (*City Rises*, Figure 12.3), by Unto Pusa, painted in 1953 for the Pohjoismaiden Yhdyspankki (Nordic Union Bank) in Lahti, is an example of an explicit depiction of reconstruction. The painting refers to the post-war industrial development and urbanization with a masculine image of reconstruction: the protagonists are all male, and heavy machinery plays an important part in the composition. Lahti is depicted as a great city with complex urban architecture with the City Hall as its center of attention.[47] Often, the post-war reconstruction is symbolized in public paintings with scaffolding or a father building a new home for his family. But how does the theme of reconstruction in public paintings relate to the past wars and their remembrance?

Figure 12.3   Unto Pusa, *Kaupunki nousee* (*City Rises*), 1953, Nordic Union Bank (now Nordea Bank), Lahti. Photo by Seppo Hilpo/Merita Art Foundation. © 2011 Artists Rights Society (ARS), New York/KUVASTO, Helsinki.

The repeated theme of (re)construction in public paintings can be seen as an emblem that encourages forgetting. It emphatically shifts the focus to future affairs. The symbolism of incomplete buildings and construction sites draws attention to the future at the expense of the past. In schools, these works were painted for children, the "future citizens." At a moment when the country was going through a rapid phase of urbanization, the paintings commonly depicted an agrarian environment. The agrarian world was presented as an ideal way of living for the city dwellers that were the main audience of these works. They presented an ideal world, rooted in traditional values. With the depiction of the family as the central unit, and reconstruction as a collaborative national goal, these paintings portray an official narrative of national unification. Finnish post-war depictions of reconstruction presented the current reality of the society by ideologically appealing to its idealized, agrarian past as a template for its future.

WAR IN PUBLIC PAINTING

Direct depictions of war, especially the traumatic civil war, have been to a large degree absent from Finnish public painting in state and municipal locations. A few cases can be found in corporate public painting that can more easily take sides. During the interwar period various companies, such as banks and industrial entrepreneurs, wanted to demonstrate right-wing patriotism also through their art acquisitions, and with imagery resonating with the White remembrance of the civil war. In 1933, Eric O. W. Ehrström painted a fresco series depicting "War of Freedom"—as the Whites called the civil name—for the lobby of an auditorium of the Kymi Paper Corporation in Kuusankoski. The series consists of eight paintings with emphatically patriotic subject matters, such as children waving flags and flowers to a regiment of (White) soldiers marching by in a Finnish landscape. The narrative recreates the civil war as a victorious battle of the Whites. As a consequence, the frescos were covered in the post-war years and not revealed until 1983.[48] The strong support for the White cause could not be manifested at the moment of the post-war unanimity talk.

Because of widespread mobilization of the Finnish people during World War II, many artists served and died on the front. Experiences of the front, however, rarely translated explicitly into the artistic works of those who survived. Artists depicting war focused on issues on the home front, on loneliness and grief, and the rare scenes from the front often depicted moments before or after the battle. As war scenes were hardly depicted in post-war Finnish painting, it is not surprising that in officially produced public paintings there were even fewer of them. Soldiers were depicted in the murals painted for military environments, as the subjects of public paintings have often been created to match the function of the building they are located in. However, even in these locations the works do not depict military action.

Jenni Kirves has addressed the culture of silence that prevailed in Finland after the World War II. According to Kirves, men returning from the war wanted both to guard themselves from the painful memories and also to spare their children from the terrors of war. In public, those who spoke about war were frequently labeled warmongers. Even the word "war" (*sota*) was avoided, and different euphemisms were used instead. Kirves suspects that one reason for the silence was the lack of words: it was better to remain silent about something so difficult to address.[49] As Paul Connerton writes, such silencing may be, besides a form of repression, also a form of survival. The desire to forget may be essential for this process of survival.[50]

Kirves discusses the refusal of Finnish novelists to deal with war in their works but this seems to be the case also with other artists. According to Olli Valkonen, the refusal to depict the war in art—even in order to oppose it—implied a complete resignation from it.[51] On a broader political level, the losing party of the war, Finland, remained cautious on issues which could have affected its relations towards the Soviet Union. Also for this reason, the subject of war was likely easiest dealt with when completely avoided in officially produced art. Monuments were designed in conventional ways, which did not aim to entice ambiguous readings or problematic recollections from the viewing audience. In public painting, artists mostly refrained from remembering the war at all.

Figure 12.4   Kimmo Kaivanto, *Tori* (*Market Square*), 1976, Tampere City Office Building. Photo by author. © 2011 Artists Rights Society (ARS), New York/ KUVASTO, Helsinki.

A rare example of officially commissioned public paintings referring to the civil war is Kimmo Kaivanto's *Tori (Market Square,* 1976). It was commissioned for the main lobby of the Tampere City Office Building and depicts the history of Tampere through events taking place on the square (Figure 12.4). Tampere's industrial and working-class roots defined the city from the late nineteenth century forward, and during the civil war, Tampere was a markedly "Red city" and the site of the war's bloodiest battles.[52] In *Market Square,* references to civil war are subtle but nonetheless evoke memories of the war for local spectators. The war is depicted in a succession of events, preceded by the General Strike of 1905, which was an important moment in the Finnish workers movement. The civil war is referred to with a violent figure of a horse falling on its head, while the sky looms in red behind a turn-of-the-century building on the south side of the square. The symbolic shades of red in this case are numerous.

Although Kaivanto also refers to World War II, he does not paint a heroic picture of the "Spirit of the Winter War" or reconstruction. Instead, he depicts the First of May celebration of the year 1939, the moment before the war, and an ashen factory pipe refers to the wars and bombings. The distance in time to even this conflict made the imagery possible in a publicly commissioned painting. *Market Square* takes the viewpoint of the worker in relation to the history of the city, suggesting new memories made possible in an official, public context. The division of the work into various scenes depicts the many facets of city life and shifts the focus from universal to individual experiences. Furthermore, the reflecting surface makes the viewer and the present-day environment a part of the work. The work, thus, distances in many ways from the conventions of the public painting—and also of the official memories—of the earlier decades.

COMMEMORATION AND FORGETTING

By resigning Finnish twentieth-century history to these two wars, I have taken the risk of continuing the traditional history writing, which has evaluated wars over other events in history. However, my intention is not to glorify the wars or undervalue the actual losses of lives by focusing on the production of art. These wars are the focus of my study precisely because they have been defined as key events of the Finnish national experience.[53] By examining the depiction of the wars in public paintings, my goal is not to suggest the existence of a shared national memory or correct interpretation; but to illuminate the complex and controversial nature of the wars and changing role of public paintings as a form of public remembrance.

These wars are, in many ways, still present in Finnish society and memories of the civil war in particular continue to be sensitive and debated. Even today, people tend to relate to one side of the war, and only three of the 500 Finnish civil war monuments commemorate both sides.[54] In regards to World War II, the narratives of unity are widely accepted, and the "Spirit of the Winter War" is still used to refer to Finland as a unified and uncompromising nation. The national narratives have emphasized the separate nature of Finnish struggle and the noble character of Finnish warfare. In recent studies, these official histories and seemingly shared experiences have been revisited and questioned.[55]

As this chapter demonstrates, officially produced art is used in the complex process of remembering and forgetting in a society in various ways. After 1918, memorial monuments had a visible role in portraying ruling social and political power in Finland. Depicting the civil war in public painting proved nearly impossible; in the 1929 Parliament House competition memories of the civil war were too sensitive to be even remotely suggested. The demand of forgetting was imposed especially on the losing party by the victors, among other ways, by preventing the creation of public memorials. Later, at the wake of World War II, the whole society needed to forget the past wrongs. Following the war, the bettering of the spiritual state of the nation was strived with public art, which implied desires for national unification: monuments celebrating brothers-in-arms, and public paintings suggesting an idyllic Finnish life.

Often the city- and state-level authorities may decide the appropriate subjects for memorial monuments and other public artworks. Public art suggests what is worthy of remembering in the society, while many other subjects are being omitted. At the same time, with the erecting of a monument, the memories are "stored" seemingly visibly, and do not need to burden the society.[56] Public art may serve as a form of forgetting, and forgetting as an essential tool for the creation of a functioning society, or a nation with a national sentiment.

NOTES

1. Riitta Kormano, "Punaisten hautamuistomerkit—vaiettuja kiviä," in *Taidehistoriallisia tutkimuksia 23*, ed. Renja Suominen-Kokkonen (Helsinki: Taidehistorian seura, 2001), 40.
2. See Liisa Lindgren, *Monumentum: Muistomerkkien aatteita ja aikaa* (Helsinki: Suomalaisen kirjallisuuden seura, 2000) and Kormano, "Punaisten hautamuistomerkit" on Finnish memorial monuments.
3. W. J. T. Mitchell, "The Violence of Public Art: Do the Right Thing," in *Art and the Public Sphere*, ed. W. J. T. Mitchell (Chicago and London: The University of Chicago Press, 1992), 35.
4. Large numbers of murals have been painted for example in Northern Ireland for the Republican hunger-strike victims during the Troubles, and on the walls of Tehran for Iranian martyrs during the Iran-Iraq war. See Bill Rolston, *Politics and Painting: Murals and Conflict in Northern Ireland* (London and Toronto: Associated University Press, 1991); Christiane J. Gruber, "The Message is on the Wall: Mural Arts in Post-Revolutionary Iran," *Persica* 22 (2008): 15–46.
5. See Patrick H. Hutton, *History as an Art of Memory* (Hanover and London: University Press of New England, 1993), 9.

6. Alan Gordon, *Making Public Pasts: The Contested Terrain of Montreal's Public Memories, 1891–1930* (Montreal: McGill-Queen's University Press, 2001), 3.
7. James E. Young, "Memory/Monuments," in *Critical Terms for Art History*, ed. Robert S. Nelson and Richard Shiff (Chicago and London: The University of Chicago Press, 2nd ed., 2003), 234–37.
8. Jay Winter and Emmanuel Sivan, "Setting the Framework," in *War and Remembrance in the Twentieth Century*, ed. Jay Winter and Emmanuel Sivan (Cambridge: Cambridge University Press, 1999), 6–10. On collective memory, see Maurice Halbwachs, *The Collective Memory*, trans. Francis J. Ditter, Jr., and Vida Yazdi Ditter (New York: Harper & Row, 1980).
9. Young "Memory/Monuments," 237–38. See also Pierre Nora, "Between Memory and History: Les Lieux de Mémoire," *Representations*, 26 (1989), 7–24.
10. Petri Karonen, "Johdanto: kun rauha tuo omat ongelmansa," in *Kun sota on ohi: sodista selviytymisen ongelmia ja niiden ratkaisumalleja 1900-luvulla*, ed. Petri Karonen and Kerttu Tarjamo (Helsinki: Suomalaisen Kirjallisuuden Seura, 2006), 12, 18–20.
11. Ibid., 12.
12. Paul Connerton, "Seven Types of Forgetting," in *Memory Studies* vol. 1, no. 1 (Sage Publications, 2008), 59–71.
13. Seppo Hentilä, "Itsenäinen Suomi idän ja lännen välissä: Väli-Euroopan maa," in *Suomi: Outo, pohjoinen maa? Näkökulmia Euroopan äären historiaan ja kulttuuriin*, ed. Tuomas M. S. Lehtonen (Jyväskylä: PS-kustannus, 1999), 91–94; Tuomas Hoppu, "Tampereen vankileiri," in *Tampere 1918* (Tampere: Vapriikki, 2008), 176.
14. Paloma Aguilar, "Agents of Memory: Spanish Civil War Veterans and Disabled Soldiers," in *War and Remembrance in the Twentieth Century*, ed. Jay Winter and Emmanuel Sivan (Cambridge: Cambridge University Press, 1999), 86.
15. Ulla Peltonen, *Muistin paikat: Vuoden 1918 sisällissodan muistamisesta ja unohtamisesta* (Helsinki: Suomalaisen kirjallisuuden seura, 2003), 236–43; Kormano, "Punaisten hautamuistomerkit," 34.
16. Kormano, "Punaisten hautamuistomerkit," 36–37.
17. Eeva-Maija Viljo, "Suomen kuvanveistäjäliitto 1910–1940," in *Taidehistoriallisia tutkimuksia 23*, ed. Renja Suominen-Kokkonen (Helsinki: Taidehistorian seura, 2001), 5–6, 19–25.
18. Peltonen, *Muistin paikat*, 222; Viljo, "Suomen kuvanveistäjäliitto," 19–21.
19. Liisa-Maria Hakala-Zilliacus, *Suomen eduskuntatalo: kokonaistaideteos, itsenäisyysmonumentti ja kansallisen sovinnon representaatio* (Helsinki: Suomalaisen kirjallisuuden seura, 2002), 217, 321–22.
20. Titles such as *Oikeus ja työ* (Justice and Labour), *Lain historia* (History of Law) and *Työ—Laki—Uskonto* (Work—Law—Religion) were included in the competition. Palkintolautakunnan pöytäkirja (minutes of the jury) 1930, §3. Archives of the Finnish Parliament, Helsinki.
21. Hakala-Zilliacus, *Suomen eduskuntatalo*, 321.
22. Ibid., 217–220. The jury consisted of five members: architects Onni Tarjanne, Lars Sonck, as well as J. S. Sirén, the designing architect of the building, represented the building committee in the jury, painters Gabriel Engberg and Ilmari Aalto, the Finnish Artists Association.
23. Ibid., 220–21.
24. Ibid., 119–20, 225.
25. Målarna mot arkitekterna, *Svenska Pressen*, February 19, 1930; O. O-n, [Onni Okkonen] Eduskuntatalon maalauskilpailu, *Uusi Suomi*, February 28, 1930.

26. Hakala-Zilliacus, *Suomen eduskuntatalo*, 224–25, 229, 319.
27. In my ongoing research, I have been able to map roughly seventy public paintings between 1900 and 1945. The number naturally depends on the definitions of "public painting": which locations, commissioners, and techniques are included, for example.
28. "Vetoomus," *Uusi Suomi*, November 1, 1938. All translations of quotes from Finnish are by the author.
29. "Percent for Art" refers to the allocation of a percentage (often 1–2%) of the construction costs to the artistic decoration of the building.
30. Romy Golan, "From Monument to Muralnomad: the Mural in Modern European Architecture," in *The Built Surface*, vol. 2, *Architecture and the Pictorial Arts from Romanticism to the Twenty-first Century*, ed. Karen Koehler (Hants: Ashgate Burlington, 2002), 186.
31. "Kilpailu Suomen Taiteilijoille," December 2, 1932. Archives of the Art for School association, Finnish National Archives, Helsinki.
32. See also Michelle Facos, "Educating a Nation of Patriots: Mural Paintings in Turn of the Century Swedish Schools," in *Art, Culture, and National Identity in Fin-de-Siècle Europe,* ed. Michelle Facos and Sharon L. Hirsh (Cambridge: Cambridge University Press, 2003), 236–38.
33. Tuomas Tepora, "'Elävät vainajat'—kaatuneet kansakuntaa velvoittavana uhrina," in *Ruma Sota: Talvi- ja jatkosodan vaiettu historia,* ed. Sari Näre and Jenni Kirves, (Helsinki: Johnny Kniga Publishing, 2008), 104–05.
34. Kormano, "Punaisten hautamuistomerkit," 38.
35. Peltonen, *Muistin paikat*, 235; Tepora, "Elävät vainajat," 104–05.
36. Lindgren, *Monumentum*, 197–98.
37. Kormano, "Punaisten hautamuistomerkit," 38.
38. Petri Raivo, "'This Is Where They Fought': Finnish War Landscapes as a National Heritage," in *Politics of War Memory & Commemorations,* ed. T. G. Ashplant, Graham Dawson, and Michael Roper, (Florence, KY: Routledge, 2000), 155.
39. Olli Vehviläinen, *Finland in the Second World War: Between Germany and Russia* (New York: Palgrave, 2002), 70, 113.
40. Unlike many European countries, Finland did not receive Marshall Plan assistance. By 1952, Finland had paid off its war indemnity, amounting to 444.7 million U.S. dollars. Vehviläinen, *Finland in the Second World War,* 157–58.
41. Kormano, "Punaisten hautamuistomerkit," 40, 46–47.
42. Lindgren, *Monumentum*, 205–09.
43. Lennart Segerstråle, *Suomen Pankin Finlandia-freskomaalausten esityöt* (Helsinki: Taidehalli, 1943), 6.
44. Aimo Reitala, *Suomi-neito: Suomen kuvallisen henkilöitymän vaiheet* (Helsinki: Otava, 1983), 144.
45. Segerstråle, *Suomen Pankin Finlandia-freskomaalausten esityöt*, 6–8.
46. Antti Karisto, "Suuret ikäluokat kuvastimessa," in *Suuret Ikäluokat,* ed. Antti Karisto (Tampere: Vastapaino, 2005), 17–23.
47. On Pusa, see Kerttuli Wessman, *Unto Pusa, monumentaalimaalari: Rengas taiteen ketjussa* (Helsinki: Otava, 1997).
48. Anna-Lisa Amberg, "Käsityön mestari ja taideteollisuusmies," in *Eric O. W. Ehrström 1881–1934,* ed. Katja Hagelstam, et al. (Helsinki: Kustannus W. Hagelstam, 1998), 63, 106.
49. Jenni Kirves, "'Sota ei ollut elämisen eikä muistamisen arvoista aikaa'— kirjailijat ja traumaattinen sota," in *Ruma sota: Talvi- ja jatkosodan vaiettu historia,* ed. Sari Näre and Jenni Kirves (Helsinki: Johnny Kniga Publishing, 2008), 381–82, 417–18.

50. Connerton, "Seven Types of Forgetting," 68.
51. Olli Valkonen, "Modernismin 50-luku," in *1950-luku: vapautumisen aika,* ed. Pirjo Tuukkanen and Timo Valjakka, (Helsinki: Suomen taideyhdistys, 2000), 8–9.
52. See Tuomas Hoppu, ed., *Tampere 1918* (Tampere: Vapriikki, 2008).
53. See, for example, Raivo, "This Is Where They Fought."
54. Peltonen, *Muistin paikat*, 236.
55. See, for example, *Ruma sota: Talvi- ja jatkosodan vaiettu historia,* ed. Sari Näre and Jenni Kirves (Helsinki: Johnny Kniga Publishing, 2008); Oula Silvennoinen, *Salaiset aseveljet: Suomen ja Saksan turvallisuuspoliisiyhteistyö 1933–1944* (Helsinki: Otava, 2008).
56. See Connerton, "Seven Types of Forgetting," 65–66.

13 Making Memories
Tragic Tourism's Visual Traces

Emily Godbey

Before me, I have what is undoubtedly a marooned object of memory, unmoored from maker, owner, and story. A professionally-made photograph, mounted on stiff board, shows an elaborate brick building with sweeping arches and a wide, cone-shaped roof at one end. Except for the rounded rooms underneath the cone-shaped roof, all is in ruins: massive piles of debris, individual bricks on the ground, near-leafless trees. A framed picture, strangely, still hangs squarely on a second floor wall. In the foreground are passers-by, some carrying umbrellas or parasols, many blurred because of the lengthy exposure time. The photographer's scratched-in label, "Union Club[,] Lafayette + Jefferson" is scrawled at the bottom. In the mid-ground, at the edge of the debris field, however, are four dark-skirted women pressed closely together who appear in crisp, immobile relief. One woman holds a baby in a white frock. Why would they be standing at this place and in that arrangement? They can only be posing for a photographer, perhaps the person who appears furthest left in the foreground. The four women have paused in front of a devastated building in order to create a souvenir, a visual trace of individual lives in the aftermath of a very public catastrophe. The anonymous photographer of the scene now in my hands has, in turn, made an image of their posing for a picture. This anonymous photograph in the Missouri History Museum's archives showing the aftermath of a devastating 1896 tornado is thereby a sort of meta-picture about encapsulating a traumatic moment: one unseen photographer catches another anonymous photographer in preserving the memory.

Tragedy, memory, and visuality are intimately related. The phenomenon of "flashbulb memory"—the spontaneous, highly-visual mental recording of where an individual was when that person heard that Abraham Lincoln was assassinated, John F. Kennedy was shot, the Challenger exploded, or the September 11th attacks took place—is one aspect of this weaving together of personal history with traumatic, public events. Americans have an established social-technological history of making memories after tragic events, by making and taking souvenirs of various kinds. In *Tourists of History: Memory, Kitsch, and Consumerism from Oklahoma*

Figure 13.1   Union Club, St. Louis, Missouri, after the cyclone May 1896. Southeast corner of Lafayette and Jefferson, 1896. Photo courtesy of Missouri History Museum, St. Louis.

City to Ground Zero, Marita Sturken has deftly analyzed these practices using examples from September 11th and the Oklahoma City bombing, but these activities have a much longer—if relatively unexplored—history.[1] This chapter posits that in taking steps to remember a terrible occurrence, turn-of-the-century Americans reformulated disaster and tragedy into the rhetoric of both consumption and leisure. After devastating events like the St. Louis tornado of 1896 or the Johnstown Flood of 1889, people flocked to the scene and did what tourists to Niagara Falls or the Grand Canyon would do—they bought train tickets, gaped at the awesome sights, had their pictures taken, assembled photo albums, and collected or purchased mementos and souvenirs. Natural disasters of the period offer a unique opportunity to examine modernity's growing investment in commodified memory practices simply because those very events they document seem so intense and unforgettable.

Natural disasters and other shocking events are prime candidates for the phenomenon of "flashbulb memory." Researchers Brown and Kulik first coined the term "flashbulb memory" to refer to that almost-blinding moment when a surprising and sudden cultural or deeply personal event becomes encoded and seemingly engraved with minute detail.[2] Where people were, what they were doing, perhaps even what they were wearing or eating all comes flooding back. Flashbulb memories are incredibly vivid, often highly emotional, and seem highly resistant to erasure. They exist in high definition against the grey, forgettable backdrop of everyday occurrences. John F. Kennedy's assassination is the classic example. People testify that their memories of this event have lasted decades, and visitors to the Sixth Floor Museum at Dealey Plaza describe highly detailed memories from long ago:

> I was in 6th grade in November of 1963. It was a Friday and I had walked to school that morning, as was my usual routine. It was Girl Scout-meeting day and I had on my crisp green scout uniform. For some reason our principal and teachers at W. C. Warren Elementary in Garland, Texas had decided not to tell us about the tragedy. We were protected from the surreal events. The children who had gone home for lunch (and more than likely had heard the news) were stopped at the school's door and instructed not to tell the rest of us what had happened at Dealy [sic] Plaza. As I walked home that afternoon, a boy in my class rode by on his bicycle. I was almost at the corner, where Mr. Parrot, our crossing guard was standing. Mike, the boy on the bike, called out to me that the President had been shot.[3]

The incredible personal specificity—green scout uniform, Girl-Scout meeting day, the odd name of the crossing guard—are all characteristic of what the researchers termed "flashbulb memory."[4] The memory combines personal history with momentous public events.

Although these memories seem "photographic" and incredibly accurate, an interesting study conducted with Duke University students after September 11th contends that flashbulb memories are not special in terms of accuracy. However, they do seem to be coded visually. Subjects were asked how they remembered the events of September 11th. In images or in words? Coherent or fractured? Flashbulb memories came as coherent mental pictures, not words.[5] Similarly, the original flashbulb theorists, Brown and Kulik, had hypothesized that these flashbulb memories were most often retained as image-based, affective representations rather than word-based narratives. This "core" non-verbal image becomes the basis for many different verbal retellings. Another study, specifically about memories of traumatic events, contends that certain memories cannot be integrated on a semantic/linguistic level but are coded as visual and somatic sensations.[6] It is understandable why many researchers would have made the analogy to photography or printing, as the image-based memory seems complete and can be revisited and "re-read." The extensive use of photographic and printmaking metaphors relate that the recalled memory is a visual record. Here phenomenology of memory is conceptualized as being a flash photograph—a split-second of time that becomes visible and seemingly indelible.

Natural disasters offer a perfect opportunity for flashbulb memory creation, whether a person experiences the event directly or finds out the shocking news from afar, but they have also demonstrated that people have made significant efforts to remember terrifying events. Ordinary Americans, ones who have left only fragmentary parts of their lives recorded in newspaper reports, bits of ephemera donated to collections, postcards found in attics, and other partial records can inform this study. What these imperfect records say is that after a disaster or traumatic event both aid workers and gawkers rush in. Visitors—many with cameras—cross into a disaster zone as soon as they are able to do so. It is relatively common to see news coverage describing curiosity seekers. The reality of crowds drawn to and fascinated by sites of pain and suffering is quite telling. Sites of tragedy become inadvertent tourist attractions that beckon people to visit them in person, even if media coverage has been comprehensive. Terminology for these people at sites of tragedy usually relates to the external sense of vision: they are sightseers, gawkers, voyeurs, and rubberneckers. Less often are they called mourners or pilgrims, terms that deal with the invisible inner disposition of the visitors.

The 1990s saw a flurry of writing about the idea of sites of pain and tragedy as tourist attractions. The largest body of work responds to twentieth century events like the Holocaust, celebrity deaths, the Oklahoma City bombing, and September 11th, but nineteenth century people paved the way for contemporary sightseers.[7] Historians and sociologists have given the phenomenon a variety of names. Lucy Lippard coined the term "tragic tourism" to refer to tourism which brings people to celebrity murder sites, concentration camps, and sites of natural disaster.[8] Tony Seaton effectively harnesses Thomas De Quincy's *On Murder Considered as One of the Fine Arts* (1827) as a touchstone and uses the word "thanatourism" (from the Greek "thanatos" for "death") to address the tourism at sites of tragedy. He argues that violent death is a commodity of modernism and advocates that a revival of the term "thanatopsis" [from the Greek for "a sight or view of death"] would be useful.[9] Malcolm Foley and John J. Lennon coined the term "dark tourism" to characterize "visits to battlefields, murder and atrocity locations, places where the famous died, graveyards and internment sites, memorials, and events and exhibitions featuring relics and reconstructions of death."[10]

This essay explores the roots of contemporary memory practices (explored elsewhere in this volume) at sites of tragedy and disaster as they emerged in American popular culture. In short, Americans began to treat sites of tragedy as a kind of visual commodity and tourist attraction. By treating sites of suffering and destruction as a commodity and attraction which was ripe for memory-making, nineteenth century visitors purposefully interwove their own personal memories with disaster events which were singularly memorable because of the perceived sense of reality and genuineness.

We are living in an era in which remembering trauma is a national obsession. Almost from the moment that the World Trade Center towers fell and the magnitude of the loss was clear, commentators began discussing what would happen with this wounded piece of land. The towers' falling was clearly an occasion for a searing flashbulb memory, yet slogans asking people to "Never Forget" began appearing on kitschy souvenir objects for sale soon afterwards. It might be easy to think of these commercial souvenirs surrounding the trauma of September 11th as products of post-modernity, but this chapter asserts that contemporary practices in tragic tourism are rooted in early modern American history.

TOURISM AS VISUAL COMMODITY

The European Grand Tour of the eighteenth and nineteenth centuries catered to the elite. What is particularly interesting, as Judith Adler so elegantly details, is that traveling undergoes a shift into an experience for the eye. Whereas elite and elegantly-clothed men once would have described in journals which people they met and what they discussed, written travel journals began to change, roughly in the seventeenth century. Instead of recording memories of what the writer said or thought, scribbling travelers began to focus on what they saw.[11] John Frow concurs that what developed was "an investigative art of travel, governed by an ideal of objectively accurate vision."[12] Therefore, collecting sights and visual memories, not verbal stories, becomes a chief goal, and Urry has written about what he calls the "generalized tourist gaze."[13] The *Bildungsreise*, or educational travel adventure, which depended upon highly active verbal skills (learning language, meeting people, hearing stories), becomes the more passive sightseeing tour, where the primary goal is to see the sights.

As wealth spread to the middle class, touring became available to a much wider group. With the model of "sightseeing" firmly in place, the European Grand Tour was supported by a large volume of travel guidebooks which told the reader what to see: the ruins of Pompeii, the Alps, Venice, and Rome. On the other side of the Atlantic, a kind of American Grand Tour sprang up. Instead of the Alps, Venice, and Rome, the American Grand Tour included the Hudson River, the Catskills, Lake George, the Erie Canal, Niagara Falls, the White Mountains, and the Connecticut Valley.[14] Notably, a visit to the White Mountains mandated seeing the Willey House, a small inn and home where an entire family was killed in a rockslide in 1826, yet the house (supposedly with an open Bible on the table) remained untouched.[15] In one sense, the Willey House site can be seen as a highly miniaturized and Americanized version of Pompeii as a sightseeing destination of tragedy. As at Pompeii, humans were obliterated by an absolutely unforeseen natural disaster while the built environment was preserved. The difference in scale—one Christian family compared to thousands of ancient Romans—perhaps makes the comparison laughable, but the Willey house was a "must see" stop for any well-traveled, nineteenth century American. Different too is the accompanying moralistic mythology;

many nineteenth century Americans deemed the volcano's eruption as a consequence of pagan activities in ancient Roman cities (the popularity of Bulwer-Lytton's *The Last Days of Pompeii* is just one outgrowth of this sentiment), the Willey family members were cast as pious Christians bravely living in the American wilderness who were struck down in a tragic natural disaster.

This early example of tragic or disaster tourism is directly connected to contemporary practices; the Willey family had tremendously bad luck to be in the path of a rockslide, but the family's legend became one of brave, God-fearing Americans attempting to tame a wild country. In turn, that mythology transformed the site into a point of interest for American tourists, although, quite frankly, there was not much to actually see—just an intact house and some rocks. The Willey slide example is tightly linked to contemporary cultural practices like the tremendous outpouring of patriotic rhetoric after September 11th in which those who died were lionized as exemplary Americans. Ground Zero became an instant tourist attraction and pilgrimage site.

DISASTER TOURISM

Although certain sites of tragedy became accepted parts of standard itineraries, accident and catastrophe gave rise to a more spontaneous kind of investment in leisure tourism, as in the example of the 1896 St. Louis tornado. Estimated to be an F4 tornado, the storm ripped through the city, killing hundreds of people, leaving a mile-wide path of utter devastation through St. Louis. In the days that followed the St. Louis tornado, the citizens of St. Louis went sightseeing: "Thousands followed the cyclone's path the following day, picking their way among the wreckage, and pausing to gaze horror-stricken at some of the scenes that met their gaze."[16]

Two locations were of particular interest: Lafayette Park and the Eads Bridge. The park swarmed with visitors, and "[t]he only living things in all the park, except the sight-seers, were the birds on the pond" which "swam about in an aimless, bewildered sort of fashion."[17] At the river, the bridge and waterfront destruction drew crowds. The Eads Bridge, considered a model of nearly indestructible modern engineering, showed damage, as did the smashed boats along the river's bank. Strangely, the mob seemed almost festive:

> With daylight, however, their courage returned and they thronged the levee laughing and discussing the events of the night as if nothing had occurred to upset their equilibrium, and morbidly curious, now that the danger was past, to gain all the gruesome details of the disaster. Here and there could be seen the tear-stained countenance of one who had lost a dear one in the course of the night's horrible events, but the majority of that motley crowd seemed unconcerned and even gay.[18]

Even several hundred girls employed at the local bag factory came out *en masse* to see what remained of their former workplace. Some had been injured, yet "[t]he next morning the girls assembled about the factory in droves and discussed innumerable hair-breadth escapes they had experienced. Then they went sight-seeing with evident enjoyment, regardless of the fact that they will be thrown out of employment."[19] One source says "[i]t was like a holiday" in which "all the stores were closed and thousands lounged in the streets. Men and women stood moodily in sheltered places watching the crowds."[20] "Holiday," a word deriving from "holy day," is a provocative term as, in this sense, holidays were for pilgrims and penitents. In contrast, the behavior described by contemporaneous reports was anything but pious. Those crowds, quite evident in pictures preserved at the Missouri Historical Society, swelled as outsiders read the news of the St. Louis disaster.

The result was remarkable. Instead of staying away from the disaster area, some made a special trip to see it, many spending hard-earned cash to see with their own eyes. The disaster zone quickly became something to be consumed as an attraction. Only a few days after the tornado, railroads offered special excursion fares to view the ruined city, and tourists arrived in droves, nearly collapsing what remained of the crippled infrastructure. Instead of a problem, railroad companies saw a capitalist's opportunity. Sunday, the traditional day of rest, seems to have brought more out-of-towners to view the destruction. Thousands of "visitors and Sunday idlers" participated in "sight-seer's day" coming "by railway, in wagons, in street cars, and on foot. Unmindful of the drizzling rain and sloppy streets they tramped through the whole region of the wreck, uttering one continuous chorus of expressions of horror and amazement at the terrific power of wind and its awful consequences."[21] Reports put the total number of "sight-seers" and "excursionists" at in the thousands (estimates range from 5,000 to 140,000).[22]

Sightseeing days at St. Louis seem quite similar to behavior after other tragedies, like the much more publicized Johnstown Flood. On May 31, 1889, a dam broke and literally swept the working-class town of Johnstown, Pennsylvania, off the map, killing some 2,200 people.[23] A few days later, a newspaper article entitled "Spectators in the Way" announced that the railroad station in Pittsburgh was crowded with "applicants [that] were either of the bogus order or merely of the curiosity order."[24] Newspapermen and relief workers complained that the curious crowd took the available seats on the trains to Johnstown. The Superintendent in charge posted a notice at the station that the train was unable to get all the way to Johnstown as the track was washed out and said,

> We have practically had to close our doors against hordes of people who are clamoring for transportation to the scene of the wreck. We want it to be distinctly understood that sight-seers are not wanted. If the Pennsylvania railroad desired to make a play on death and sorrow, we could run continuous trains to the scene of the disaster. We do not want a single person of such a class. Workers are wanted—none else.[25]

But the vacation-minded travelers were not to be dissuaded by a simple sign because on June 5th, the *Pittsburgh Commercial Gazette* ran yet another article entitled "Please Keep Away: Sight-seers Are Regarded as a Perfec [sic] Nuisance at Johnstown," which described "people who come from no other motive but curiosity" and who were "literally underfoot."[26] Newspaper articles in the *Philadelphia Inquirer* complained about sightseers who could have been put to work if they had had the inclination.

The distinction here between working and sightseeing is important—and not just in this instance where officials were frustrated by the lack of workers to do Johnstown's clean-up—as it marks the difference between the traveler and the tourist. "Tourism" is defined as the practice of traveling for pleasure, and the word arose during the nineteenth century. It is a non-work activity. The term "traveler," in contrast, comes from the word "travail" and is more associated with mental and verbal work, as in the Bildungsreise, or educational journey.[27] In addition, tourism also places great emphasis on the act of *looking* above all other sense perceptions, something marked by the associated term "sight-seeing." It seems that the desire to physically view a site of tragedy or destruction attracts crowds, and, eventually tourists. The desire to "see for oneself" seems to govern the strong impulse to make a long journey to the site of tragedy, or, as with the girls from Johnstown's bag factory, to return immediately to the place where they experienced disaster first-hand.

A little more than two weeks after the disaster, the B&O Railroad was selling round-trip excursion tickets for $2.35 to allow tourists to see the town for four hours. The railroad sagely advised the gawkers, "Those who desire to go on this excursion should provide themselves with lunch baskets as provisions cannot be procured at Johnstown."[28] Renowned humanitarian Clara Barton, who had come to help at Johnstown, noted the "thousands of excursionists" in the city and saved in her diaries an article cut from the *Pittsburgh Commercial Gazette*, entitled "Excursionists' Day" which described "morbid curiosity displayed by sight-seers." When the railroad officially allowed outsiders to board trains to Johnstown, a new flood—this time, not water, but people—arrived.[29] The demands placed on the railroads were extreme, "as the pressure to get [there] demanded several sections of nearly every scheduled train and taxed the capacity of the road to convey the thousands who wanted to see."[30] Others came on horseback and in festively-decorated horse-drawn conveyances, complete with picnic baskets: "They came, men, women and children, of all colors and nations, many decked out in holiday attire and laden down with huge lunch baskets. Farmers drove in from surrounding villages with horses and wagons decorated with bunting and evergreens."[31] The mention of "bunting and evergreens" offers a clue to the visitors' attitude, as this decoration would have been common for a parade. While it is true that decorations were also part of the nineteenth century funeral procession, one would expect to hear the words "black crape (or crêpe)" had they been decorated in a funereal fashion. Bunting is a lightweight material often used for flags and festive decorations, while crape is a slightly crinkled material used in the period almost exclusively for black mourning wear. Both from the rather unequivocal descriptions in the newspapers and within the more subtle evidence, it seems that these visitors went sightseeing on Sunday, a day which was often set aside for church, rest, and a drive in the country. In these examples, turn-of-the-century tragedy becomes the occasion for tourist activities that involved consumption—from purchasing train tickets, buying special provisions for the excursion, and even decorating vehicles. Consuming disaster has in today's culture become even more prominent and rapid; the tragedies at Oklahoma City and Ground Zero quickly became tourist attractions which involve consumption. As of this writing, the Ground Zero Museum and Workshop currently ranks tenth in popularity on Tripadvisor's list of "Things to Do," right after a slew of walking, biking, and eating tours of New York.[32] Sturken rightly comments on the presence of the Oklahoma memorial gift shop, where one can purchase kitchy objects like snow globes and teddy bears.

VISIBLE TRACES: RELIC CRANKS

What did these sightseers at St. Louis and Johnstown do besides consume the thrilling sights? Many made sure to take something home in the form of a souvenir, memento, or keepsake, and these came in two main forms: physical objects and images. Not all of these reminders had to be bought, however, since almost any object could serve as a memento to someone daring enough to go in person to the disaster scene. In St. Louis "[t]housands of persons visited the park and commiserated with each other on the ruin of what had been justly called the prettiest spot in St. Louis. They cut canes from the branches of the trees and carried away parts of benches as mementoes of the storm."[33] This is certainly not the first time nor the last time that the curious came in search of objects to remember a stupendous event. After the terrible Galveston hurricane in 1900, Alice Easton wrote about picking up a piece of marble: "I think I will keep it as another souveneer [sic]."[34] The message on one San Francisco earthquake postcard mailed in 1906 in my own collection reads, "Will search the above places for relics for you soon."

After turn-of-the-century disasters, "relic cranks" also set up for business, charging customers for objects taken from the wreckage. Apparently, in Johnstown, there were a great many of them:

> One enterprising man has opened shop for the sale of relics of the disaster, and is doing a big business. Half the people here are relic cranks. Everything goes as a relic, from a horseshoe to a two-foot section of iron pipe. Buttons and little things like that, that can easily be carried off, are the most popular.[35]

After the San Francisco earthquake of 1906, individuals as well as entrepreneurs collected relics and vendors quickly mobilized. Another San Francisco Earthquake postcard in my own collection offers a glimpse into this selling of memory objects. The postcard depicts a mustachioed vendor at his makeshift shop (more like a shack) in an earthquake-damaged building with a sign that says "Souvenirs and Relics from Chinatown for Sale Here." The objects for sale are not entirely legible, although most appear to be broken Chinese pottery; however, the sender's message (in Esperanto) gives more insight. The writer in San Francisco tells the card's recipient about how vendors sold strange objects that had been melted in the intense heat of the ensuing fires. The card, postmarked in 1909, concludes by reflecting upon the "recent earthquakes" in Italy, a remark that must refer to the 1908 Messina earthquake. One might surmise that the postcard's author was subtly encouraging his Parisian correspondent to strike now to claim a reminder of the Messina quake. Picture postcards, invented in the late nineteenth century, were quite quickly incorporated into commercialized sightseeing and tourism. See the sights; buy the postcards. Or, as some commented, dispense with the actual sightseeing and just buy the cards. Although postcards were made on every topic imaginable, the scenic view ("Wish you were here") and its darker cousin, the disaster view, were dominant. In this regard, the postcard of the souvenir vendor is entirely self-reflexive; it is a souvenir image *about* souvenirs.

The seemingly overwhelming desire to own a memento or souvenir, whether free or sold, is worth examining in more detail. These objects stand as signs or traces of authenticity, of the lived experience as well as of the wish to remember it in the future. Those taking home pieces of the event affirmed two things: that the event was real and that they were (living) witnesses. Of course, as Susan Stewart says, the souvenir's function as a sign of authenticity is only meaningful when accompanied by the narrative of the experience.[36] Without the narrative, the purchased melted bit of metal from Chinatown was just a metal tchotchke, destined to be tossed in the garbage bin by some descendent. However, with the linkage to the narrative of lived experience, that tiny shard became a marker of nature's power.

Souvenir collecting at sites of disaster was in keeping with behaviors in other places thought to be worthy of remembering, both for early modern tourists and their contemporary counterparts. A nineteenth century museum guidebook gives some indication of the pull of the souvenir impulse. The owners complained about the "apparently uncontrollable propensity of visitors to carry away souvenirs [which was] very costly and annoying."[37] The manager counted how many visitors took something away: in thirty minutes, twenty of 100 visitors claimed a "free" souvenir. The guidebook urged visitors to purchase photographic views available at the gift shop instead of grabbing shells, tree branches, and other objects. One of the shocking stories from Ground Zero concerns souvenirs taken from the Fresh Kills landfill; FBI agents removed objects as mementoes—like a Tiffany globe that ended up in the Minneapolis FBI office and the metal shard from the crashed Washington, D.C. plane in the possession of former Defense Secretary Donald Rumsfeld.[38] Not surprisingly, victims' families complained; the mother of the Tiffany globe's former owner (an AON employee who had perished) wrote to Attorney General John D. Ashcroft to request its return. This embarrassing episode for the FBI led to stricter observation of crime scene protocol, and one wonders whether those FBI agents now wish that they had taken a photograph or resisted the impulse altogether.

VISIBLE TRACES: SILVER SALTS

Photographs are a second form of souvenir collecting. Where there is a site of trauma and mass casualty in modernity, the camera has been an important memory device that, like the object taken from the scene, maintains a physical trace of its creation. Photography, because it is allied with physics, optics, and the machine, has been characterized (though improperly) as an ideal tool for preserving memory. Earliest reports of daguerreotypes called the shiny, wondrous objects "mirrors with a memory." In fact, because of the fidelity to mechanics and physics, photographs have often been considered the most realistic representation possible, better than human memory. Photography's proliferation marks a crucial shift to the eye, much as the way that "sightseeing" and "tourism" (leisure activities primarily for the eye) mark a change from concepts like "Bildungsreise" or "travel" (work activities incorporating more senses). As in the metaphorical use in the term "flashbulb memory," the camera seems to be an integral part of the trip to sites of disaster and tragedy.

Unlike the flashbulb memory phenomenon (unintentional and absolutely free of charge), the producing, buying, keeping, and exchanging of photographs involves both the intention to remember a terrible event and a modern world filled with commodities. Commercial photographers transformed the real life views into two-dimensional, easily-transportable souvenirs that consumers could buy in the form of individual prints, illustrated books (which often compared the "before" to the "after"), and in postcards. All these commercially-available images allowed consumers to combine personal recollection with dramatic, memorable public events.

One manifestation of this impulse to record an already unforgettable public event as a personal one comes in the form of pictures taken specifically to record "I was there," even before the influx of consumer-friendly cameras, and the image of the ladies getting their picture taken in front of the Union Club is a direct and dramatic meta-picture of this desire to get this image recorded. Other fragmentary records offer support for this touristic impulse. For example, the images preserved in the Missouri Historical Society, from different photographers and donated by different people, show that certain areas of the city were more likely to be photographed than others. It seems that the area right around the Union Club was one of St. Louis' prime "picture spots." Like designated "scenic overlooks" at national parks or clearly labeled "picture spots" at Disneyland, this was a site with a dramatic backdrop appropriate for picture-making. Ordinary and now anonymous modern Americans were looking for a way to, literally and metaphorically, "put themselves into the picture" of the intense events which made lasting memory impressions.

The image below is a compelling photograph taken by Ivan G. Mitchell of three women, a man, and a boy standing in front of a small structure which has had a brick wall torn away in the St. Louis tornado. The building is turned inside out—with its normally private interior bizarrely on display. The people are gathered along a picket fence and gaze unsmilingly at the camera, very aware that they are being photographed. The authorship of the photograph is patently clear, as the photographer has tacked a sign to the fence: "Photographed by Ivan G. Mitchell." Other evidence of Mr. Mitchell's photographic activities has not come to light, but it seems reasonable to infer that Mitchell hung out his mobile canvas shingle in order to make this kind of picture to be sold to the sitters and other consumers.[39]

Figure 13.2   Ivan G. Mitchell, 1896, Unidentified boy, Anna Fay, Jennie Thurmann, Alice Bawn, Mr. Mathews standing in front of a wrecked dwelling. Photo courtesy of Missouri History Museum, St. Louis.

Exactly how and why Ivan G. Mitchell operated is not clear; his name does not even appear in contemporaneous city directories as a photographer. Did he put up the sign in front of this ruin and then invite passers-by to pose in front of it? Or, was he the mobile one, traveling around the ruined district and offering to photograph residents?

These images, like so many others in the archives, demonstrate how individuals and their wishes to remember are joined to larger narratives. Even the act of purchasing and archiving can be seen as part of this process. The reality is that many of these images, both those taken by individuals' cameras and those commercially produced, *will* end up in contexts that blend public and private images, personal and collective stories. The recent exhibit *Snapshot Chronicles: Inventing the American Photo Album* is one example of this blending of personal and public stories intertwined in the family album.[40] In just one album, the viewer moves through the 1906 San Francisco Earthquake, an ocean-side picnic, a child's first steps, a husband's machine shop, a drawing room interior, a political rally, and the death of a loved one.[41] The Baur-Kuester family chronicler, on the other hand, mounted St. Louis cyclone photos along with bucolic pictures of the picnicking family; a print made from a cracked glass negative of the wrecked Union Club building is on the same page as a snapshot of a happy family in a park.[42]

Disaster's consumers were drawn to see destruction that is awesome, vast, strange, terrible—and very real. Dean MacCannell's thought-provoking study probes the connection between the experiences of modernity and the function of the sign of authenticity. MacCannell says that "[t]he rhetoric of tourism is full of the manifestations of the importance of the authenticity of the relationship between tourists and what they see" and it is this sense of disaster's breathtaking reality and genuineness which, I believe, drew these turn-of-the-century people to consume disaster experiences and objects as tourists.[43] The opportunities presented also allowed them to certify their own lives through experiences and objects connected to these reality-filled public events.

Although there is no way to go back and interview many of these anonymous and nearly anonymous people whose fragmentary, but fascinating, records inform this paper, it seems reasonable to infer from today's research about shocking natural disaster that such occurrences offered the impression of intensity and authenticity. Recent research suggests that flashbulb memories are no more accurate than everyday memories; however, flashbulb memories do differ in intensity and belief in the accuracy of those memories. So, although a person may *feel* like the moment of finding out that Kennedy was shot, the Challenger exploded, or that terrorists had flown jet airliners into the World Trade Center is accurate and true-to-life, those memories turn out to be no more accurate than any other. Even months or years later, participants *think* that flashbulb memories are more accurate, more filled with reality.

Contemporary natural and man-made disasters, like Hurricane Katrina and September 11th, strongly echo the practices outlined in this paper. The fact that people were bombarded with media images these events, both moving and still, and yet felt a keen need to see it in person, is remarkable. One visitor to the site related that he had watched on television as the towers went down "but said it was a different experience to see the ruins with his own eyes."[44] Seeing, for this type of visitor, seems to outrank all the other senses, and it is often the visual memory that visitors wish to impress upon their minds. Many seem to be of the mindset of one of New York's Ground Zero's bystanders who remarked, "I feel very sad, but we must not forget. I wanted to see it, to not forget."[45] Although it seems nearly impossible for someone to forget the event, or even the thousands of images displayed since, Ground Zero quickly became one of New York's top "attractions."

These practices, however, are not—and probably should not be—immune from ethical suspicion. Susan Sontag rightly questioned the role of the camera in making people tourists of their own and other people's reality, and this uneasiness is one easily found at Ground Zero visits or in Hurricane Katrina tours. Formal bus tours in New Orleans give visitors a taste of Hurricane Katrina's deadly force, but also of the residents' indignation. A New Orleans video production company, "2-cent Entertainment," made a short, scathing video assessment of Katrina tourism. The video shows sightseers in private cars and tour buses brandishing cameras, while the video production group's members hold signs saying "Tourism $$," "You are being filmed," and "This is what you paid to see, right?" The narrator sardonically asks, "If y'all keep paying your money to see it, should we rebuild it?"[46]

In fact, many people who participate in this kind of tourism feel somewhat conflicted about their own participation. On a travel website, a visitor to the Ground Zero Museum workshop contends that he expected to find "a somewhat commercialized venture that exploited both victims and rescuers," but that he was "pleased not to find it a museum setting at all, but more of an intimate memorial to what was a terrible tragedy." The author goes on to note that there were boxes of tissues throughout the exhibit, a decidedly un-museum-like addendum.[47] Another visitor titles a post "The Highlight of Our 3 Day Get-A-Way" and reflects, "It is a must see when visiting NYC. It is not a tourist attraction, [sic] it is an experience for all. Make it your first stop and you will be talking about it for days."[48] Positioning oneself as a mourner/pilgrim visiting a shrine or memorial rather than a tourist attraction seems to be a popular strategy for dealing with the discomfort with finding oneself a tourist of tragedy.

Visitors' reactions to sites of tragedy reveal that they feel both pulled towards and repelled by the sights (and perhaps by their own behavior), but tragedy provided an irresistible moment of personal validation, intensity, and authenticity in the midst of ephemeral modern commodity culture. Andreas Huyssen reminds historians of the Holocaust that "there is no pure space outside of commodity culture, however much we may desire such a space."[49] In fact, key questions about commodity culture are located between traumatic memories and commercial attractions in a somewhat uncomfortable moral terrain. In that light, one might measure those participating in the activities considered in this paper with a somewhat more lenient moral yardstick, as it is possible that they were doing the best that they could to deal with frightening events and ephemeral memories using the tools that modernity provided.

NOTES

1. Marita Sturken, *Tourists of History: Memory, Kitsch, and Consumerism from Oklahoma City to Ground Zero* (Durham and London: Duke University Press, 2007).
2. Roger Brown and James Kulik, "Flashbulb Memories," *Cognition* 5 (1977): 73–99.
3. Laurie Windham McGill, comment on "Memory Book," The Sixth Floor Museum at Dealey Plaza, comment posted on October 19, 2006. Retrieved August 17, 2009 from http://www.jfk.org/go/about/memory-book/.
4. The history of flashbulb memory research is covered in Martin A. Conway, *Flashbulb Memories* (Hove, UK and Hillsdale, NJ: Lawrence Erlbaum Associates, 1995).
5. Jennifer M. Talarico and David C. Rubin, "Confidence, Not Consistency, Characterizes Flashbulb Memories," *Psychological Science*, 14:5 (September 2003): 458.
6. Bessel A. van der Kolk and Rita Fisler, "Dissociation and the Fragmentary Nature of Traumatic Memories," *Journal of Traumatic Stress*, 8:4 (October 1995): 14.
7. See also Dean MacCannell, *The Tourist: A New Theory of the Leisure Class* (New York: Schocken Books, 1989); Nick Stanley, *Being Ourselves for You: The Global Display of Cultures* (Middlesex: Middlesex University Press, 1998); John Urry, *The Tourist Gaze: Leisure and Travel in Contemporary Societies*, (London and Newbury Park: Sage Publications, 1990). For a discussion of the tsunami memorial in Hilo, Hawaii, see Mike Davis, "Tsunami Memories," in *Dead Cities, and Other Tales* (New York: New Press: Distributed by W. W. Norton & Company, 2002).
8. Lucy R. Lippard, *On The Beaten Track: Tourism, Art and Place* (New York: New Press, 1999).
9. Tony Seaton, "From Thanatopsis to Thanatourism: Guided by the Dark," *International Journal of Heritage Studies* 2 (1996): 234–44.
10. A. V. Seaton and J. J. Lennon, "Thanatourism in the Early 21ˢᵗ Century: Moral Panics, Ulterior Motives, and Alterior Desires," in *New Horizons in Tourism: Strange Experiences and Stranger Practices*, ed. T. V. Singh (Oxfordshire and Cambridge: CABI Publishing, 2004), 63. See also M. Foley and J. J. Lennon, "JFK and Dark Tourism: A Fascination with Assassination," *International Journal of Heritage Studies* 2 (1996): 198–211 and M. Foley and J. J. Lennon, "Dark Tourism—An Ethical Dilemma," in *Strategic Issues for the Hospitality, Tourism, and Leisure Industries*, ed. M. Foley, J. J. Lennon, and G. Maxwell (London: Cassell, 1997), 153–64.
11. Judith Adler, "The Origins of Sightseeing," *Annals of Tourism Research* 16:1 (1989): 7–29.

12. John Frow, "Tourism and the Semiotics of Nostalgia," *October* 57 (Summer 1991): 143.
13. John Urry, *The Tourist Gaze: Leisure and Travel in Contemporary Societies* (London: Sage, 1990), 82.
14. John F. Sears, *Sacred Places: American Tourist Attractions in the Nineteenth Century* (New York and Oxford: Oxford University Press, 1989), 4.
15. See Eric Purchase, *Out of Nowhere: Disaster and Tourism in the White Mountains* (Baltimore: The Johns Hopkins University Press, 1999).
16. Julian Curzon, *The Great Cyclone at St. Louis*, 76.
17. Ibid., 87.
18. Ibid., 175.
19. Ibid., 176.
20. Ibid., 127.
21. "View the Dire Scenes," *Chicago Daily Tribune*, June 1, 1896, 1.
22. Homer Bassford, "What a Cyclone's Attack on a Great Community Means," *Harper's Weekly*, June 13, 1896, 594.
23. Willis Fletcher Johnson, *History of the Johnstown Flood*, 219.
24. "Spectators in the Way," *Pittsburgh Press*, June 3, 1889, 1.
25. Ibid.
26. [Henry], "Please Keep Away: Sight-seers Are Regarded as a Perfec [sic] Nuisance at Johnstown," *Pittsburgh Commercial Gazette*, June 5, 1889, 1.
27. Daniel J. Boorstin, *The Image: A Guide to Pseudo-Events in America* (New York: Harper & Row, 1964), 85.
28. Paula Degen and Carl Degen, *The Johnstown Flood of 1889: The Tragedy of the Conemaugh* (Philadelphia: Eastern Acorn Press, 1984), 61.
29. "Excursionists' Day," *Pittsburgh Commercial Gazette*, June 24, 1889, page unknown, found in Clara Barton Papers, Library of Congress.
30. Ibid.
31. Ibid.
32. Tripadvisor.com, "Things to Do in New York City." Retrieved March 1, 2010 from http://www.tripadvisor.com/Attractions-g60763-Activities-New_York_City_New_York.html.
33. Julian Curzon, *The Great Cyclone at St. Louis,* 86.
34. Letter from Mrs. Alice "Mamie" Easton to M. H. Easton, October 14, 1900, Galveston and Texas History Center, Rosenberg Library, Galveston, Texas. Academic discourse tends to categorize the souvenir as something purchased, and the memento as something accumulated through personal experience; in everyday language of the period, this distinction in terminology is not as strict.
35. Willis Fletcher Johnson, *History of the Johnstown Flood*, 377.
36. Susan Stewart, *On Longing: Narratives of the Miniature, the Gigantic, the Souvenir, the Collection* (Durham and London: Duke University Press, 1993), 132–51.
37. *Guide to the Ridge Hill Farms: Wellesley, MA and Social Science Reform, September 1877* (Boston: Betschell Bros, 1877), 65.
38. Sturken, *Tourists of History*, 208.
39. Prints and Photographs Collection, Missouri Historical Society Box 733, Folder 7. The people are identified on the back as Anna Fay, Jennie Thurmann, Alice Bawn, Mr. Mathews, although it is not clear what their relationship might have been. The only person whose occupation and location were specified is Wade H. Mathews, a police officer (note the star on his lapel), who lived at 2313 Randolph.
40. Reyhan Harmanci, "A Candid Crisis," *San Francisco Chronicle*, April 6, 2006, H24.

41. Stephanie Snyder, "The Vernacular Photo Album: Its Origins and Genius," in *Snapshot Chronicles: Inventing the American Photo Album*, ed. Barbara Levine and Stephanie Snyder, (New York and Portland: Princeton Architectural Press, 2006), 25.
42. Baur-Kuester Family Collection, 1872–1944, Box 1923, Large Family Album, Missouri Historical Society.
43. Dean MacCannell, *The Tourist*, 14.
44. Diego Ibarguen, "Trade Center Ruins are Now a Grim Attraction for Sightseers," The Associated Press State & Local Wire, September 21, 2001, Friday, BC cycle.
45. Jessica McBride, "9–11: One Year Later," *Milwaukee Journal Sentinel*, September 8, 2002, 1A
46. 2-Cent Entertainment, "New Orleans for Sale." Retrieved October 17, 2009 from http://2-cent.com/Watch.html and http://www.youtube.com/watch?v=DgbyoBLnln0.
47. Jahnick of Saskatchewan, comment on Trip Advisor for the Ground Zero Museum and Workshop, June 4, 2009. Retrieved October 17, 2009 from http://www.tripadvisor.com/ShowUserReviews-g60763-d626630-r33060400-Ground_Zero_Museum_Workshop-New_York_City_New_York.html#TOPC.
48. lopezfam12 of Miami, comment on Trip Advisor for the Ground Zero Museum and Workshop, October 7, 2008. Retrieved October 17, 2009 from http://www.tripadvisor.com/ShowUserReviews-g60763-d626630-r33060400-Ground_Zero_Museum_Workshop-New_York_City_New_York.html#TOPC, 7 October 2008.
49. Andreas Huyssen, *Present Pasts: Urban Palimpsests and the Politics of Memory* (Stanford: Stanford University Press, 2003), 19.

Contributors

Kingsley Baird is a visual artist and Associate Professor in the School of Visual and Material Culture, College of Creative Arts, at Massey University. His primary research activities concern memory, cross-cultural memorialization, and public art. His national and international exhibitions and works include Diary Dagboek (Belgium), The Cloak of Peace Te Korowai Rangimarie (Japan), The Tomb of the Unknown Warrior Te Toma o Te Toa Matangaro (New Zealand), and The New Zealand Memorial (Australia).

Robert M. Bednar is Associate Professor of Communication Studies and American Studies at Southwestern University. His work as a photographer, ethnographer, and theorist focuses on the ways that people perform their identities visually and materially as they inhabit public landscapes. He is the author of several works on snapshot photography in the U.S. National Parks as well as several works on roadside car crash shrines.

Dee Britton is an Assistant Professor and academic area coordinator in Social Sciences and Social Research at the State University of New York's Empire State College. She has also taught at Syracuse University, Colgate University, and Hamilton College. Her primary research areas include the construction and deconstruction of collective memory, the sociology of disaster, and visual representations of memory and disaster.

Anne Teresa Demo is an Assistant Professor in the Department of Communication and Rhetorical Studies at Syracuse University. Her scholarship has appeared in the *Quarterly Journal of Speech*, *Critical Studies in Media Communication*, *Rhetoric & Public Affairs*, *Environmental History*, and *Women's Studies in Communication*. She is a recipient of the Golden Monograph Award from the National Communication Association and the most outstanding essay prize in *Women's Studies in Communication*.

Paul Duro is Professor of Art and Art History/Visual and Cultural Studies at the University of Rochester, New York. He is the author of *The Academy* *and the Limits of Painting in Seventeenth-Century France* (Cambridge University Press, 1997), editor of *The Rhetoric of the Frame: Essays on the Boundaries of the Artwork* (Cambridge University Press, 1996), and co-author of *Essential Art History* (Bloomsbury, 1992). His recent work on the institutions of art, travel writing, the sublime, and the theory of imitation has appeared in *Art Journal*, *Word and Image*, and *Art History*.

Margaret Ewing is a Ph.D. Candidate in Art History at the University of Illinois, Urbana-Champaign, and a Berlin-based contributor to *Artforum*. Her dissertation analyzes Hans Haacke and German national identity after 1989.

Emily Godbey is an Assistant Professor of Art and Design History at Iowa State University. Her research concerns photography, early film, material culture, and American painting. She has published articles in *American Studies*, *Encyclopedia of American Material Culture,* and *Pennsylvania History*. Her work has been supported by a National Endowment for the Humanities Chairmanship, a Deutscher Akademischer Austausch Dienst Summer Fellowship, and a grant from the Society for the History of Technology.

Frances Guerin is currently a Marie Curie Fellow at the Instititut für Medienwissenschaft, Ruhr University. She is the author of *A Culture of Light: Cinema and Technology in 1920s Germany* (University of Minnesota Press, 2005) and *Through Amateur Eyes: Film and Photography in Nazi Germany* (Minneapolis: University of Minnesota Press, 2011). She is co-editor of *The Image and the Witness: Trauma, Memory and Visual Culture* (Wallflower Press, 2007). Her articles have appeared in *Cinema Journal*, *Screening the Past*, and *Film and History*.

Kevin Hamilton holds appointments in the Department of Media and Cinema Studies and in the School of Art and Design at the University of Illinois, Urbana-Champaign, where he is an Associate Professor and Chair of the New Media Program. Current artistic and research projects include visualization research for health and energy conservation applications, a critical archive of American nuclear propaganda and training films, a performance series on race and religion in the Colorado Rockies, and a timeline mural on cybernetics research. Recent awards include a grant from the National Science Foundation, a National Endowment for the Humanities Summer Fellowship through Vectors/IML at University of Southern California, and an invited fellowship with the Cornell University Society for the Humanities.

Andrea Hammer is a Senior Lecturer of Landscape Architecture at Cornell University. She is the founder and director of SlackWater Center and the

Southern Maryland Documentation Project. She is project director and executive editor of *SlackWater Journal*. Hammer is the recipient of an Andrew W. Mellon Foundation Grant. Her work has appeared in such publications as *Jump Cut* and *SlackWater Journal*.

Ekaterina V. Haskins is an Associate Professor of Rhetoric in the Department of Language, Literature, and Communication at Rensselaer Polytechnic Institute. She is the author of *Logos and Power in Isocrates and Aristotle* (University of South Carolina Press, 2004). She has published numerous articles and essays on the history of rhetoric, visual culture, and public memory. She is a recipient of the Karl R. Wallace Memorial Award from the National Communication Association, the Everett Lee Hunt Award for Outstanding Scholarship in recognition of her book, and the Kneupper Award for Best Article from the Rhetoric Society of America.

Ned O'Gorman is an Assistant Professor of Communication at the University of Illinois, Urbana-Champaign. He is the author of *Spirits of the Cold War: Contesting Worldviews in the Classical Age of American Security Strategy* (Michigan State University Press, 2011). His research has appeared in *Communication and Critical/Cultural Studies*, the *Quarterly Journal of Speech*, *Rhetoric and Public Affairs*, *Rhetoric Society Quarterly*, *Philosophy and Rhetoric*, the *Millennium Journal of International Studies*, and elsewhere. He has served as President of the American Society for the History of Rhetoric and has been a faculty fellow of the Illinois Program for Research in the Humanities, a National Endowment for the Humanities fellow, and winner of the Religious Communication Association's top prize for a journal article.

Ernesto Pujol is a site-specific performance artist and social choreographer. He stages performance art as the psychic portrait of a people and their landscape. His collective durational performances serve as ephemeral monuments through silence, solitude, and reflection. He believes that art is critical to the sustainability of democracy in a diverse society. Pujol is based in New York but works regionally across the United States as the founder and director of UteHaus Associated Performers and The Field School Project. Pujol has a Bachelor of Arts degree in Humanities and Visual Arts from the University of Puerto Rico, and a Master of Fine Arts degree in Interdisciplinary Practice from The School of The Art Institute of Chicago. He has also pursued graduate work in education, art therapy, media theory and communications.

Johanna Ruohonen is a Ph.D. Candidate in Art History at the University of Turku, Finland. She has previously served as a Visiting Scholar in the Graduate Center of the City University of New York. She has published various articles on public art and also works as a freelance art critic.

Bradford Vivian is an Associate Professor of Communication and Rhetorical Studies at Syracuse University. He is the author of *Public Forgetting: The Rhetoric and Politics of Beginning Again* (Pennsylvania State University Press, 2010) and *Being Made Strange: Rhetoric beyond Representation* (State University of New York Press, 2004). His work has appeared in the *Quarterly Journal of Speech, Philosophy and Rhetoric, Rhetoric & Public Affairs, JAC,* the *Journal of Speculative Philosophy,* and the *Western Journal of Communication.* His research grants include a National Endowment for the Humanities Summer Stipend, and he is a recipient of the Karl R. Wallace Memorial Award from the National Communication Association and the B. Aubrey Fisher Award.

Malcolm Woollen is an architect and Adjunct Professor in the Department of Architecture at Pennsylvania State University. He was educated at Middlebury College and Yale University School of Architecture. He has written about modern European landscape architecture, including projects by Dieter Kienast, Bernard Lassus, and Peter Latz.

Index

Note: Numbers in *italics* indicate figures.

80581104R00152

Made in the USA
Lexington, KY
04 February 2018